WORMWOOD

The little book from Revelation

HANNAH ORION

BALBOA.
PRESS

A DIVISION OF HAY HOUSE

Balboa Press books may be ordered through booksellers or by contacting:

Balboa Press
A Division of Hay House
1663 Liberty Drive
Bloomington, IN 47403
www.balboapress.com.au
1 (877) 407-4847

Print information available on the last page.

ISBN: 978-1-4525-3095-6 (sc)
ISBN: 978-1-4525-3096-3 (e)

Balboa Press rev. date: 09/11/2015

And the name of the star is called Wormwood:
and the third part of the waters became
wormwood; and many men died of the waters,
because they were made bitter. Re:8:11

CONTENTS

INTRODUCTION

Below is a short list of some of the ancient gods that were worshipped during the time of Jesus Christ. His new religion, that we now call Christianity, was instrumental in eliminating these ancient beliefs and replacing these old worships with that of the new Christianity. One of the first tasks of the early Christians was to travel to every village and country they could, preaching the Word. The aim was to eradicate all these ancient beliefs. This practice is still in use today, and many doctrines of Christianity still send missionaries to a variety of lands and countries to do exactly this. The belief is that "there are no such things as gods!" The poor tribes in New Guinea or in South America as in other places have all had their belief systems challenged if not totally overwritten by modern day missionaries.

Unfortunately Christian doctrines only ever succeeded in replacing one belief system with another just as intolerant and inane as the cult it replaced. After saying that 'there are no such things as gods' they then claim that there really **is** such a thing as a god, but only on their terms. However one can't say on one hand that 'there are no such things as gods' and then contradict it by saying "hang on, there is one god!"

There are many things Christ said that show if not prove that "There really are no such things as gods!"

The intent of Christ's Christianity was to destroy or prove that these other gods were nothing more than delusions set up by the high priests or

Shamans of the day, who had a vested interest in reaping a harvest off the followers. Jesus set about revealing this TRUTH and this sums up His ministry. It was not that He wanted to destroy other people's beliefs, but more importantly, He wanted to show the world the TRUTH, that there are no such things as gods period and all sin is irrelevant. Worshipping gods that don't exist pollute the mind with delusion and dogma and leave the follower vulnerable to exploitation, which was exactly the case. He was a healer who not only treated physical complaints the best way He could, but also attempted to purge people's minds, by informing them of the TRUTH about the types of delusions they were labouring under.

Jesus was not teaching monotheism; a belief in only one god. The Jews already had monotheism. Monotheism was already well known at the time of Christ. Contrary to popular belief the world at the time of Christ, was not amazed by the concept of one god monotheism.

Jesus came up against the Pharisees and Sadducees of His religion and confronted their beliefs in god. He said they had turned from the truth and had changed the truth of god into a lie. Jesus came to them teaching Atheism! There is no god at all He suggested! His version of God and religion was based on an Ideal. He made this IDEAL into a Father figure and all mankind was seen as His Family and to this end He named Himself the 'Son of Man' or the 'Son of Mankind'. He was a visionary and His vision was to make people free by explaining His truth about all religions, that there actually are no such things as gods. The following list outlines a few of the deities of the ancient world that the new Christian sect battled against.

Joh:8:32: And ye shall know the truth, and the truth shall make you free.

MAIN ROMAN GODS	
	Jupiter - King of the Gods
Juno - Queen of the Gods	Neptune - God of the Sea
Pluto - God of Death	Apollo - God of the Sun
Diana - Goddess of the Moon	Mars - God of War

Venus - Goddess of Love	Cupid - God of Love
Mercury - Messenger of the Gods	Minerva - Goddess of Wisdom
Ceres - The Earth Goddess	Proserpine - Goddess of the Underworld
Vulcan - The Smith God	Bacchus - God of Wine
Saturn - God of Time	Vesta - Goddess of the
Home Janus - God of Doors	Uranus and Gaia - Parents of Saturn
Maia - Goddess of Growth	Flora - Goddess of Flowers
Plutus - God of Wealth	

EGYPTIAN GODS	
Amun is Thebes, king of gods in the New Kingdom.	Anput is the wife of Anubis and the mother of Kebechet.
Anubis is god of funerals and death.	Anuket is the goddess of river Nile.
Apophis is the god of chaos.	Aten is the monotheistic sun god.
Babi is the god of baboons.	Bastet is the cat goddess.
Bes is the dwarf god of children.	Geb is the god of the earth.
Hathor is the goddess of the love and children.	Heket is the goddess of childbirth and fertility.
Horus is the god of war and son of Osiris.	Isis is the goddess of marriage, healing and motherhood.
Kebechet the goddess of purification	Khepri is the god of scarab beetles.
Khmun is the ram-headed god.	Khonsu is the god of the Moon.
Ma'at is the goddess of justice and of order.	Mafdet is the god of justice
Nephthyrs is the river goddess.	Nekhbet is the vulture goddess.
Nut is the goddess of sky and stars.	Osiris is the god of the underworld and the afterlife. Husband of Isis.
Ptah is the god of creation.	Ra is the god of the Sun and king of the gods until Horus took over his throne.
Sehkmet is the goddess of lions and fire.	Serqet is the goddess of scorpions.
Seshat is the goddess of writing and measurement.	Seth, or Set, is the god of deserts, storms, evil, and chaos.

Shu is the god of wind and air.	Sobek is the god of crocodiles and alligators.
Tawaret is the hippopotamus goddess.	Thoth is the scribe god and the god of wisdom.
Wadjet is a goddess of protection.	

NORSE GODS	
Baldr - God of beauty, innocence, peace, and rebirth. Consort: Nanna	Borr - Father of Óðinn, Vili and Ve. Consort: Bestla
Bragi - God of poetry. Consort: Iðunn	Búri - The first god and father of Borr.
Dagr - God of the daytime, son of Delling and Nótt.	Delling - God of dawn and father of Dagr by Nótt.
Eir - Goddess of healing.	Forseti - God of justice, peace and truth. Son of Baldr and Nanna.
Freyja - Goddess of love, sexuality, fertility and battle. Consort: Óðr	Freyr - God of fertility. Consort: Gerð
Frigg - Goddess of marriage and motherhood. Consort: Óðinn Can also be pronounced Frigga	Fulla - Frigg's handmaid.
Gmot - God of the moon. Brother of Re`es andWeth.	Gefjun - Goddess of fertility and plough.
Hel - Queen of Neifelheim, the Norse underworld.	Heimdallr (Rígr) - One of the Æsir and guardian of Ásgarð, their realm.
Hermóðr - Óðinn's son.	Hlín - Goddess of consolation and protection.
Höðr - God of winter.	Hœnir - The silent god.
Iðunn - Goddess of youth. Consort: Bragi.	Jörð - Goddess of the Earth. Mother of Þórr by Óðinn.
Kvasir - God of inspiration.	Lofn - Goddess of love.
Loki - Trickster and god of mischief. Consort: Sigyn (also called Saeter)	Máni - God of Moon.
Mímir - Óðinn's uncle.	Nanna - An Ásynja married with Baldr and mother to Forseti.

Nerþus - A goddess mentioned by Tacitus. Her name is connected to that of Njörðr.	Njörðr - God of sea, wind, fish, and wealth.
Nótt - Goddess of night, daughter of Narvi and mother of Auð, Jörð and Dagr by Naglfari, Annar and Delling, respectively.	Odin The "All Father" (The Ruler of the gods)
Sága - An obscure goddess, possibly another name for Frigg.	Sif - Wife of Thor.
Sjöfn - Goddess of love.	Skaði - Goddess of winter Njörðr's wife.
Snotra - Goddess of prudence.	Sol (Sunna) - Goddess of Sun.
Thor (Donar) - God of thunder and battle. Consort: Sif.	Tiki- God of Stone
Tree-Goddess of life	Tyr- God of War Also the God of the Skies.
Ullr - God of skill, hunt, and duel. Son of Sif.	Váli - God of revenge.
Vár - Goddess of contract.	Vé - One of the three gods of creation. Brother of Óðinn and Vili.
Víðarr- Son of Odin and the giantess Gríðr.	Vör - Goddess of wisdom.
Weth-Goddess of anger	
GREEK GODS	Theogony
Chaos	The Titans
Aphrodite	Apollo
Ares	Artemis
Athena	Demeter
Dionysus	Hades
Hephaestus	Hera
Hermes	Hestia
Poseidon	Zeu

This is by no means an exhaustive list as there were hundreds of past gods and cults. Christianity has abolished most of these religions and this has not been achieved without bloodshed. The major religions that are left are either Eastern ones or the main monotheistic ones such as Islam, Judaism and Christianity. This book deals only with Christianity and looks critically at the New Testament to do so. It is written in defence of what Jesus Christ taught. This book is only interested in revealing clarity of thought with regard to belief systems. The only knowledge that should be accepted and trusted is that which has been ratified by the scientific process in the spirit of revealing truthfulness.

CONCEPT ONE

SIGN OF THE TIMES

At the time of Christ, some two-thousand years ago, the superpowers of the day, namely Egypt, Greece and Rome, all worshipped a plethora of gods. Jesus recognised that such belief systems were a folly that corrupted the minds of the followers, with dogma that led to delusion and misconception. Religions which held onto false ancient beliefs, also observed a number of wrongful practices such as sacrificing animals and sometimes even people. The governing bodies of priests, Shamans and powerful religious leaders including His own religion also made many corrupt laws and taxes aimed at enriching the powerful elite by subjugating the poor.

Jesus felt it was time the modern world and the Pharisees learned the truth about religion. He came to the Middle East with a new message from the ancient religion. The Jews had practiced monotheism for centuries prior to Jesus' time. Monotheism, the worship of just one god, was nothing new to Jesus or the ancient world, but even this one-god viewpoint, was incorrect as far as Jesus was concerned. He was not bringing monotheism to a world that already had monotheism. Instead, He went on to as many villages as he could, suggesting such things as; "Why do you worship a plethora of gods? Don't you know that there are no such things as gods? He said the kingdom of god was within you.

> Lu:17:21: Neither shall they say, Lo here! or, lo there! for, behold,
> **the kingdom of God is within you.**

More of his actual words are recorded in the four gospels and His verses will be repeated here for the convenience of the reader, taken from King James Version of the Bible. There are many Bibles around these days many of which have been edited by people with rigid viewpoints and by those who believe the common concept that God exists. These corrected editions cause conflict when examined earnestly because there are many heretical passages to be found in the New Testament. Since people who believe that a god exists cannot fathom why there should be heretical phrases in their Bible, they simply alter or delete them or change the wording in order to make such phrases conform to their own opinion to be more appealing to an authoritarian viewpoint. Even the modern Bible is not free of such editing so that only one perspective should be drawn, which is that god exists. Therefore the King James Version has been chosen as an authority to be examined, as it is mostly untouched and free of modern day corrections

> *Re:22:19: And if any man shall take away from the words of the book of this prophecy, God shall take away his part out of the book of life, and out of the holy city, and from the things which are written in this book.*

The words of Jesus Christ are everlasting and the message is clear, that there are no such things as gods. This is said to purge the human mind of preconceived ideas and notions about god. This is also the most fundamental teaching of all from which stems all the insights and benefits to mankind that truthfulness and purity of mind can afford. Jesus taught His disciples the same message, and they continued His work, preaching this illumination long after His demise. They went from village to village teaching 'There are no such things as Gods' and the new Christian effort of Baptism that arose, purged most of the Middle East and Europe of polytheism and perverted worship. We see evidence of this heretical teaching in verse, for example the following from Luke. Jesus' words are concise and simple as He intimated that we the people were as Gods ourselves.

*Joh:10:34: Jesus answered them, Is it not written in your law, **I said, Ye are gods?***

He said very clearly that God was an ideal.

*Lu:17:20: And when he was demanded of the Pharisees, when the kingdom of God should come, he answered them and said, The kingdom of God cometh **not with observation:***

*Lu:17:21: Neither shall they say, Lo here! or, lo there! for, behold, **the kingdom of God is within you**.*

In this verse Jesus reveals two major concepts the first is that god cannot be found anywhere that you might seek Him and the second is that god dwells within us. Stating that the Kingdom of God dwelt within people, meant that God was not a super being seated on a throne in a place called Heaven at all, but was actually an IDEAL within us that Jesus and His followers clung to and believed in. God was NOT a supernatural BEING but was instead a belief in TRUTHFULNESS and Honesty and a commitment to do good work.

If there were no such things as gods then Jesus must have reasoned that there was no such thing as a singular God period. A true belief in god was a belief in the ideals and morals that one would expect if god were real. Seeing that god was an imaginary archetype, Jesus then set about teaching the types of behaviours people should adopt, in order to reflect such a belief. In other words, the followers themselves portrayed a type of godliness, through their beliefs and behaviours, without the need for an actual god. God was merely the personification of this behaviour. This is the truth.

Joh:1:12: But as many as received him, **to them gave he power to become the sons of God**, even to them that believe on his name:

God was an adopted Father in heaven. Through this adoption as many as received Him became also the adopted children or sons of God. This was considered to be heretical according to the Pharisees of the time. The

Bible is full of heretical sayings that offend people who strictly believe that God exists in Heaven. Therefore many Bibles are heavily worded to reflect such a belief but the real evidence actually points to Jesus teaching the freedom of atheism to the Pharisees. Jesus recognised that He could not just come out with claims that the imagined god did not actually exist; He had to prove to people, that what they read in their Bibles, and their interpretation of that reading, was in fact altogether misunderstood. The basic premise that a god existed, corrupted the mind with a false belief or delusion that sullied every other thought and decision the person held. The problem was how does one achieve such a goal as proving atheism? In fact this very problem still exists today, even in the face of such overwhelming evidence as the theory of evolution, not to mention all the other sciences, chemistry, physics, astrophysics and quantum mechanics; some people continue to argue for spontaneous creation by a creator. To argue that Dinosaurs did not exist, even while holding a dinosaur bone in your hand, is to demonstrate bigotry. To say that God is larger than the universe which He must have created, then to say He dwells on Mount Zion is ludicrous

> *Isa:8:18: Behold, I and the children whom the LORD hath given me are for signs and for wonders in Israel from the LORD of hosts, which dwelleth in mount Zion..*

Most people are unaware of the barefaced but truthful nature of Jesus' teachings, because most doctrines do not teach it, in fact no-one teaches it. Having been influenced since the beginning of time by the imagined presence of a god, the case for a secular, truthful lifestyle, threatens the established theologies with losing their grip on the congregation. This was true in Jesus' day as well; synagogues and churches were trapped by their own dogma.

If a person's mind is affected by a basic delusion such as religious idiom, how can they ever come to the knowledge of truthful teachings such as science? At least this is what it was like during the middle-ages when science was a struggling notion in the minds of a few geniuses like Galileo. The difference of believing in science, as opposed to religion, is that with science the beliefs are constantly changing and being corrected as new definitions are found, but with religious dogma one believes the same unchanging myth, as the ancestors did, forever, and such a mindset is incapable of accepting new change; new challenges and new truths, for fear of being proved wrong or perhaps fear of being dammed.

Jesus said nobody has ever seen any such thing as a god.

> *Joh:1:18:* **No man hath seen God at any time**; *the only begotten Son, which is in the bosom of the Father, he hath declared him.*

Saying that "No man or person has ever seen God at any time" is stating the obvious, that there is no evidence that a god exists at all. People of Jesus' day had only the word of the priest (who also had never seen any god) as evidence that there actually is a god, and this word of the priest was only an account of that one priest's imagination. In fact all interpretation emanates from the imagination of the men at the top of the hierarchy who had a vested interest in perpetrating the delusion. Because of the nature of imagination and personal interpretation of scripture, there have been countless disputes over what is the most perfect doctrine of all. Hence we now have a plethora of Christian denominations, all of whom fall under the same God-spell.

Nobody has ever seen any god or any such things as gods. The notion that god created the earth is problematic to say the least; as such a creation implies that the whole universe was created by a god. God therefore would need to be bigger than the universe itself, if such a god existed. Not only that but all the Laws governing science, nature and mathematics in both microcosms and macrocosms, would have been created by the same god and so would all the parallel universes. The big bang itself would have been such a creation, and the list goes on and on until the very thought of someone or something being so enormous but still focusing on the earth and on individual people, becomes totally preposterous.

Jesus said explicitly to His disciples, that **God was within us**. God was an IDEAL. This IDEAL was a belief in good as opposed to a belief in evil. A belief in goodness required a commitment to do good work, in all aspects of life. This public commitment was demonstrated and became known as the Baptism. This teaching was that we should help others, and to turn the other cheek when someone wronged us.

> M't:5:39: But I say unto you, That ye resist not evil: but whosoever shall smite thee on thy right cheek, **turn to him the other also**.

> Lu:6:29: And unto him that smiteth thee on the one cheek **offer also the other**; and him that taketh away thy cloke forbid not to take thy coat also.

Jesus taught us to love thy neighbour as thyself, this concept was termed the second great commandment and it reflects the notion that God dwells within us or indeed in all people, as the first great commandment states, that we should love god (the Ideal) with all our heart.

> *M't:22:39: And the second is like unto it,* **Thou shalt love thy neighbour as thyself**.

However Jesus' God was an Ideal of doing good deeds. Imagine it this way; if you add an 'O' to the word 'GOD', you get 'GOOD'. To love God is to love Good. A decision to serve God should be a decision to serve Good. Life presents us with a simple but critical choice, either we promote goodness or we choose evil, which is to be uncaring and unmindful of others. This is the great choice all people are faced with sometime during their life; to serve 'Good' (God) or Evil.

> M't:6:24: **No man can serve two masters**: for either he will hate the one, and love the other; or else he will hold to the one, and despise the other. Ye cannot serve God and mammon.

> Lu:16:13: **No servant can serve two masters**: for either he will hate the one, and love the other; or else he will hold to the one, and despise the other. Ye cannot serve God and mammon.

It is stated in the Bible that to serve Evil is to be unaware of moral standards and such people live their lives in darkness not knowing or understanding the value of promoting goodness or morals for the benefit of society.

Planting the seeds of goodness in young children will see them grow into reliable and caring parents themselves but the alternative only produces selfish and uncaring adults.

These teachings were far superior and vastly different, from the teachings of the Jewish Hierarchy at the time, which were only trumpeting monotheism, as well as vain repetitions of dogma. Not only that, but as Jesus taught that there are no such things as gods (or indeed a God) the hierarchy realised that such teachings would soon turn people away from the established synagogues, which earned their income. Therefore He was hated by the hierarchy because He was seen as being an anti-god heretic. He was in fact just being truthful and honest in all His attempts at verbalising the enlightenment of truth. To this end he said such things as the Pharisees and Sadducees were **vain** to believe that a god created all things. Not only this, but that they knew the truth once, and had turned this pure secular truth into the philosophy of lies and rituals that perpetuated the delusion that god actually exists.

> Romans1:21: *Because that, when they knew God, they glorified him not as God, neither were thankful;* **but became vain in their imaginations**, *and their foolish heart was darkened.*

He said that the hierarchy were vain in their imaginations and that they had turned the TRUTH into a lie. This of course meant that instead of worshipping god as an IDEAL they worshipped god as an 'omnipotent being' which was in fact idolatry which affected their mindset.

Being vain in their imaginations refers to the vanity of worshipping an imagined god – any god – or all gods. It doesn't stop at gods either. The imagination fills heaven with any number of creatures such as angels and cherubim. Then people start to believe in ghosts and before you know it there are soothsayers and diviners and a host of other spinoffs. This is called IDOLATRY. Since there are no such things as gods, then by definition worshipping any god was vain. Jesus knew this truth well. To say that there even was <u>one</u> god above all others was also a deception that Jesus often referred to as the covering or veil of heaven. This is the Dark Confession of Christ's knowledge. When Jesus spoke of God (His adopted

The whole of Jesus' teachings proclaim this very issue. The notion that the truth is hidden by a 'covering' is consistent from Genesis to Revelation. It is central to understanding the message against idolatry. Idolatry was the one colossal sin that Israel always resorted to, even after being severely admonished, time and time again by the Prophets. They always continued to worship god. Idolatry is basically interpreted as worshipping idols as gods but the biblical interpretation is that of worshipping any gods at all. To give one's mind over to worshipping god or gods is to surrender one's own discerning ability, to oppression of thought by others. Gods do not exist, so to worship something that does not exist, or to worship anything at all, is to surrender one's own will power. This is offensive to those who cherish holistic viewpoints of the self. Such surrender always commits the individual's viewpoint to oppression of thought by others.

Below is an extract from Exodus concerning the idolatry of the Jews even whilst Moses was on the Mountain receiving the Ten Commandments?

> *Ex:32:22: And Aaron said, Let not the anger of my lord wax hot: thou knowest the people, that they are set on mischief.*
>
> *Ex:32:23: For they said unto me, **Make us gods**, which shall go before us: for as for this Moses, the man that brought us up out of the land of Egypt, we wot not what is become of him.*
>
> *Ex:32:24: And I said unto them, Whosoever hath any gold, let them break it off. So they gave it me: then I cast it into the fire, and there came out this calf.*
>
> *Ex:32:25: **And when Moses saw that the people were naked; (for Aaron had made them naked unto their shame among their enemies:)***
>
> *Ex:32:26: Then Moses stood in the gate of the camp, and said, Who is on the LORD's side? let him come unto me. And all the sons of Levi gathered themselves together unto him.*
>
> *Ex:32:27: And he said unto them, Thus saith the LORD God of Israel, Put every man his sword by his side, and go in and out*

*from gate to gate throughout the camp, **and slay every man his brother, and every man his companion, and every man his neighbour.***

*Ex:32:28: And the children of Levi did according to the word of Moses: and there fell of the people that day **about three thousand men**.*

Moses saw that the people were NAKED in their worship of god. This nakedness implies spiritual nakedness (the fear that Moses was not returning and they would be left without a god). You have heard of the "Naked Truth" well the naked truth is truth that is not covered by misleading description that hides the real facts from our minds.

*The fable of the **naked truth** says that Truth and falsehood went bathing. Falsehood came first out of the water and dressed herself in Truth's garments. Truth being unwilling to take the garments of Falsehood went naked. "Dictionary of Phrase and Fable – Brewer"*

It was said that Moses was the only person who could "talk with God" because only he knew the secret of how to do this. The Truth is that Moses invented his own impression of God. Therefore Aaron was used as a mouthpiece to intercede for Moses and the people.

Ex:4:14: And the anger of the LORD was kindled against Moses, and he said, Is not Aaron the Levite thy brother? I know that he can speak well. And also, behold, he cometh forth to meet thee: and when he seeth thee, he will be glad in his heart.

*Ex:4:15: And thou shalt speak unto him, **and put words in his mouth**: and I will be with thy mouth, and with his mouth, and will teach you what ye shall do.*

*Ex:4:16: And he shall be thy spokesman unto the people: and he shall be, **even he shall be to thee instead of a mouth, and thou shalt be to him instead of God**.*

Ex:4:17: And thou shalt take this rod in thine hand, wherewith thou shalt do signs.

God (Moses's conscience) confided in Moses; Moses told Aaron; Aaron told the people and somewhere in the retelling the truth became distorted. The scripture said that instead of God, Aaron had Moses. Aaron disguised the things that Moses told him. Whether he knew that there was no such thing as god as Moses did because he was a Levite or whether he believed that there actually was a god we do not know. All we know is that Moses (being spiritually naked) knew there are no such things as gods (the naked truth) but the people continually resorted to idolatry which is worshipping god, or clothing their beliefs with fables; traditions and worship; obviously they believed that God existed hence the motivation for their idolatry.

Today many people choose atheism or agnosticism, not because of anything that is written in the Bible but because of the stockpile of true knowledge that we have today with Universities and Schools, Book stores and Libraries, the Internet and Television and much more. These resources are so overwhelming that there simply is no room for out-dated concerns such as god worship. The Grace of God which is simply the covering of stories and fables and rituals such as feasts and fasts is seen as nothing more than mortal services and ceremonies. People still get married in churches but just as many choose Celebrants and civil marriages instead of Pastors and churches. The ambivalence demonstrated by some modern societies for religion in general signifies a movement away from traditional religious attendance. Some churches these days admit that the numbers of attendees is dropping off. Therefore religious movements this century have attempted to re-invent Christianity with the advent of charismatic movements such as New-Age Christian Outreach Worship which include the 'speaking in tongues' and the 'Laying on of Hands to heal the sick' and 'fervent prophecy' as well as other infatuations of the spirit. All these 'Born Again' methodologies appeal to those people seeking solace in such emotive methods of worship but isn't this exactly what the covering or veil or mystery of God is for? Isn't it designed to be their comforter? Isn't it called the Grace of God?

Fortunately there are some people who are not enticed by such charismatic and passionate cults as these for very long and the thirst for knowledge and hunger for truth usually lead such people into other truthful, honest and sincere expressions of doctrine or scholastic endeavours.

Jesus was adamant about truth. He took every opportunity to teach truthfulness. It was as if there was nothing more important on earth than being sincere, honest and truthful.

> Joh:8:32: And ye shall know the truth, and the truth shall make you free.

Even for Pontus Pilate all Jesus said in His own defence was I seek the Truth.

> Joh:18:37: Pilate therefore said unto him, Art thou a king then? Jesus answered, Thou sayest that I am a king. To this end was I born, and for this cause came I into the world, that **I should bear witness unto the truth**. Every one that is of the truth heareth my voice.

So it is with this in mind that we accept scripture not so much for the comfort of the veil which we now understand to be nothing more than a psychological unguent for a longing soul but for the stringent quality of the truth that God is **within** us.

It is this same truth that reveals to us the 'cloak' or 'veil' of god which constitutes the 'mystery of god' referred to so often throughout the New Testament.

> Re:10:7: But in the days of the voice of the seventh angel (messenger), when he shall begin to sound, the **mystery of God** should be finished, as he hath declared to his servants the prophets.

> Joh:15:22: If I had not come and spoken unto them, they had not had sin: but now **they have no cloke for their sin**.

We witness that the 'mystery of God' is finished or at least revealed by doctrines such as the little book spoken of in Revelations, and others like it, that show that vain worship is a sickness of the mind which leads mental health astray with inspirations of grandeur, that are in fact hollow. New Age doctrines which promote such ill motivated behaviour and strong infatuation risk losing credence. In this day and age it is difficult to find people who value the bare truth and even old fashioned morals.

Hence we see that a dying away of traditional churches is taking place, and a somewhat rise and fall of new age church revivals is happening as attendances surge to and fro with new worshippers being baptised and older ones leaving as the novelty wears off. Such worship is solidly pushed via pamphlet drops and promoted on early morning TV shows.

Fortunately such schools of gospel enterprise are coming to an end. All religious fads eventually die out by virtue of the momentum of truth that may be slow but is persistently revealing the falsehoods that misguide the public. The New Testament predicts this gradual decline and uses metaphor to disclose it to those who can understand the sign of the times.

The little book that speaks of such things is not a spiritual book. The book is about spiritual things but in itself is not spiritual. Revealing the truth is academic and secular. It remains truthfully and brutally objective in order to express sincere lessons on what actually exists and not on what can be imagined.

By revealing the code that underwrites the Bible, the little book by nature fulfils many prophetic statements in the Bible. Both the Old and New Testaments record prophecies of the end times. Jesus Himself gave us signs to look out for in anticipation of the end times. It must be pointed out that the Bible always refers to the End Times as a REVEALING of truths that reassert that Jesus taught fact.

> Lu:12:2: **For there is nothing covered, that shall not be revealed**; neither hid, that shall not be known.

> Lu:17:30: Even thus shall it be in the day when the Son of man is **revealed**.

Jesus called Himself the 'Son of Man' in order to get across the notion that He was a visionary born of mankind first 'Son of Mankind' then only after this had been explained was he called the 'Son of God' because of the adoption of the Ideal of God as a Father figure.

> Joh:1:12: But as many as received him, to them gave he power **to become the sons of God**, even to them that believe on his name:

So the first lesson is to realise that God was an Ideal and always had been an Ideal even from Adam and Eve days.

This book will be revealing all the hidden things and scripture that has been covered up by religious and even spiritual code since the beginning of time.

> M'r:4:22: For there is nothing hid, **which shall not be manifested**; neither was any thing kept secret, but that it should come abroad.

It is the aim of this writing not to interpret the Bible but to outline the scripture passages to show the reader literary devices where the reader can interpret the passage for themselves. In order to do this the Biblical verse must be cited so that the reader can see that nothing has been altered.

Naturally there will always be people who will decry such work. This is especially referring to those who have the most to lose through any Biblical study. These of course are those under the biggest delusion of power just as it was in Jesus' day. The revealing of truthful things pertaining to the Bible always comes as a shock to fundamentalists and extremists. This reaction has been seen throughout history as scientists reveal new knowledge in astronomy and biology that expose false concepts held by worshippers and the church in general. We now know truthfully that the Earth is not flat; it is not the centre of the universe and that all creatures on Earth evolved over millions of years. We know that Adam and Eve do not represent the first homo-sapiens and that human evolution has taken millions of years to develop.

The behaviour of worshippers and also that of some churches can be predicted because their mindset being focused on god is opposed to all things of a secular nature. Science and knowledge generally is atheistic in nature. Therefore it often goes against long nourished dogma. So predictably there will be groups of people that will always bewail the expositions and prophecies of such a book as this. Incredibly their very reactions can be and has been predicted and it even forms the basis of knowing that the end time is truly at hand. In this book a number of hidden truths which will give the reader a new understanding of the New Testament and more to the point a new appreciation for the life of Jesus Christ will be revealed.

Truthfulness is key to this understanding.

> Re:10:7: But in the days of the voice of the seventh angel (messenger), when he shall begin to sound, **the mystery of God should be finished**, as he hath declared to his servants the prophets.

The reader will see that verse is used to underscore the concepts written about. In this way these things can be revealed and the reader will readily see these associations themselves. However there will be many groups in the world that will abhor such a book and will proceed to condemn it vehemently. Nevertheless this is only one of the prophecies foretold of the end time and as there are many prophecies we will outline them as we explore the hidden things of the gospels. It is amazing that prophecies foretell the things in the book but these are not illumined in order to magnify anybody's reputation. The revealing of parable and prophecy is only done in the interest of discovering another possible meaning to ancient verse. In 2 Timothy 3:16 Paul writes that "All scripture is given by inspiration of God, and is profitable for doctrine, for reproof, for correction, for instruction in righteousness:" We also believe this and therefore write of the New Testament and of the life of Jesus Christ from a new point of view namely an Holy albeit secular standpoint wherein God is an Adopted Father Ideal. This Ideal is adopted in order that we can perfect our own behaviour toward one another and of course to the well-being of the planet and all eco systems. We adopt God as our Father and we become the adopted children of God. This new attitude of atheism (but with the adopted **Ideal** as a Father of our spirit and livelihood) is seen as a more perfect condition than any bigoted way as we were when we were under idolatry; when we only ever wanted spiritual gifts and flatteries.

With secularism we have found self-responsibility and have stopped wanting spiritual blessings and gifts. Therefore being less needy we have discovered what God is really all about through the teachings of Jesus Christ. Jesus is also seen for the first time as a real person; as a man with the same frailties as us all. Jesus is seen as an honest and truthful person with a pure heart and this makes His sacrifice all the more revered.

So it is time that the general public see this also. It is time that all these wonderful things were written down, before those who know them pass away into obscurity taking this knowledge with them. The mystery of God is a treasure that can only be revealed through such secular work. It is unfortunate that we must use the words like 'atheist' in places but there is no other word that will suffice to mean exactly what this word means. The fact is that god is only an 'Ideal' but a living IDEAL. This is what is meant when the prophet says 'And God said unto Moses, I AM THAT I AM: and he said, Thus shalt thou say unto the children of Israel, I AM hath sent me unto you. Ex:3:14:' It is also noted that a similar vague description of God is worded in Revelations; 'I am he that liveth, **and was dead**; and, behold, I am alive for evermore, Amen; and have the keys of hell and of death. Re:1:18:' God is an Ideal.

The word Amen is interesting, is said to mean '*so be it*' in Hebrew but remember that Moses was raised by Pharaoh as a High Priest, and at that time the Egyptians worshipped many gods the chief of whom was the oldest of all gods 'Amen' the '*Hidden One*'. The ending of prayer with the name of God "Amen" was the custom of the Egyptians and who is to say that this custom did not transfer to us with the Pentateuch. It should be pointed out that Amen was a self-created god. He created Himself and His name meaning 'Hidden One' or 'One that is hidden from gods and man' indicate that there was not a word that could describe his existence either.

According to Egyptian tradition he is the oldest of the gods and was called the "The Hidden One" the "Divine God" the "Self-Created", the "Maker of the Gods". The "Creator of Men", "He who stretched out the heavens", "who illuminated the Tuat (other world) with his eyes (the right eye meant the Sun or 'imagination' and the left eye meant the Moon or 'truth"). The form he existed in is not known but he created for himself, as a place to dwell, the great mass of Celestial Waters to which the Egyptians gave the name Nu (meaning the Subconscious). In these Celestial Waters he lived quite alone for a long time but then in a series of efforts of thought he created, through inspiration, the heavens and the celestial bodies in them, and the gods and the earth, and men and women, animals, birds and creeping things in his own mind. These thoughts or ideas of creation were translated into words by Thoth (God of Writing) who was known as the Scribe of the gods. With writing came the BOOK or Bible.

The history of Egyptian religion is not all that different from Judaism which is not surprising really since Judaism grew out of the former. Moses who was responsible for the establishment of Judaism grew up as Pharaoh's son and became a high priest in Egyptian religion. We should not be surprised therefore to discover similarities. The concept that the truth (atheism) is our spiritual nakedness which needs to be covered up in order to protect us from such emptiness.

This covering is called "The Grace of God". It is also interesting to note that the Egyptian god AMEN, (The Hidden One) is still impossible to describe today. Moses called Him "I AM THAT I AM" and Revelations says "I am he that liveth, **and was dead**; and, behold, I am alive for evermore". We might think of an IDEAL as only a CONCEPT of the mind and doesn't exist in the real world, but everything about Jesus and His religion is about the mind and concepts. The Baptism is a Concept which develops into a full Conception. Everything that is about God is a Concept of the Mind. All the teachings of Jesus are for the improvement of individual people so that society in general can be improved. All this is a concept of the mind. Life and the way we interpret the world around us, is all only a concept of the mind. Is it too difficult to believe that God is also a concept of the mind?

If God is only a Concept of the mind then how can we be saved?

Jesus informs us that religion is a concept that all societies invent according to their own needs. If we know and understand this **we are saved** from the MISCONCEPTION that gods are real people with extraordinary powers to grant our every wish. If we believe that gods are real people we fall into the trap called IDOLATRY. Worshipping god is a delusion. Delusions deceive the mind and corrupt all thought processes so that the person under the delusion is unable to make any reasonable decision. A deluded person certainly cannot tell right from wrong or fact from fiction. Some people devalue themselves by calling themselves sinners and are then oppressed by the nightmare of sin. Everything is seen as a sin. Such people are therefore burdened with guilt which then leads them into all the horrible aspects of unhealthy mental dilemmas.

Jesus freed us from such a life when He forgave all sin.

> Lu:5:23: Whether is easier, to say, Thy sins be forgiven thee; or to say, Rise up and walk?

> Lu:5:24: But that ye may know that **the Son of man hath power upon earth to forgive sins,** (he said unto the sick of the palsy,) I say unto thee, Arise, and take up thy couch, and go into thine house.

He confessed that there was no such thing as god. He said that God was a concept.

> "**Neither shall they say, Lo here! or, lo there! for, behold, the kingdom of God is within you.** Lu:17:21".

> "**But as many as received him, to them gave he power to become the sons of God, even to them that believe on his name:** Joh:1:12:"

> "**Jesus answered them, Is it not written in your law, I said, Ye are gods?**" Joh:10:34:

> **"No man hath seen God at any time; the only begotten Son, which is in the bosom of the Father, he hath declared him**. Joh:1:18."

So if god is only a concept or an ideal then what is sin? Sin does not exist either. It has all been forgiven by Jesus and hence has no more influence on us. Sin is only a concept which Jesus showed to be unworthy of our time, our thoughts and our conscience. No animal on earth sins. Animals behave according to the rules of the wild, kill or be killed, eat or be eaten. Humanity is no different. Behaviour is just behaviour, there is no sin. Evolution is blind and does not sin. Humanity however has the power to lift itself above the wild and become humane. This is the premise of our religion that we can be better humans than we have been in the past.

To be a sinner one must first believe in sin. If one does not believe in sin there is no way that such a one can be a sinner. Jesus could never be convinced of sin.

> Joh:8:46: **Which of you convinceth me of sin**? And if I say the truth, why do ye not believe me?

Those who don't think of themselves as sinners are not sinners. You are what you believe.

CONCEPT TWO

THE SPIRIT OF NUMBERS

In order to understand the hidden meaning of the Bible we need to know the hidden meaning of names and also of numbers. Name meanings can usually be found in a good concordance but number meanings are a little more complex. A clue for discovering the meanings behind biblical numerology can be found by examining the Hebrew counting words themselves. Without belittling their origins we will attempt to present a very simplified breakdown of their role. Each number is given an alphabetical letter as a name which has its own special meaning;

One for example is *Aleph* which means ox. The ox is a beast of burden and is hitched to a yoke in order to plough the field. This represents a laborer in 'sowing the seed of God' e.g. perhaps a missionary.

Two is *Beth* which means *House*. This word appears in many places including place names such as Bethel (House of God) but with regard to numerology its inference is a place where people and family struggle together. Its emphasis is on the family and partnerships.

Three is *Gimel* which means *Camel*. This is probably one of the most important numbers of all signifying the absolute truth i.e. the atheistic and heretical knowledge that God is an ideal. The reason it means Camel is because Camels being the 'Ship of the Desert' are able to go without water. Water represents the Spirit of Life. To be without this spirit then is to be as the dry ground and hence atheistic. **THREE is also the absolute Truth** explained by darkness and the colour Black.

In exodus;

> Ex:20:21: And the people stood afar off, and Moses drew near unto the thick darkness where God was.

> *Ex:10:22: And the LORD said unto Moses, Stretch out thine hand toward heaven, that there may be **darkness** over the land of Egypt, **even darkness which may be felt.** Ex:10:21:*

> *And Moses stretched forth his hand toward heaven; and there was **a thick darkness** in all the land of Egypt **three** (truth) days:*

In Acts we see an association which combine three with darkness;

> *Act:9: And he was **three days without sight**, (i.e. in darkness) and neither did eat nor drink.*

In Jonah the same insinuation applies;

> *Now the LORD had prepared a great fish to swallow up Jonah. And Jonah was in the belly of the fish **three** (darkness) days and **three** (darkness) nights. (Out of sight from God, i.e. without God) Jon:1:17:*

In Matthew there is a reference to the above;

> *For as Jonas was **three** (darkness) days and **three** (darkness) nights in the whale's belly; so shall the Son of man be **three** (darkness) days and **three** (darkness) nights in the heart of the earth (in darkness). M't:12:40:*

In Revelations

> *And when he had opened the **third** seal, I heard the third beast say, Come and see. And I beheld, and lo **a black** horse; and he that sat on him had a pair of balances in his hand. Re:6:5:*

Four is *Dalet* which means *Door,* This number represents Teaching or Preaching the word of God. More precisely Door signifies *'seed for the field';* just as a door is an opening for opportunity so too is teaching or sowing a field.

Five is *He* which means *Window* and in some places it means *Armed*. The significant thing about this number is a bit obscure. One would think that a window would signify view or light which it does but the tricky ancients also saw the window as a place for a curtain. Therefore the meaning of five stands for the **curtain** or **veil** or **covering**. It represents therefore, qualities such as mercy or the grace of God.

Six *is Vau whose* meaning is *Nail*. This is a very interesting number. It represents man under sin or more accurately *'laborers under the veil'*. It signifies IDOLATRY and delusion and therefore the biggest threat to the Truth that there is. The concept *of Nail* as a meaning shows how a delusion can 'hold fast' to a person's belief system.

Seven is called *Lain* which means a *Sword*. This is the Sword of God or what we have come to know as the WORD *of* GOD. Just put the letter 'S' in front of 'Word' and you have 'SWord'. The *sword* of God is a two edged sword, having one edge in truth and the other in deception. It is therefore very powerful for it can change sides at a whim depending on who wields it.

> *Re:2:16: Repent; or else I will come unto thee quickly, and will fight against them with the **sword of my mouth**.*

Eight is *Cheth* which is a *Fence*. This number is one for protection and its meaning is for RIGHTEOUSNESS. It is interesting to note that the ritual of circumcision was carried out on the **eighth** day of life. The concept of *'cutting off* the foreskin, i.e. that which **covers** the reproductive organ where the *seed* is produced signifies how the *'seed of truth'* (atheistic knowledge) has no covering and hence *'cuts us off'* from committing idolatry. If our seed is righteous then our fruit also will he righteous. To be circumcised therefore indicates an associate to the Truth of God. Also for this reason monks shave their heads to show that they too have no covering for the truth that they know. Hair is always seen as a covering Remember Samson's strength lay in his hair the covering of his truth.

Nine is *Teth* which means *Serpent*. No marks for guessing this one which signifies the **search for truth**. The reference you will find in the Bible will more than likely point to the hour of prayer which is the Ninth hour, the truth hour.

> *Ac:3:1: Now Peter and John went up together into the temple at the hour of prayer, being the **ninth** hour.*

CONCEPT THREE

ADAM AND EVE

Let's begin by looking at the various literary devices throughout the Bible that are used in order to disguise the truth behind the parables and stories. Perhaps the most talked about example of all Biblical stories is the creation of mankind; Adam and Eve. This story has been cited as the beginning of the evolution of humans on earth in contrast and opposition to Charles Darwin's famous theory of Evolution. Bible proponents say that God created Adam and Eve exactly as it is stated in Genesis and further to this they say that this creation took place only 4000 years ago. The truth is that science has evidence of fossils that date back millions of years and history that can show that people began to evolve some 4 million years ago and that by 100,000 years ago were exactly like we are today. There is a mountain of evidence supporting this knowledge.

The story of the creation of Adam in the Bible seems short and uncomplicated but this is in fact a ruse.

> Ge:2:5: And every plant of the field before it was in the earth, and every herb of the field before it grew: for the LORD God had not caused it to rain upon the earth, and there was not a man to till the ground.

> *Ge:2:6: **But there went up a mist from the earth, and watered the whole face of the ground.***
>
> *Ge:2:7: **And the LORD God formed man of the dust of the ground, and breathed into his nostrils the breath of life; and man became a living soul***.

The story depends on one major insight; the reference to the word '**ground**'. The use of this word is not just convenient reporting, but instead a whole world of interpretation depends on its exact meaning. Jesus makes it clear what this reference is all about. The parable that reveals these insights is one of the first parables that Jesus taught us. It is no coincidence that Jesus wanted only His disciples to know the meaning. He says He would tell them the meaning but not tell the general public. This is because the true meaning was sensitive information, not to mention that He could have been put to death for heresy, by the utterance.

Now although it is verbose, it is necessary to reprint the exact verses from the King James Bible New Testament, so that the reader can readily see that nothing has been taken out of context. The parable of the sower is repeated in three of the Gospels. Here they are verbatim.

Matthew's account: Matthew begins with describing that Jesus would not tell the general public the secret locked up in the parable. This is important but sensitive information given only to the disciples.

> *M't:13:10: And the disciples came, and said unto him, Why speakest thou unto them in parables?*
>
> *M't:13:11: He answered and said unto them, **Because it is given unto you to know the mysteries of the kingdom of heaven, but to them it is not given***.

After the parable He gives us the meaning (the same meaning He said He would not give to the public). So we are left wondering what on earth He is really holding back. We will come to that soon but first must look at all the evidence. If you are familiar with these verses then please skip over them.

M't:13:36: Then Jesus sent the multitude away, and went into the house: and his disciples came unto him, saying, Declare unto us the parable of the tares of the field.

M't:13:37: **He answered and said unto them, He that soweth the good seed is the Son of man;**

M't:13:38: **The field is the world; the good seed are the children of the kingdom; but the tares are the children of the wicked one;**

M't:13:39: **The enemy that sowed them is the devil; the harvest is the end of the world; and the reapers are the angels.**

M't:13:40: As therefore the tares are gathered and burned in the fire; so shall it be in the end of this world.

Now Mark's account:

M'r:4:3: Hearken; Behold, there went out a sower to sow:

M'r:4:4: And it came to pass, as he sowed, some fell by the way side, and the fowls of the air came and devoured it up.

M'r:4:5: And some fell on stony ground, where it had not much earth; and immediately it sprang up, because it had no depth of earth:

M'r:4:6: But when the sun was up, it was scorched; and because it had no root, it withered away.

M'r:4:7: And some fell among thorns, and the thorns grew up, and choked it, and it yielded no fruit.

M'r:4:8: And other fell on good ground, and did yield fruit that sprang up and increased; and brought forth, some thirty, and some sixty, and some an hundred.

M'r:4:9: And he said unto them, He that hath ears to hear, let him hear.

M'r:4:10: And when he was alone, they that were about him with the twelve asked of him the parable.

M'r:4:11: And he said unto them, **Unto you it is given to know the mystery of the kingdom of God: but unto them that are without, all these things are done in parables***:*

M'r:4:12: That seeing they may see, and not perceive; and hearing they may hear, and not understand; lest at any time they should be converted, and their sins should be forgiven them.

M'r:4:13: And he said unto them, Know ye not this parable? and how then will ye know all parables?

M'r:4:14: The sower **soweth the word***.*

M'r:4:15: **And these are they by the way side, where the word is sown***; but when they have heard, Satan cometh immediately, and taketh away the word that was sown in their hearts.*

M'r:4:16: And these are they likewise which are sown on stony ground; who, when they have heard the word, immediately receive it with gladness;

M'r:4:17: And have no root in themselves, and so endure but for a time: afterward, when affliction or persecution ariseth for the word's sake, immediately they are offended.

M'r:4:18: And these are they which are sown among thorns; such as hear the word,

M'r:4:19: And the cares of this world, and the deceitfulness of riches, and the lusts of other things entering in, choke the word, and it becometh unfruitful.

M'r:4:20: And these are they which are sown on good ground; such as hear the word, and receive it, and bring forth fruit, some thirtyfold, some sixty, and some an hundred.

M'r:4:21: And he said unto them, Is a candle brought to be put under a bushel, or under a bed? and not to be set on a candlestick?

M'r:4:22: For there is nothing hid, which shall not be manifested; neither was any thing kept secret, but that it should come abroad.

M'r:4:23: If any man have ears to hear, let him hear.

Now Luke's account:

Lu:8:5: A sower went out to sow his seed: and as he sowed, some fell by the way side; and it was trodden down, and the fowls of the air devoured it.

Lu:8:6: And some fell upon a rock; and as soon as it was sprung up, it withered away, because it lacked moisture.

Lu:8:7: And some fell among thorns; and the thorns sprang up with it, and choked it.

Lu:8:8: And other fell on good ground, and sprang up, and bare fruit an hundredfold. And when he had said these things, he cried, He that hath ears to hear, let him hear.

Lu:8:9: And his disciples asked him, saying, What might this parable be?

*Lu:8:10: And he said, **Unto you it is given to know the mysteries of the kingdom of God: but to others in parables; that seeing they might not see, and hearing they might not understand.***

*Lu:8:11: Now the parable is this: **The seed is the word of God.***

*Lu:8:12: Those by the way side are they that hear; then cometh the devil, and taketh away the **word out of their hearts**, lest they should believe and be saved.*

Lu:8:13: They on the rock are they, which, when they hear, receive the word with joy; and these have no root, which for a while believe, and in time of temptation fall away.

Lu:8:14: And that which fell among thorns are they, which, when they have heard, go forth, and are choked with cares and riches and pleasures of this life, and bring no fruit to perfection.

*Lu:8:15: **But that on the good ground are they, which in an honest and good heart, having heard the word, keep it, and bring forth fruit with patience**.*

Lu:8:16: No man, when he hath lighted a candle, covereth it with a vessel, or putteth it under a bed; but setteth it on a candlestick, that they which enter in may see the light.

Lu:8:17: For nothing is secret, that shall not be made manifest; neither any thing hid, that shall not be known and come abroad.

The meaning of the parable as Jesus explains it is this. The sower is the Son of Man (Jesus); the seed is the Word of God (The Bible); the field are the people in whose hearts the word is sown (The Population of the world otherwise known as the field of God which is the **ground** wherein the seed is sown).

It is beautiful in its simplicity. God's FIELD or GROUND is MANKIND in whose hearts the WORD of GOD is sown by the Son of Man. This is very easy to understand. Now we must apply it to Adam. God's field or ground as mankind.

In Corinthians there is a beautiful statement that provides insight as to what Adam really is.

1Co:15:45: And so it is written, The first man Adam was made a living soul; the last Adam was made a quickening spirit.

If the last Adam was Christianity as Paul indicates then the first Adam must be the Hebrews. In other words the first Adam was not one person but instead was a whole society of Hebrews just as the last Adam is not one Christian but indeed is a whole society of Christians.

So now we are able to look at ADAM and his creation in a fresh new light.

> *LORD God had not caused it to rain upon the earth* **(Evangelising)**, *and there was not a man to till the ground* **(sow the word in Gods Field or mankind)**.

> *Ge:2:6: But there went up a mist from the earth, and watered the whole face of the ground* **(evangelising to mankind)**.

> *Ge:2:7: And the LORD God formed man of the* **dust of the ground (the population where the Word was sown)**, *and breathed into his nostrils* **the breath of life**; *and* **man became a living soul**.

The Lord God formed MAN from the **dust** of the GROUND (god's field). This is saying that God's ground is mankind (learned above) and MAN (e.g. ADAM which means 'of the ground') was formed or taken from the dust (or a small portion) of that population. This was achieved by a "watering" of the ground. A "watering" refers to teaching or spreading the word of God throughout mankind. A BAPTISM or Evangelising would be considered such a "watering". Therefore ADAM was not one man but was in fact a **SOCIETY** separated from the main population of mankind by this Baptism or by holding a new belief in God. This society consisted of both **male and female** persons and this explains why in chapter one of Genesis the creation of man is given both genders.

> "*Ge:1:27: So God created* **man** *in his own image, in the image of God created he him;* **male and female created he them**."

Jesus tells us through the parable of the sower that Gods field is mankind. It is this field or mankind that Adam was made from by a 'watering' or baptism or evangelising. Adam constitutes the first group of Hebrews or the beginning of Israel, male and female.

Corinthians is plainly stating that the First Adam (who were Hebrews) were made a **living soul** as it states in Genesis and that the Second Adam (who were Christians) were made a quickening spirit. If these two **Adam's** are referring to a populace rather than a single person, what then are they referring to?

> *Ge:5:1: This is the book of the generations of Adam. In the day that God created man, in the likeness of God made he him;*
>
> *Ge:5:2: **Male and female created he them; and blessed them, and called their name Adam, in the day when they were created**.*

Even in this statement above from Genesis the plural form was used to describe Adam as male and female (and called **their** name Adam) so that we know without mistake that <u>Adam is not one singular man but is instead a community</u>, male and female, called Hebrews. The creation of Eve (not a singular person either but instead the "mother of all Living") is therefore quite different from that which is taught by traditional schools of theology. Eve is not a singular woman.

This creation of Adam is mentioned in chapter one of Genesis long before any mention of EVE. In fact the creation of Eve has to wait until the naming of all the creatures of the earth by Adam is complete, only then does God see fit to give man a 'help meet'.

The creation of EVE is also not what a shallow reader expects it to be. In fact EVE is not a physical woman at all. It stands to reason that if ADAM is a **society** comprising both male and female genders, then EVE must be something altogether different and so it is.

First let us look at the exact scripture.

> *Ge:2:21: And the LORD God caused a deep sleep to fall upon Adam and he slept: and he took one of his ribs, and closed up the **flesh** instead thereof;*

Ge:2:22: And the rib, which the LORD God had taken from man, made he a woman, and brought her unto the man.

*Ge:2:23: And Adam said, **This is now bone of my bones, and flesh of my flesh: she shall be called Woman, because she was taken out of Man**.*

*Ge:2:24: Therefore shall a man leave his father and his mother, and shall cleave unto his wife: and **they shall be one flesh**.*

Ge:2:25: And they were both naked, the man and his wife, and were not ashamed.

The verse states that God took one of Adam's RIBS in order to make EVE. The word 'RIB' is actually 'TSELA' in the original Hebrew and Tsela for example according to Young's Concordance can mean anything from Tsel = defence, shade, shadow to Tsela = beam, board, chamber, corner, halting, leaf, plank, rib, side, side chamber, another, one and adversity.

So to make woman; (wo-man means 'Taken out of man'); from Adam's rib (Tsela) That which covers the heart but it could be any of the above meanings. If we are paraphrasing ancient writings it would not be unreasonable to assume that **'leaf'** is just as possible a meaning as rib, which the ancients had in mind, because at least this would point to Adams **'covering'** or 'sacred apron', for his spiritual nakedness. Nevertheless the rib is that part which is covering the heart. In other words their scripture, doctrine or belief system is what was taken 'out of man'; remember that we are not talking about a physical woman, (physical women were created as part of Adam). What was taken "Out of Man"; out of that society called Adam, were their beliefs or more precisely their Doctrine. This is reinforced by the statement *'and closed up the **flesh** instead thereof'* which is an exact reference to their doctrine. Jesus said;

Joh:1:14: And the **Word was made flesh**, and dwelt among us, (and we beheld his glory, the glory as of the only begotten of the Father,) full of grace and truth.

33

The WORD of course is doctrine and it was made flesh which means that the metaphor of flesh was applied to represent doctrine. Early doctrine was written on Parchment which is goats hide or 'flesh' so the two became synonymous. Jesus also said that He was the Flesh or doctrine of God.

> Joh:6:51: I am the living bread which came down from heaven: if any man eat of this bread, he shall live for ever: and **the bread that I will give is my flesh**, which I will give for the life of the world.

So we see that **bread is flesh is doctrine**. When Eve was made from Adams rib, God said he closed up **the flesh** instead thereof meaning that doctrine had been utilised in the making of Eve. Further to this the scriptures record that Adam and Eve then became one flesh!

> Ge:2:23: And Adam said, This is now bone of my bones, and **flesh of my flesh**: she shall be called **Woman, because she was taken out of Man**.

> Ge:2:24: Therefore shall a man leave his father and his mother, and shall cleave unto his wife: and they shall be **one flesh**.

Adam was the society of Hebrews and Eve was His wife who was in fact his flesh or doctrine. In other words Eve was Adam's religion. Hebrew society created religion.

Every society on Earth has created its own religion. This is a truth that only the Bible will confess. Every tribe, every society, every civilisation, has invented their own version of God, Gods, Spirits, witchcrafts, witchdoctors, Shamans and Gurus as it pleased them. In the Middle-East Baal was a favourite. Baal simply means 'Lord' so this religion caused a great deal of confusion because all religions at the time called God 'Lord'. In fact the Tower of Babel simply means the 'Gateway to the Lord' or 'Gate of God' and Babylon where the Jews were imprisoned for so long, is interpreted to mean 'Gate of Bel' or 'Gate of the Lord'. We see by these names and name meanings that there remain some inconsistencies when it comes to proper meaning of scripture.

When the Hebrews went from an oral tradition to a written tradition they created something new. The first writing allowed for these beliefs to be coded in tablet form for the first time in history. The knowledge on how the oral tradition of the Hebrews was developed into a Holy and awe-inspiring written form is insightful research. Such traditions demonstrate that the magical written form of the stories made them rigid and unchangeable. Unlike the flexibility of an oral tradition, the wording of written stories could not be changed by the storyteller. Not a single letter could be changed. The hard copy of the written form remained exactly the same and could be copied by others exactly the same verbatim. Therefore beliefs or doctrine that made the society of Adam (Hebrews) different from the rest of the population came about as the beginning of a Holy Book or Holy Record.

The general uneducated public saw this 'written' form as a magical thing that those few special people of God (the educated priests) could look at and know what was said by somebody else from deep in past history. Magic of this kind reinforced the priests position and in the case of Israel the Levites who were entrusted with the mystery of God.

It has always been intriguing that the city Byblos also known as Gerbil, or in ancient Greek Byblos or Biblon which means 'Book' from which the Bible takes its name is in fact the oldest known continuously inhabited city in the world. It dates back at least 8000 years even before writing was invented and was a chief port on the Mediterranean Sea. From this Greek word we have the title to our Holy word the Bible. The Bible or 'Book' was and still is a collection of documents written by a number of authors who were enlightened into the knowledge of god. These people were often considered to be prophets because of their unique understanding of scripture. The Bible writers all understood a certain code that scripture conforms to. This metaphorical code can be seen in all the books of the Bible. There are some recent new discoveries of ancient texts such as the 'Dead Sea Scrolls' and other testaments and gospels recorded at the time of Christ. Most of these newly discovered gospels do not seem to conform to the same code easily found in both Old and New Testaments. The fact that the Bible was ratified at the request of Emperor Constantine at the

Council of Nicea in 320 A.D. and was sanctioned by a group of ordinary men without due training or insight into Biblical code amazes us who know of such things. How did they get it right is the obvious question. Obviously something guided their hand, because the Bible as it stands (at least the Approved King James Version) seems to be in harmony with this invisible code the same code that Jesus described as the Veil of Heaven.

The point of all this is that ancient writers understood this code. This is the same code that the Levites used in all their communication. It is the same code that all the prophets used. Moses also uses this code in the Pentateuch, the first five books of the Old Testament which he is accredited with writing. Finally John the Baptist knew this code as did Jesus who then taught it to the disciples.

> M'r:4:11: And he said unto them, **Unto you it is given to know the mystery of the kingdom of God**: but unto them that are without, all these things are done in parables:

Returning to Adam; he was the first SOCIETY of Hebrews and these Hebrews had developed the written form of their Holy Records. Studies show that the written language of Ur existed around Abraham's time and at least some of the writings of Job, dated to the Patriarchal period (2100-1800 B.C.) which give credence to Moses as author of the Torah or Pentateuch. Moses was raised by Pharaoh and taught in linguistics of not only Egyptian but also surrounding cultures. This knowledge provides evidence that at some time in the ancient past the Hebrew Doctrine was written down and became fast or unchangeable. Such is the beginning of dogma. Most of the Hebrew population were illiterate at that time and were absolutely amazed by writing. They thought it to be magical, and the few who could write, namely the educated few Priests used this power to impress their religious control over them all the more.

So we see and understand how the Doctrine of the Hebrews was recorded in writing for the first time. This was called EVE (Foundation of Life). Spiritually EVE means 'the Foundation of Life' just as it says in the verse

*Ge:3:20: And Adam called his wife's name Eve; **because she was the mother of all living.***

Eve therefore was the first Bible of the Hebrews the Torah and as such she was 'taken out of man'. The fact that She was 'Taken Out of Man' tells us that Eve (the Religion) was invented by the Hebrew society and by definition God also was invented by the same process. God therefore became known as the "Creature' of the creation story and not Adam.

Ro:1:25: Who changed the truth of God into a lie, and **worshipped and served the creature more than the Creator**, who is blessed for ever. Amen.

Eve was also viewed as 'Foundation of Life'. This is not too different from Jesus calling Himself the' 'foundation of Life'.

Joh:14:6: Jesus saith unto him, **I am the way, the truth, and the life**: no man cometh unto the Father, but by me.

She also was seen as 'wife' of mankind or 'wife of Adam' just as Christians are to be seen as 'wife' of Jesus.

Re:19:7: Let us be glad and rejoice, and give honour to him: **for the marriage of the Lamb is come**, and **his wife hath made herself ready.**

So the information we glean from this story is this; Woman means 'out of man' Adam means 'of the ground' (God's ground or population) Eve means 'Foundation of Life'. Eve was made from Adam's (Hebrew society) Rib, (covering of the heart). This Rib (covering) refers to the Hebrews doctrine. Eve therefore is the doctrine which is the 'Foundation of Life' and 'wife' for the Hebrews; in other words their Bible known as their 'Flesh' the Torah.

Joh:6:53: Then Jesus said unto them, Verily, verily, I say unto you, **Except ye eat the flesh of the Son of man**, and drink his blood, ye have no life in you.

When Eve was made, the scripture says they were both naked. "***They were both naked*** *the man and his wife but were not ashamed*". This is also an important statement hinting that this new society (The Hebrews) knew the **truth** about the non-existence of God. To be naked before the Lord is to be atheist i.e. not believing that there is a God at all. There are no such things as gods. This truth makes us spiritually naked. Therefore the very first society of Hebrews knew this truth. This is the nakedness of Adam and Eve after they ate of the tree of knowledge of good and evil (the truth).

> Ge:3:10: And he said, I heard thy voice in the garden, and I was afraid, **because I was naked**; and I hid myself.

> Ge:3:11: And he said, Who told thee that thou wast naked? **Hast thou eaten of the tree**, whereof I commanded thee that thou shouldest not eat?

This is also the same nakedness of Noah.

> *Ge:9:20: And Noah began to be an husbandman, and he planted a vineyard:*

> *Ge:9:21:* ***And he drank of the wine, and was drunken; and he was uncovered within his tent.***

> *Ge:9:22: And Ham, the father of Canaan,* ***saw the nakedness of his father***, *and told his two brethren without.*

This story of Noah makes no sense at all unless we understand the nature of being 'naked'. It simply refers to being without a belief (atheist or agnostic) or to be in a state of expounding ones beliefs. In the story, Noah was drunk and probably mouthing off his naked viewpoints or a naked truth.

And the nakedness of Moses; this happened immediately after Moses was given the Ten Commandments. The Commandments explain social rules which the Hebrews were expected to live by. These were considered to be Laws that were not part of worship methods but were bare laws. It is noteworthy to point out that Moses stood in the "**thick darkness where**

God was" which also hints at an empty or naked belief. In verse 23 and 24 the allusion to idolatry is undeniable.

> *Ex:20:20: And Moses said unto the people, Fear not: for God is come to prove you, and that his fear may be before your faces, **that ye sin not**.*

> *Ex:20:21: And the people stood afar off, and Moses drew near unto **the thick darkness where God was.***

> *Ex:20:22: And the LORD said unto Moses, Thus thou shalt say unto the children of Israel, Ye have seen that I have talked with you from heaven.*

> *Ex:20:23: Ye shall not make with me **gods of silver**, neither shall ye make unto you **gods of gold**.*

> *Ex:20:24: An altar of earth thou shalt make unto me, and shalt sacrifice thereon thy burnt offerings, and thy peace offerings, thy sheep, and thine oxen: in all places where I record my name I will come unto thee, and I will bless thee.*

> *Ex:20:25: And if thou wilt make me an altar of stone, thou shalt not build it of hewn stone: for if thou lift up thy tool upon it, thou hast polluted it.*

> *Ex:20:26: Neither shalt thou go up by steps unto mine altar, **that thy nakedness be not discovered thereon**.*

To say that their Nakedness shall not been seen when they are at the Altar, refers to their worship as something that covers their spiritual nakedness.

And also the nakedness of Job; The Book of Job is a long winded story about how Job was tested by God and Satan. In all of the afflictions that God sent upon him he never turns against God. The real story is that Job has the insight to know that God does not actually exist and therefore cannot be blamed for any of the torments that befall him. Unless this code is known about the book of Job, reading the whole 42 chapters makes little sense.

Job's ability to not deny God is the same strength of character and courage shown by the early Christians as they were tortured or thrown to the lions. Once somebody knows the truth "that there are no such things as gods" then it is impossible to return to the former state of gullible worship. This is why there is so much emphasis placed on idolatry throughout the Bible – the worship of gods – all gods – any gods – none of which exist. All god worship is idolatry and a pollution of thought.

> *Job:1:21:* ***And said, Naked came I out of my mother's womb,*** ***and naked shall I return thither:*** *the LORD gave, and the LORD hath taken away; blessed be the name of the LORD.*

And the nakedness of Peter the disciple; In this story in John 21 Peter the disciple goes fishing *in the nude* in the company of Thomas, Nathanael, John and a couple of others. While he is fishing in the nude John says to him "here is the Lord" at which time Peter wraps his fishers coat around himself and then casts himself into the sea because he was naked. The story is pointless and ridiculous unless it was making a decisive point regarding nakedness. Nakedness is to be atheistic (a pure state of mind) but this atheistic state of mind, needs to be covered and camouflaged (fishers coat), so that less informed people, do not become confused or think that you are an hypocrite.

> *Joh:21:7: Therefore that disciple whom Jesus loved saith unto Peter, It is the Lord. Now when Simon Peter heard that it was the Lord,* ***he girt his fisher's coat unto him, (for he was naked,) and did cast himself into the sea.***

There are many other prophets and people said to be naked, culminating in Revelations, telling us that we are also naked, but are not aware of it. This verse means we are not aware that there are no such things as gods.

> *Re:3:17: Because thou sayest, I am rich, and increased with goods, and have need of nothing; and knowest not that thou art wretched, and miserable, and poor, and blind,* ***and naked****:*

Nakedness is spiritual emptiness. To be without god or in fact to be without all spiritual concepts is to be spiritually naked. To believe in some spiritual concept is to clothe your mind with beliefs. People do this as some form of emotional protection against spiritual emptiness, but to do it invites disappointment or even fear at some point in the future, when you are confronted with the ultimate truth that we are all naked whether we admit to it or not.

> *Job:1:21:* **And said, Naked came I out of my mother's womb, and naked shall I return thither:** *the LORD gave, and the LORD hath taken away; blessed be the name of the LORD.*

Job is saying that a newborn baby is not indoctrinated with belief systems and so is naked. It depends on where in the world a person is born as to what belief system they are indoctrinated into. We Christians have many denominations all variations of a general theme that says that Jesus is a god – Son of a God. Of course, if this was so then Jesus would not have feared anything or any treatment by mere mortal men. If He knew He was a God with real godly powers over miraculous things then crucifixion would be absolutely meaningless to Him. He would therefore be totally unaware of the frailty of mortality. This is the dilemma faced by religious leaders who attempt to account for Jesus' humanness. The truth is that Jesus was not a god He was a person just like any other person on earth. He was just a man like any other man. He called Himself the Son of Mankind long before the title of Son of God (God is always *adopted as a Father figure* as a preferred belief system therefore by adoption we all are sons or daughters of God). As the Son of Mankind he saw himself as a prophet or a visionary whose ancestors were all the generations that went before him. In other words he saw himself as a visionary and the son of mankind. He knew the truth that there are no such things as gods, and he knew that he had no powers of magic or miracles. This is why He said that no signs shall be given, mainly because miraculous signs only showed how corrupted a person's mind could really get. A pure mind knows that miracles don't happen and can't be worked. Magic does not exist. Therefore Jesus was as fearful of pain and crucifixion as any man alive. He was as powerless as any man. He was as vulnerable as any man. He was just a man who sought to know the truth.

Re:16:15: Behold, **I come as a thief**. Blessed is he that watcheth, and **keepeth his garments, lest he walk naked**, and they see his shame.

Returning to Eve the 'Foundation of Life" that which was 'taken out of man' is our belief system. More precisely Eve represents the Bible actually the Old Testament or Pentateuch itself. She is the wife and the belief system of Adam. She is Doctrine. She is the written form of the word of God. She is the Bride of Adam just as Christianity is the Bride of Jesus. Jesus likened Himself to Eve in this way.

*Joh:14:6: Jesus saith unto him, **I am the way, the truth, and the life: no man cometh unto the Father, but by me.***

He sees Himself as the foundation of truthfulness within the religion but Woman (that which was taken out of man e.g. Doctrine) is also depicted in Revelations as a corrupt woman (out of man or religion).

*Re:12:1: And there appeared a great wonder in heaven; a **woman(out of man)** clothed with the sun, and the moon under her feet, and upon her head a crown of twelve stars:*

This woman (out of man or religious doctrine) in Revelations is a far cry from the perfect state of Jesus' realm. She represents the corruption of doctrine that has come about by worshippers adopting the vain belief that a god actually exists; in other words idolatry, and all the false beliefs that follow, such as believing in miracles and the denying of truth, knowledge and science. Therefore 'Woman' is seen in two lights; the Mother of all and the foundation of faith as well as the Mother of all Idolatry. This twofold nature of 'Woman' (Out of Man or religion) is easily seen. One side is the gentle Mother figure, the nurturing and feeding and protecting blessed mother religion who gives birth via the baptism. The other aspect is the mother of idolatry wherein her doctrine is so corrupt that it corrupts the minds of those who fall into her nets and snares so that those who are baptised are swallowed up by her indoctrination.

In the story of the creation of Eve, it is said that Adam and Eve became one FLESH.

> *Ge:2:24: Therefore shall a man leave his father and his mother, and shall cleave unto his wife: and they **shall be one flesh**.*

The term 'Flesh" is also explained by John the disciple in opening his testament;

> *Joh:1:14: And the **Word was made flesh**, and dwelt among us, (and we beheld his glory, the glory as of the only begotten of the Father,) full of grace and truth.*

He says it plainly "the word was made flesh" which simply means the "word of God" was made "flesh" (or scripture). In other words the New Testament was written down. The word of god was written down as truthfully as Jesus revealed it to the disciples. So we see in Adam and Eve that these two also became one flesh! This is to say that Adam (a society of Hebrews) became one Flesh (Doctrine) with the people through their newly created Bible or Holy Writings the Torah. Religious doctrine became the wife of humanity. God was invented just as religion was invented by society. God is the creature of creation.

> Ro:1:25: Who changed the truth of God into a lie, and worshipped and served the creature more than the Creator, who is blessed for ever. Amen.

Christianity has the same metaphor. Jesus said unless you eat my flesh and drink my blood ye have no life.

> Joh:6:51: I am the living bread which came down from heaven: if any man eat of this bread, he shall live for ever: and **the bread that I will give is my flesh**, which I will give for the life of the world.

> Joh:6:52: The Jews therefore strove among themselves, saying, How can this man give us his flesh to eat?

> Joh:6:53: Then Jesus said unto them, Verily, verily, I say unto you, **Except ye eat the flesh of the Son of man, and drink his blood, ye have no life in you.**

> Joh:6:54: Whoso eateth my flesh, and drinketh my blood, hath eternal life; and I will raise him up at the last day.

Of course Jesus was referring to His doctrine. We eat our 'Daily Bread' and digest its meaning. His doctrine is the flesh of the New Testament.

Although Jesus was known as the Son of God it is written that anybody can also be the Son or Daughter of God through the adoption of the principles of God. This of course is achieved via a public display or commitment such as the Baptism.

> *Joh:1:12: But as many as received him,* **to them gave he power to become the sons of God, even to them that believe on his name:**

> Ro:8:15: For ye have not received the spirit of bondage again to fear; but ye have **received the Spirit of adoption**, whereby we cry, Abba, Father.

The way to become a son of god was to believe in the truth (the truth is that gods do not exist). If you believe that gods exist then it follows that Satan also exists and Sin exists which makes people into sinners. Therefore the person begins to tie themself in knots with a host of imaginary restraints and condemnations. This can then become rampant and one might populate heaven with angels and cherubim's and Hell with all manner of gargoyles and beasts. Further to this people start having inanimate objects blessed as if that makes any difference to their working or blessing a boat improves the fisherman's catch. The whole gambit of false, ridiculous and unnecessary habits like eating fish on Friday or going without pork or some other kosher diet; all because of corruption in the way one thinks.

A secular viewpoint is far better and more pure to hold than the god-delusion because it enables the acceptance of knowledge and is not hindered by long held dogma. One is also not oppressed by food regulations either and is enabled to eat any desired foodstuff rather than being dictated to by a 5000 year old opinion that one should not eat any cloven footed animal or some similar dictate.

> 1Co:8:4: As concerning therefore the eating of those things that are offered in sacrifice unto idols, **we know that an idol is nothing in the world**, and that there is none other God but one.

> 1Co:8:5: For though there be that are called gods, whether in heaven or in earth, (as there be gods many, and lords many,)

> 1Co:8:6: But to us there is but one God, the Father, of whom are all things, and we in him; and one Lord Jesus Christ, by whom are all things, and we by him.

> 1Co:8:7: Howbeit there is not in every man that knowledge: for some with conscience of the idol unto this hour eat it as a thing offered unto an idol; and their conscience being weak is defiled.

> 1Co:8:8: **But meat commendeth us not to God: for neither, if we eat, are we the better; neither, if we eat not, are we the worse.**

> 1Co:8:9: But take heed lest by any means this liberty of yours become a stumblingblock to them that are weak.

To be whole, a person needs to know the truth. The realisation that there are no such things as gods is old news, yet the god delusion continues to hog-tie a good proportion of the population. The problem with this is that such people then force it onto others including their own children. This is called a secondary delusion when it happens because it is taught to others by the person who holds the primary delusion. The misguided clergy teach it to as many as they can, thus infecting the whole society with false knowledge. Some doctrines even go door to door spreading the delusion as far afield as they can. Others send missionaries to afar lands to witness to societies in distant countries. The truth is, there are no such things as gods.

> *Joh:4:23: But the hour cometh, and now is, when the true worshippers shall worship the **Father in spirit and in truth**: for the Father seeketh such to worship him.*

> *Joh:4:24: **God is a Spirit**: and they that worship him must worship him in **spirit and in truth**.*

Only by knowing this truth can a person truly be free to explore the knowledge of the universe. Only through this knowledge can people be deemed to be equal. As long as the god delusion remains, there will always be religious discrimination. Only the truth as Jesus Christ taught it, can free people of the conflict of sin and guilt and free people to eat as they please and free people from racist thoughts toward others belief systems. All this requires a certain purity of thought that is not possible while the mind is deluded.

> *Joh:8:32:* **And ye shall know the truth, and the truth shall make you free.**

> *Ti:1:15:* **Unto the pure all things are pure**: but unto them that are defiled and unbelieving is nothing pure; but even their mind and conscience is defiled.

The doctrine of Jesus was therefore written down and became known as the FLESH of Christ. It is also known as the BREAD of life. This was in fact the New Testament. Jesus says that His words were the bread of life and that His Flesh was doctrine. This is not the same doctrine of the Pharisees. Jesus was telling the population not to worship a plethora of gods. He also revealed that His idea of God was a personification of good behaviour that if adopted by society would benefit every individual. This is how God was seen to be real. It was in the sense that the culmination of society's benefits in helping and supporting each of its individuals; while the society was alive so too was God.

> *Joh:6:51:* **I am the living bread** *which came down from heaven: if any man eat of this bread, he shall live for ever: and the bread that* **I will give is my flesh**, *which I will give for the life of the world.*

So this is the Bible which we eat by way of reading and digesting the things it tells us. This is our "Daily Bread" or daily scripture to ponder on. Flesh and Bread are two words that basically mean the same thing and Jesus gives us the interpretation of these, as with all Biblical interpretation. No Biblical interpretation is correct unless it takes into account these metaphors. Unless a person knows the truth about god; that gods do not exist, then there is no way of knowing or understanding the lessons written in the Bible and all translations are meaningless.

So when it comes to 'Flesh' we see the use of this metaphor way back in the Old Testament with Adam and Eve Genesis 2:23; And Adam said, This is now bone of my bones, and flesh of my flesh: she shall be called Woman, because she was taken out of Man.

So Flesh is Doctrine and Adam was not one man but in fact was the first society of Hebrews therefore Adam's 'Flesh' was Adam's 'Doctrine' which of course was 'Taken Out Of Man' as we discovered earlier.

> *Ge:2:23: And Adam said, This is now bone of my bones, and flesh of my flesh: she shall be called Woman, because she was **taken out of Man**.*

Eve was Adams religion or 'Foundation of Life' just as Jesus was the 'Foundation of Life' for Christians.

> *Joh:14:6: Jesus saith unto him, **I am the way, the truth, and the life**: no man cometh unto the Father, but by me.*

But Jesus also said that God was a **Spirit**, but by this He meant that people should adopt the same enthusiasm of the Idea of a community effort to portray behaviours that are godlike rather than corrupt one's mind with imagined phantasms and ghosts and other supernatural things that don't exist.

> *Joh:4:24: God is a Spirit: and they that worship him must worship him in spirit **and in truth**.*

Jesus says god is a spirit but this word spirit does not imply that god is a ghost or any kind of creature or being. God is a spirit means that we should adopt the same spirit or enthusiasm in order to behave like a good person or good Christian. The term "spirit" in this sense is an agreement to behave the same way. It simply means to have the same outlook or temperament. There is nothing supernatural about it. Jesus goes on to say that we must worship god in spirit and in truth. This truth is the knowledge that gods do not exist in fact God was invented when Eve was created. Without accepting this knowledge and this honesty, one cannot have a clear mind.

> *2Tm:1:7: For God hath not given us* **the spirit of fear; but of power, and of love, and of a sound mind.**

If we believe that common delusion that gods exist, we reduce our own competency. We cannot be competent if we have a deluded mind. We cannot be taught anything of a truthful nature if we are deluded by dogma. We are also unable to accept new knowledge if our head is clouded. Look at the trouble stirred up over Darwin's theory of Evolution. When I say that knowledge is hampered by a delusion or misconception I mean it. All our 21st Century knowledge was hard won; not because of difficulties with nature but because of the misconception of the church in general. The scientific method which we rely on today to ensure that new knowledge is trustworthy; has been painfully honed in order to inspire in us **a** Spirit of honestly seeking out Truth. The scientific method **is the Spirit of Truth**.

> *Joh:14:16: And I will pray the Father, and he shall give you another Comforter, that he may abide with you for ever;*
>
> *Joh:14:17:* **Even the Spirit of truth;** *whom the world cannot receive, because it seeth him not, neither knoweth him: but ye know him;* **for he dwelleth with you,** *and shall be in you.*

This Spirit of Truthfulness can be said to be like the Spirit of Science. It is an attitude of testing knowledge in order to ensure that what we believe in is not folly. We have a responsibility to pass on to our children an education in all things not just religion or dogma. We have a responsibility to ensure as correct a teaching as possible. Through our education system in the Western World we have conquered many misconceptions about the world we live in so that in this 21ˢᵗ century we are sitting at the pinnacle of knowledge. This would not have been possible if we remained shackled by dogma, delusion, deceit and misconception.

Before we go too much further, it should be pointed out that the ultimate truth, that there are no such things as gods, is referred to as the Holiest of all Holy things in fact Jesus calls this veil of heaven the Holy Ghost. This knowledge is so damming to religion, that it becomes an object of reverence itself. It is the most Holy thing ever, which has to be treated with the strictest security and secrecy. Only the very highest of the hierarchy are entrusted with the knowledge, for example the Pope; in the Old Testament it was the Levites. However judging by the exploitation of Christianity today, this secret fact of religion has probably been lost somewhere in history. It was because of this secret that the Bible is full of references to the holiest of Holies or the Holy Ghost.

It is first seen in Genesis in the story of Adam and Eve who are told that they must not eat of the **forbidden fruit lest they die.**

> *Ge:3:1: Now the serpent was more subtle than any beast of the field which the LORD God had made. And he said unto the woman, Yea, hath God said, Ye shall not eat of every tree of the garden?*
>
> *Ge:3:2: And the woman said unto the serpent, We may eat of the fruit of the trees of the garden:*
>
> *Ge:3:3: But of the fruit of the tree which is in the midst of the garden, God hath said, **Ye shall not eat of it, neither shall ye touch it, lest ye die**.*
>
> *Ge:3:4: And the serpent said unto the woman, Ye shall not surely die:*
>
> *Ge:3:5: For God doth know that in the day ye eat thereof, then your eyes shall be opened, and ye shall be as gods, knowing good and evil.*

The important deciphering in these verses is simply the fact that God says they will die if they eat or even touch the fruit of knowledge in the midst of the garden. The Serpent however contradicts this and says to them that they won't die but would instead have their eyes opened and be **as gods** knowing good and evil. There is no mistaking that the tree of knowledge of good and evil is a reference to the truth, that there are no such things as gods. The ancient Jews, Levites all, knew this principle well but hid it from the general public. The interesting thing to this story is the fact that *God tells the lie* and the serpent actually tells the truth here. God said that they would die if they eat or even touch the fruit whereas the serpent says you won't surely die but instead will become as Gods knowing the truth. True enough they eat the fruit and don't die just as the serpent predicted.

Of course now we can understand what this death really signifies. If the apple represents the holiest of holies or the truth that gods do not exist, then to die would be seen as becoming atheist – a spiritual death. Only by accepting this Truth can a worshipper be made dead (become atheist) which of course is not only dead to god but also dead to delusion. Therefore to be made dead in this fashion is actually to be raised to a newness of life; one free from misconception and delusion. They become as gods knowing truth and are above sin. Jesus says exactly this.

Ro:6:7: **For he that is dead is freed from sin**.

What is meant by this is that to be dead to worshipping gods is to be free of sin. An atheist sees no sin. Jesus' whole ministry was aimed at making people free and forgiving Sin. It is not the physical death of the body but the spiritual death of misconception. He saw that people who were oppressed by the religion of the day were stifled and could not move freely in their life. The Pharisees and Sadducees governed everything and dictated everything to do with living. Sin was the greatest hurdle of them all, because Jesus had to get people to believe who He said He was, in order to forgive Sin. However, He also resorted to explaining the truth about religion, to certain people, in order to get them to believe that their sins were actually cancelled out.

M't:9:5: For whether is easier, to say, **Thy sins be forgiven thee**; or to say, Arise, and walk?

Jesus viewed those who worshipped god already dead. They were dead to the Truth.

M't:8:21: And another of his disciples said unto him, Lord, suffer me first to go and bury my father.

M't:8:22: But Jesus said unto him, Follow me; **and let the dead bury their dea**d.

The dead who bury their dead are obviously those who believe in god else why go to the trouble of a burial?

Atheists have no problem with sin. Such people usually are aware that laws are made by ordinary people. In particular, society creates laws and rules so that the population can live in harmony. This only works if everybody follows the same idea. Therefore police are recruited in order to enforce society's rules. Atheists don't usually count breaking these rules a mortal sin. Nobody goes to Hell because of a parking ticket. Therefore their conscience is usually reasonably clear and they don't spend a lot of time agonizing over sin.

Religion however has other intentions for people. Religions dictate that breaking a rule is against god and therefore is a mortal sin that follows the person to Hell forever. This type of oppression is well known, and we hardly need to describe it. We know from history, that the religion has often condemned people for trivial errors and expelled them from Heaven or excommunicated them. People have been persecuted throughout the millenniums, even innocent people like Galileo. Further to this is the subjugation of women because it was claimed they are the original sinners (Eve and the apple fame). This of course is blatant misuse of power and wrong in every sense of the word. Then there are the Inquisitions and the torment inflicted on innocent lives by the same corruption and witch-hunts and Holy Wars and the list goes on.

It is only the religion that preaches sin. Religion is the father, and inventor of sin. No other body of people blame others like religion does. Sin is the weapon and flagstaff. Such persecution is neither of God nor of Jesus.

> Re:2:13: I know thy works, and where thou dwellest, **even where Satan's seat is**: and thou holdest fast my name, and hast not denied my faith, even in those days wherein Antipas was my faithful martyr, who was slain **among you, where Satan dwelleth**.

Jesus said

> *Joh:8:42: Jesus said unto them, If God were your Father, ye would love me: for I proceeded forth and came from God; neither came I of myself, but he sent me.*

> *Joh:8:43: Why do ye not understand my speech? even because ye cannot hear my word.*

> *Joh:8:44: **Ye are of your father the devil, and the lusts of your father ye will do. He was a murderer from the beginning, and abode not in the truth, because there is no truth in him. When he speaketh a lie, he speaketh of his own: for he is a liar, and the father of it.***

> *Joh:8:45: And because I tell you the truth, ye believe me not.*

> *Joh:8:46: **Which of you convinceth me of sin? And if I say the truth, why do ye not believe me?***

Jesus could not be convinced of sin because as an atheist He knew sin was irrelevant. It did not exist. **This is how He was able to forgive sin** and why people believed that their sin had been forgiven once Jesus spoke to them. Only one who is free of sin knows what sin is. He informed them of the truth. He explained the Holy Ghost to them. The Pharisees piled sin onto people; Jesus removed it and in the removing made people free and whole.

Joh:8:7: So when they continued asking him, he lifted up himself, and said unto them, **He that is without sin among you, let him first cast a stone at her.**

The entire notion of sin (idolatry - believing in gods) binds people and restricts their thoughts and imaginations. Jesus said that such people were already dead; which is meaning dead to truth.

> Ro:6:11: **Likewise reckon ye also yourselves to be dead indeed unto sin,** but alive unto God through Jesus Christ our Lord.

When Jesus heard that Lazarus was sick He responded this way;

> *Joh:11:4: When Jesus heard that, he said, **This sickness is not unto death,** but for the glory of God, **that the Son of God might be glorified thereby.***

Stating that the sickness was not unto death, meant that Lazarus's sickness was not monotheism; but it was instead a turning toward atheism that Lazarus was wrestling with. Sometimes the journey from monotheism to atheism is difficult to grasp, how do we worship a non-god? Some people are so dismayed by the truth that they are afflicted with confusion.

Jesus said that it was for the glorification of the Son of God. In other words Jesus could use this sickness of doubt to His advantage.

> *Joh:11:11: These things said he: and after that he saith unto them, Our friend Lazarus sleepeth; but I go, that I may awake him out of sleep.*

> *Joh:11:12: Then said his disciples, Lord, if he sleep, he shall do well.*

> *Joh:11:13: **Howbeit Jesus spake of his death**: but they thought that he had spoken of taking of rest in sleep.*

> *Joh:11:14: Then said Jesus unto them plainly, **Lazarus is dead.***

Here Jesus tells the disciples what is meant by being dead. It is not sleep but death of misconception that Jesus is describing. Lazarus was troubled in spirit, he wanted to be a good Christian believing in God but he had heard enough of the Holy Secret (which is called the Holy Ghost) and the mystery of god, that his countenance was troubled, by his now conflicting thoughts. He wondered was god real or not?

> *Joh:11:16: Then said Thomas, which is called Didymus, unto his fellow disciples, Let us also go, that we may die with him.*

> *Joh:11:17: Then when Jesus came, he found that he had lain in the grave four (four is the number for **preaching the word of God**) days already.*

> *Joh:11:18: Now Bethany (house of figs) was nigh unto Jerusalem, about fifteen furlongs off:*

> *Joh:11:19: And many of the Jews came to Martha and Mary, to comfort them concerning their brother.*

> *Joh:11:20: Then Martha, as soon as she heard that Jesus was coming, went and met him: but Mary sat still in the house.*

> *Joh:11:21: Then said Martha unto Jesus, Lord, if thou hadst been here, my brother had not died.*

> *Joh:11:22: But I know, that even now, whatsoever thou wilt ask of God, God will give it thee.*

> *Joh:11:23: Jesus saith unto her, **Thy brother shall rise again.***

Jesus reassures Martha that Lazarus will rise again but it is not stated that Lazarus will rise as a Christian knowing truth because he had died as a Hebrew under a misconception. This story is not repeated in other gospels, and since John always spoke of the spirit and not of the carnal, we may infer that this whole episode with Lazarus is contrived as a spiritual lesson.

The whole business of dying and being dead and rising again has a huge preoccupation in the New Testament. There are a multitude of references alluding to it in one form or another. It would almost seem that it is the main topic of Jesus' intent, but of course it isn't. The name 'Lazarus" means 'without help' according to Young's Concordance but I see other meanings on the Internet that contradict this. Some say that the meaning is "God has helped'. In both cases it seems to be a strange name to call ones child knowing the meaning but not knowing that one day Christ would use him as an example of the baptism and raise him from the dead. We see also by the code that Lazarus had been preaching the word of god for days before this event i.e. he had lain in the grave four (four is the number for preaching the word of God) days already. It is also noted that Bethany means 'House of figs' which we know refer to followers of god.

Everything therefore hinges on the Baptism. Jesus did not introduce the Baptism. His cousin John the Baptist did.

> M'r:1:4: *John did baptize in the wilderness, and preach the baptism of repentance **for the remission of sins**.*

> Joh:4:2: (Though Jesus himself **baptized not**, but his disciples,)

Now the Baptism was preached for the remission of sins. This means that the purpose of the Baptism was to inform people of the atheistic nature of the truth, that there are no such things as gods. If one is made into an atheist, they are slain in the spirit and become dead to god. This is true. That is why the Baptism is seen not only as a death but also as a resurrection.

> Ro:6:3: *Know ye not, that so many of us as were baptized into Jesus Christ were **baptized into his death**?*

> Ro:6:4: *Therefore we are **buried with him by baptism into death**: that like as Christ was **raised up from the dead** by the glory of the Father, even so **we also should walk in newness of life.***

So when a person is Baptised they are also told the truth or Holy Secret of the doctrine or the mystery of God, namely that there are no such things as gods, this constitutes what is meant by the Holy Ghost. The word Ghost means 'a nothingness' and so we are saying that the Holy Nothingness is what we believe in. This of course represents the belief of an atheist. So then through the baptism the person who believes in something at first is informed that there is no such thing as god. Therefore their mind is cleansed by this education and from then on they believe in nothing or the Holy Ghost.

By this method people die but could then be raised up again or resurrected into the secret privileged few who knew the truth about religion. They then knew of the 'covering' or 'veil' of parable and stories and practices of ritual and worship. Jesus gave them the Holy Ghost to replace the emptiness of spirit left when god-stuff is purged.

> M't:12:43: When the **unclean spirit is gone** out of a man, he walketh through dry places, seeking rest, and findeth none.

> M't:12:44: Then he saith, I will return into my house from whence I came out; and **when he is come, he findeth it empty, swept, and garnished**.

> Lu:11:23: He that is not with me is against me: and he that gathereth not with me scattereth.

> Lu:11:24: When the **unclean spirit is gone** out of a man, he walketh through dry places, seeking rest; and finding none, he saith, I will return unto my house whence I came out.

> Lu:11:25: And when **he cometh, he findeth it swept and garnished**.

This is why the early Christians went out into the world to preach the word, not of monotheism but of atheism. Even so, the way Jesus wrapped the doctrine up, and presented it as a community spirit and movement for the betterment of mankind, caused those early Christians to keep the school going. At that time they had very few religious observances to keep.

Really, the only one was the Lords supper or communion in remembrance of Jesus. These days' people have created so many duties that it makes a mockery of sensibility. The ideal of God was adopted as a Father image and the community was administered in such a fashion as to support every individual. Donations were freely given toward this cause.

So the Baptism was a public demonstration or Vow of service to humanity.

The point is that Christianity and Baptism caused people to be classified as being dead to the misconception that they were previously under. Knowing the truth makes a person fiercely adamant about knowledge and their state of mind. Once they are so indoctrinated it is impossible to go back to the old corrupt ways, just as it is impossible for some scientists to accept spontaneous creation over the theory of evolution. Knowing truth is enlightening. For this reason early Christians were adamantly unable to deny their doctrine, because it was so superior to all other enlightenments.

> *Heb:6:4:* **For it is impossible for those who were once enlightened,** *and have tasted of the heavenly gift, and were* **made partakers of the Holy Ghost,**
>
> *Heb:6:5: And have tasted the good word of God, and the powers of the world to come,*

To be made partakers of the Holy Ghost as it states above, means that we finally understand what the Holy Ghost actually is. We of truth do understand that there is no state of mind more pure than atheism replaced by a vow to serve humanity. Atheism on its own is selfish but if the Ideal of Jesus Christ is observed then that selfishness turns into generosity.

Returning to Adam and Eve and the forbidden fruit which was the Holiest of Holies of the story we see that God said they would die but the serpent said that they would be **as** gods knowing good and evil. So Adam and Eve ate of the tree of knowledge of good and evil in other-words they saw the truth that there are no such things as gods and by this they then knew their nakedness.

> Ge:3:7: And the eyes of them both were opened, **and they knew that they were naked**; and they **sewed fig leaves together, and made themselves aprons**.

The sewing of fig leaves to make aprons is the writing of the doctrine or the creation of the Bible. These fig leaves represent the stories of the Old Testament which form a covering for our spiritual nakedness.

Just as Jesus taught, their spiritual nakedness was a realisation that gods do not exist. Remember Eve was not a person. Eve was the religion and Bride of Adam just as Christianity is the Bride of Jesus.

> Re:21:2: And I John saw the holy city, **new Jerusalem**, coming down from God out of heaven, **prepared as a bride adorned for her husband**.

> Re:21:9: And there came unto me one of the seven angels which had the seven vials full of the seven last plagues, and talked with me, saying, Come hither, I will shew **thee the bride, the Lamb's wife.**

At first Adam and Eve knew their nakedness but were not ashamed.

> Ge:2:25: And they were both naked, the man and his wife, and **were not ashamed**.

So after tasting the fruit of good and evil, clothing was necessary to hide their nakedness which now made them feel shame.

> Ge:3:21: Unto Adam also and to his wife did the LORD God make coats of skins, and clothed them.

> Ge:3:22: And the LORD God said, Behold, the man is become as one of us, to know good and evil: and now, lest he put forth his hand, and take also of the tree of life, and eat, and live for ever:

Remember that Adam is the first society of Hebrews and that Eve was his wife or doctrine, the clothing is a metaphorical covering for their spiritual nakedness or atheism. In other words their Bible or Holy Book the Torah which was written on Parchment or goat skins.

But wait! If Adam is a society and Eve is their Religion or Doctrine what is Cain and Abel?

> *Ge:4:1: And Adam knew Eve his wife; and she conceived, and bare Cain, and said, I have gotten a man from the LORD.*

> *Ge:4:2: And she again bare his brother Abel. And Abel was a keeper of sheep, but Cain was a tiller of the ground.*

CAIN AND ABEL

Adam, as we have seen was not an individual but was a unique society separated by his religion and spiritual wife (Eve). They had children; Cain and Abel. Of course these are not real people either so just what are they? In order to answer this we once again turn to Christianity. Jesus created Christianity but it was some 300 years before the Roman Catholic Church was born. After a time Christianity begat Catholic, then Lutheran, then Anglican, then Protestant then Methodist and so forth all these denominations and many more are all children of the one Mother; Christianity! Every offshoot of the religion is viewed as offspring. Each has a name and each a particular curriculum which differs from the parent. Cain and Abel are just such offspring. The Bible tells us all we need to know in order to resolve their mystery. For example their name meanings are freely given to us, in fact the Bible always tells us the name meaning of important people especially if the name meaning is crucial to understanding the meaning of their story as are Cain and Abel.

Abel (Abel means 'vanity') he was a keeper of sheep. A keeper of sheep is called a shepherd. Ever since Jesus called himself the 'good shepherd', pastors have likewise been referring to themselves as shepherds and their flock as being the congregation.

> Joh:10:14: **I am the good shepherd**, and know my sheep, and am known of mine.

So from this insight we learn that Abel (vanity) was not a man but was a doctrine (a congregation) born from the Mother religion Eve (Foundation of Life). If this is so then what is Cain?

The text says that Cain (Cain means 'Possessions') was a tiller of the ground. Remembering that the ground is God's field (the population) we can assume that a 'tiller' of mankind must be some form of worldly business based doctrine or theory. This would tie in nicely with his name meaning "possessions" a business could have worldly possessions.

Both Cain (Possessions) and Abel (Vanity) are doctrines because they were both born from the mother religion, Eve. They were called sons because Eve knew the dark truth that there are no such things as gods. Cain (Possessions) is even worldlier than Abel (Vanity) because he was a 'Tiller of the ground-population'. God is Truth and a worldly doctrine born of atheistic truth can be likened to a scientific attitude (the theory of evolution would be a good example of this belief). Seeking knowledge is good but people also need to appreciate their spirituality, consciousness and moral obligations. Science has no morals and promotes atheism which denies a person's right to spiritual comforting. Religion gives us morals as well as a comforter.

So we have this scenario.

> Ge:4:1: And Adam knew Eve his wife; and she conceived, and bare Cain, and said, I have gotten a man from the LORD.
>
> Ge:4:2: And she again bare his brother Abel. And Abel was a keeper of sheep, but Cain was a tiller of the ground.
>
> Ge:4:3: And in process of time it came to pass, that Cain brought of the fruit of the ground an offering unto the LORD.
>
> Ge:4:4: And Abel, he also brought of the firstlings of his flock and of the fat thereof. And the LORD had respect unto Abel and to his offering:

Ge:4:5: But unto Cain and to his offering he had not respect. And Cain was very wroth, and his countenance fell.

Ge:4:6: And the LORD said unto Cain, Why art thou wroth? and why is thy countenance fallen?

Ge:4:7: If thou doest well, shalt thou not be accepted? and if thou doest not well, sin lieth at the door. And unto thee shall be his desire, and thou shalt rule over him.

Ge:4:8: And Cain talked with Abel his brother: and it came to pass, when they were in the field, that Cain rose up against Abel his brother, and slew him.

Abel (Vanity) - a keeper of sheep - the shepherd and his flock offered a sacrifice to the Lord and is blessed because of it. The Bible tells us that this sacrifice is the 'firstlings of the flock'. Does this mean the church sacrifices children? Not really. The sacrifice that a zealous following make, even today, is the sacrifice of reason. In order to bolster their faith they make it immovable in their head. This process often makes it necessary to have fixed ideas about certain things so typical in fundamentalist doctrines and dogma. The believer becomes unwilling to question his doctrine for fear of blasphemy. Such a doctrine creates and sustains a wealthy income for the religion proposing it through tithing a populous held captive in the fear of being damned eternally. Naturally, Abel's offering is blessed by God because he has a devoted congregation totally dedicated to the belief.

By contrast the Lord showed no favour to Cain's (Possessions) offering of the "Fruit of the Ground-population" which is the product of the people their atheistic reasoning, questioning and doubting. How could the Lord bless an atheist attitude? Just as the attitude does not acknowledge God, the Lord does not acknowledge the attitude. There can be no blessings from the Lord e.g. the comfort of the shroud which belief induces. Perhaps Cain also indicates a certain self-indulgence and decadence typical of materialistic attitudes.

In today's terms, Cain (evolution theory) and Abel (creation theory) are still with us, struggling one against the other to win favour over the minds of the population. Cain slew Abel; how? The Bible said they talked! Cain slew Abel with words.

> Ge:4:8: **And Cain talked with Abel** his brother: and it came to pass, when they were in the field, that Cain rose up against Abel his brother, and slew him.

It is easy to imagine this happening when one realises that the larger part of the population is agnostic, not unlike Cain. It seems that Abel just became very much outnumbered. He became a minority group whose blood (spiritual life or energy) calls out from the dust of the ground (mankind), just as it does today.

It is also interesting to note that the Lord replaced Abel with Seth (whose name means Substitute).

> Ge:4:25: And Adam knew his wife again; and she bare a son, and called his name Seth: For God, said she, hath appointed me another seed instead of Abel, whom Cain slew.

Now here is an interesting fact that reinforces the view that Cain and Abel were doctrines. Seth also was a doctrine. Seth was one of the major religions of Upper Egypt dating back as far as the fourth century B.C. and it is thought by many scholars that the Egyptian Seth is the same Seth represented in the Bible. So we see that Seth also represented a religion as did Abel. In fact Seth is one of Egypt's founder gods who battled Osiris. In the second century BC we know of the Sethites who claimed perfection as being the Son of Adam.

By this time of course religious delusion had taken hold of the world in a big way and many splinter groups developed, not to mention the great civilisations such as the Egyptians, Greeks, Persians, Minoans and many others all with their own version of gods.

CONCEPT FOUR

FOURTEEN IS PASSOVER - A FAST FROM GOD

Number fourteen signifies the Passover which is a feast whereby the first born lamb is sacrificed to God. This celebration is in remembrance from Moses' day when the Spirit of Death took the first born of Pharaoh and the Egyptians. The same Spirit of Death passed over the Jews who had doused their doorways with the blood of a firstborn lamb. They were spared the death that befell the Egyptians. The number fourteen therefore signifies the fast from God (to go without God). This is also considered to be 'dead' hence the 'spirit of death' appears.

A FAST is when you 'Go Without' this may be a fast of bread (i.e. scripture) when you go without bread or scripture. If you go without scripture you are in effect fasting from god. To truly fast from god is to become an atheist. This is also referenced as to be Fatherless. Since God is seen as our Father in Heaven to be an atheist is to be Fatherless. An atheist has no spiritual doctrine in other words an atheist has no spiritual wife. Adam's (Hebrew society) spiritual wife was Eve (doctrine or scripture) just as Jesus' spiritual wife (or Bride) is Christianity, so to not have any belief in scripture at all is to be atheist and have no wife or to be a widow.

> *Jas:1:27: Pure religion and undefiled before God and the Father is this,* **To visit the fatherless and widows in their affliction,** *and to keep himself unspotted from the world.*

This Jewish system of religion created a 'covering' for the 'Truth' that Moses held and the interpretation that Aaron gave. The people therefore had a 'covering' for their spiritual nakedness (as revealed by the apron of Adam and Eve) in that they believed whatever Aaron told them, but Moses knew and believed something altogether different. Hence the covering or veil was invented by Adam and Eve and their fig leaf apron. In commemoration of this; women (religion - out of man) wear a covering or veil or burka to this very day. Although the people thought they were worshipping the same god as Moses's god, they did not know that by doing so they were committing idolatry. Jesus pointed this out. He said that although we worship god and call Him Lord we are committing idolatry. This is verbalised in the following verse.

> *M't:7:21:* **Not every one that saith unto me, Lord, Lord, shall enter into the kingdom** *of heaven; but he that doeth the will of my Father which is in heaven.*

> *M't:7:22: Many will say to me in that day, Lord, Lord, have we not prophesied in thy name? and in thy name have cast out devils? and in thy name done many wonderful works?*

> *M't:7:23:* **And then will I profess unto them, I never knew you: depart from me, ye that work iniquity**.

Believing in the 'covering' (that which covers spiritual nakedness i.e. a belief in god; worship and all its trimmings) and not the 'fruit' or truth of scripture (that there are no such things as gods), is the misconception which is also known as the deceit of the doctrine. This 'Deceit' is named as "Satan - the Deceiver" who is so depicted from Genesis to Revelations. It is this deceit or misconception (the notion that a god exists when in fact there are no such things as gods) which leads all followers astray. This is that deceit which has misled the Church, the Church leaders and all who visit the Church. Everybody ever taught by religious schools or doctrines are told this misconception, so that now nearly everyone in the world believes some form of idolatry. So this deceitfulness becomes part of the Church's teachings.

> *Re:2:13: I know thy works, and where thou dwellest, **even where Satan's seat is:** and thou holdest fast my name, and hast not denied my faith, even in those days wherein Antipas was my faithful martyr, who was slain among you, **where Satan dwelleth**.*

So we learn that Satan's seat is with the doctrine itself. The teachings of the church, of any religion, that there is a god; is primarily a delusion at worst or a misconception at best. This of course is saying that the church is also deceived into believing in the godhead and trinity as one would worship any idol. Idolatry is rampant. Jesus received flack for His open preaching of this covering metaphor, because it revealed how the Pharisees had sinned.

> *Joh:15:22: If I had not come and spoken unto them, they had not had sin: **but now they have no cloke for their sin**.*

We see and understand that they have no cloak for their sin because Jesus revealed that this covering of myths and fables deceived them into thinking that god actually exists. The truth that there are no such things as gods implies that there is no such place as heaven but also no such thing as Satan. This is how Satan is finally cast out of heaven, by the realization that he or it, doesn't actually exist. The concept of Heaven itself is nebulous and vague in fact the very word means "rolling cloud of mystery". There is no actual place where heaven can exist, not in the atmosphere or in space or even in some ethereal mist but only in our minds. Thus Sin also is a figment of the imagination; a concept dreamed up by people who use it to oppress others.

> *Re:12:7: And there was war in heaven: Michael and his angels fought against the dragon; and the dragon fought and his angels,*

> *Re:12:8: And prevailed not; **neither was their place found any more in heaven**.*

> *Re:12:9: And the great dragon was cast out, that old serpent, called the Devil, and **Satan, which deceiveth the whole world**: he was cast out into the earth, and his angels were cast out with him.*

Now we can finally understand who the accuser of mankind really is, by this above verse. That which has deceived our minds for so long, that misconception which masquerades as enlightenment is actually a delusion that makes us err in all that we attempt to accomplish. We are dominated by the notion that we have sinned and the religion perpetuates this idea because it is a power they hold deliberately over the population or congregation. How we have suffered because of wrongful instruction; how far we have fallen without being aware that we were even deceived, and we were deceived by the perpetrated concept that god was a real person. God is not real; neither is Santa, the Easter Bunny, the Tooth Fairy, The man in the Moon and all other supernatural superstitions and inventions.

Jesus knew of the deception of doctrine concerning the miracles of the Bible and 'truth' about god. When He was asked to give a sign that god existed in Him, he refused. He said that no such sign can be given.

> *M't:12:38: Then certain of the scribes and of the Pharisees answered, saying, Master, we would see a sign from thee.*

> *M't:12:39: But he answered and said unto them, **An evil and adulterous generation seeketh after a sign; and there shall no sign be given to it**, but the sign of the prophet Jonas:*

Jesus knew that miraculous events and magical signs were further corruption of the mind. He realised too that to hold a state of purity in mind a person had to be truthful (Unto the pure all things are pure)**.** So He gave no such magical signs.

> *M'r:8:11: And the Pharisees came forth, and began to question with him, seeking of him a sign from heaven, tempting him.*

> *M'r:8:12: And he sighed deeply in his spirit, and saith, Why doth this generation seek after a sign? verily I say unto you, **There shall no sign be given unto this generation.***

*Lu:11:29: And when the people were gathered thick together, he began to say, This is **an evil generation: they seek a sign; and there shall no sign be given it**, but the sign of Jonas the prophet.*

Magical signs were not possible because there is no magical place or power in existence. Jesus said that in order to see truth and accept the frail limitations of being human then one must be as accepting as a child.

Matthew:

M't:18:1: At the same time came the disciples unto Jesus, saying, Who is the greatest in the kingdom of heaven?

M't:18:2: And Jesus called a little child unto him, and set him in the midst of them,

*M't:18:3: And said, Verily I say unto you, **Except ye be converted, and become as little children**, ye shall not enter into the kingdom of heaven.*

M't:18:4: Whosoever therefore shall humble himself as this little child, the same is greatest in the kingdom of heaven.

M't:18:5: And whoso shall receive one such little child in my name receiveth me.

M't:18:6: But whoso shall offend one of these little ones which believe in me, it were better for him that a millstone were hanged about his neck, and that he were drowned in the depth of the sea.

Mark:

*M'r:10:14: But when Jesus saw it, he was much displeased, and said unto them, Suffer the **little children** to come unto me, and forbid them not: **for of such is the kingdom of God**.*

M'r:10:15: Verily I say unto you, Whosoever shall not receive the kingdom of God as a little child, he shall not enter therein.

Luke:

> *Lu:18:16: But Jesus called them unto him, and said, Suffer little children to come unto me, and forbid them not: **for of such is the kingdom of God**.*

> *Lu:18:17: Verily I say unto you, Whosoever shall not receive the kingdom of God as a little child shall in no wise enter therein.*

The very notion of asking for a sign from heaven revealed the misconception that the hierarchy held, regarding god and heaven. There are no such things as gods or places such as heaven; therefore no sign can be forthcoming. Of course the Pharisees could not comprehend such a concept. Their minds were completely corrupted by the God delusion and Jesus knew it. It was because of this, that Jesus seemed to be able to know what they were thinking, which mystified them all the more.

> *Joh:2:23: Now when he was in Jerusalem at the passover, in the feast day, many believed in his name, when they saw the miracles which he did.*

> *Joh:2:24: But Jesus did not commit himself unto them, **because he knew all men,***

> *Joh:2:25: And needed not that any should testify of man: for he knew what was in man.*

John states that Jesus knew all men but what he was inferring was that Jesus knew that the hierarchy were under the misconception of god; mistaking God as being a real person; which had the effect of prohibiting their knowledge. They could not accept new knowledge for fear it was heresy. Jesus realized also, that this deception was necessary in order that believers would continue in their church attendance. Let's face it, knowing the 'truth' or realizing that the ideal God is just that, an ideal, destroys this attendance upon the 'word'. What need has an atheist of church? For this reason, Christ advised people not to pray openly in the street, but to lock themselves in their closets in order to pray.

M't:6:5: And when thou prayest, thou shalt not be as the hypocrites are: for they love to pray standing in the synagogues and in the corners of the streets, that they may be seen of men. Verily I say unto you, They have their reward.

*M't:6:6: **But thou, when thou prayest, enter into thy closet, and when thou hast shut thy door, pray to thy Father which is in secret; and thy Father which seeth in secret shall reward thee openly.***

M't:6:7: But when ye pray, use not vain repetitions, as the heathen do: for they think that they shall be heard for their much speaking.

M't:6:8: Be not ye therefore like unto them: for your Father knoweth what things ye have need of, before ye ask him.

M't:6:9: After this manner therefore pray ye: Our Father which art in heaven, Hallowed be thy name.

M't:6:10: Thy kingdom come. Thy will be done in earth, as it is in heaven.

M't:6:11: Give us this day our daily bread.

M't:6:12: And forgive us our debts, as we forgive our debtors.

M't:6:13: And lead us not into temptation, but deliver us from evil: For thine is the kingdom, and the power, and the glory, for ever. Amen.

This is said because firstly we really don't need to attend a church in order to pray and secondly that if we are seen to be praying, others may think that we actually believe in an imagined god, and are therefore committing idolatry, and could induce idolatry into others. Praying is good, it has psychological benefits and should never be discouraged but we should also be aware of the truth about there not being any such things as gods, to prevent us from vain faith. If we pray at all, it should be secretly to ourselves not seeking any reward just as it is in the 'Lord's prayer' which is a prayer which does not actually ask for anything. We do not pray for things because as far as we know truthfully; no-one and no god is listening. Nevertheless prayer or more precisely affirmations, bolster our own principles and ego and help to reinforce our own behaviours. In His own defence before Pilate; Jesus simply implied that all He ever did was to seek the truth.

> *Joh:18:37: Pilate therefore said unto him, Art thou a king then? Jesus answered, Thou sayest that I am a king. To this end was I born, and for this cause came I into the world, that **I should bear witness unto the truth**. Every one that is of the truth heareth my voice.*

> *Joh:18:38: Pilate saith unto him, What is truth? And when he had said this, he went out again unto the Jews, and saith unto them, I find in him no fault at all.*

Religions however require a regular attendance of people at church to ensure their income and survival. Without attendance there can be no teaching of morals, no social unity, no upbringing examples for children, no weddings, or baptisms, nor social graces or cultural improvement. Neither can there be comfort in times of grief? No funerals for example. Nevertheless only this particular truth can 'heal' people of idolatry, superstition and spiritual confusion. Only this particular 'truth' can forgive sins (which don't actually exist anyway) and free people from the shackles of guilt and so-called sin. If there is no Heaven and no God, then there is also no Satan and no Sin. Once published the little book stands as a remedy for mental health issues regarding grandiosity and god confusion; sin and guilt. People can be healed once again of these sour spirits. It only takes the revealing in the spirit of truthfulness of Jesus' veil of heaven and truth to remove the fears and confusion that some people encounter. People need to be shown the contradiction of god and pointed to the deceit which is inherent in the Bible.

Below is the justification that Paul gives for this deceit within his ministry.

> *3:1: What advantage then hath the Jew? or **what profit is there of circumcision**?*

Ro:3:2: Much every way: chiefly, because that unto them were committed the oracles of God.

Ro:3:3: For what if some did not believe? shall their unbelief make the faith of God without effect?

Ro:3:4: God forbid: yea, **let God be true, but every man a liar;** *as it is written, That thou mightest be justified in thy sayings, and mightest overcome when thou art judged.*

Ro:3:5: **But if our unrighteousness commend the righteousness of God,** *what shall we say? Is God unrighteous who taketh vengeance? (I speak as a man)*

Ro:3:6: God forbid: for then how shall God judge the world?

Ro:3:7: **For if the truth of God hath more abounded through my lie unto his glory;** *why yet am I also judged as a sinner?*

Ro:3:8: And not rather, (as we be slanderously reported, and as some affirm that we say,) Let us do evil, that good may come? whose damnation is just.

This 'truth' that god is a figment of the imagination, enlightens people to knowledge and fact, rather than the darkness of superstition and vain beliefs of an occult nature, misconception and delusion. This finally allows people to be honest with regard to what they believe. Here is knowledge, wisdom and understanding but to be 'under the shadow or the covering or veil of heaven' as it were, are bigotry, hypocrisy, prejudice and dogma.

M't:7:21: **Not every one that saith unto me, Lord, Lord, shall enter into the kingdom of heaven;** *but he that doeth the will of my Father which is in heaven.*

M't:7:22: Many will say to me in that day, Lord, Lord, have we not prophesied in thy name? and in thy name have cast out devils? and in thy name done many wonderful works?

> *M't:7:23: **And then will I profess unto them, I never knew you: depart from me, ye that work iniquity.***

Of course the iniquity that is always worked is idolatry by worshipping god even if good works are done in the name of god. The inference here is that those worshippers, who do not bear good fruit (truthfulness), are workers of iniquity even though they follow the Lord. You cannot be a follower of god and be free of sin (free of misconception), as worshipping any god is idolatry and the worst of all sins. Therefore the best Christians are those who worship nothing at all (atheists) but respect everything. Those who do good works even though they may be atheists, not seeking any reward, not even heavenly reward or everlasting life. Those who seek heavenly reward or everlasting life shall miss out, because firstly their motives are misplaced and secondly heaven doesn't exist and neither does its rewards.

> M't:19:30: But many that are first shall be last; and the last shall be first

Obviously, idolatry or worshipping idols or gods, leads to all these spiritual abominations but the 'truth' or science; or an awareness of our spiritual nakedness - can cure these illnesses. Of course to say such things as these, especially at the time of Christ, or any time previous to this century for that matter, would mean an instant death sentence for blasphemy or heresy. Even these days the church still persecutes outspoken citizens and those who hold alternative viewpoints and other belief systems. It is no different from our early history when most wars were religiously inspired.

We must know what our Spiritual Nakedness is, if we are to have a clear head and trustworthy thoughts. Spiritual nakedness simply implies that there is nothing available on a spiritual level that can magically intercede for our physical lives. Magic does not exist. Miracles do not happen. If we put our trust in a god that doesn't exist, we are leaving ourselves open to real hurt, pain, exploitation and future disappointment. Not only that but we corrupt our minds with dogma, and are then unable to judge for ourselves good actions and good conscience and truth from untruth or in fact to hold an honest opinion. The very best example of this fantasy is the ongoing argument over Darwin's Theory of Evolution. This theory forms the cornerstone of all studies of biology and has shown itself to be trustworthy even under the scrutiny of DNA research. Its opponent is classical dogma, and the religious view of spontaneous creation. Added to this is the behaviour of susceptible Christians who believe in the 'Rapture" that their souls will be instantly translated and rise into Heaven, in the midst of turmoil, as the world is being destroyed by the apocalypse. Perhaps they also subscribe to the latest movement which identify themselves as 'Preppers" or people who stock up on goods, food and water and weapons (Prepping) to be prepared when the apocalypse finally comes. The hype stirred up, especially on the Internet where anyone can voice an opinion, is that the end of the world is coming perhaps even this year. A quick search of the Internet will return countless blogs of similar delusions. The truth and fact of the matter is this, that there is absolutely no evidence, on earth or in space, that anything will happen this year or in any year in the near future. Sure, there will always be floods and drought, Volcanoes erupting and vast fires, Hurricanes and Cyclones; Earthquakes and Tsunamis. More people seem to be wounded or killed by these natural disasters these days than in earlier centuries because firstly our news reporting is vastly improved and secondly that the earth's population has grown to more than seven billion. None of this supports the corrupt idea that a god exists that either causes all these calamities or will save our souls in the midst of any such disaster. The earth is an active and changing environment as it always has been, sometimes we can avoid damage and sometimes we can't. Science gives us good predictive tools which are much more reliable than the opinion of say Nostradamus (1503-1566) or any opinion of any religion or soothsayer or astrologist on earth. All the occult disciplines are only superstition and the notion of ghosts and phantasms; ghouls and wraiths is all foolishness and Astrology and Necromancy and Alchemy have all showed themselves over the millenniums to be absurd. Religions that worship a god or multiple gods join the queue of false beliefs.

This is a reflection of the oldest Scripture, for example Deuteronomy points out;

> *De:18:9: When thou art come into the land which the LORD thy*
> *God giveth thee, thou shalt not learn to do after the abominations*
> *of those nations.*

> *De:18:10:* **There shall not be found among you any one that maketh his son or his daughter to pass through the fire, or that useth divination, or an observer of times, or an enchanter, or a witch,**

> *De:18:11:* **Or a charmer, or a consulter with familiar spirits, or a wizard, or a necromancer.**

> *De:18:12:* *For all that do these things are* **an abomination unto the LORD**: *and because of these abominations the LORD thy God doth drive them out from before thee.*

> *De:18:13:* *Thou shalt be perfect with the LORD thy God.*

> *Joh:8:44: Ye are of your father the devil, and the lusts of your father ye will do. He was a murderer from the beginning, and* **abode not in the truth, because there is no truth in him. When he speaketh a lie, he speaketh of his own: for he is a liar,** *and the father of it.*

But how can we speak such things and avoid prosecution and persecution? The way was simple as Jesus informs us.

He said that all the words and language of the scriptures were written in such a way as to hide the real truth by a veil of wonder and a covering of metaphor. This veil is referenced in several New Testament books as follows. In Hebrews we see the allusion to the real veil within the synagogue as the Holy of Holies is described which we know represents the atheistic truth that only the High Priest knew.

> Heb:9:1: Then verily the first covenant had also ordinances of divine service, and a worldly sanctuary.

> Heb:9:2: For there was a tabernacle made; the first, wherein was the candlestick, and the table, and the shewbread; which is called the sanctuary.

> Heb:9:3: And after the second veil, the tabernacle **which is called the Holiest of all**;

Heb:9:4: Which had the golden censer, and the ark of the covenant overlaid round about with gold, wherein was the golden pot that had manna, and Aaron's rod that budded, and the tables of the covenant;

Heb:9:5: And over it the cherubims of glory shadowing the mercyseat; of which we cannot now speak particularly.

Heb:9:6: Now when these things were thus ordained, the priests went always into the first tabernacle, accomplishing the service of God.

Heb:10:18: Now where remission of these is, there is no more offering for sin.

Heb:10:19: Having therefore, brethren, **boldness to enter into the holiest** by the blood of Jesus,

Heb:10:20: By a new and living way, which he hath consecrated for us, **through the veil, that is to say, his flesh**;

Heb:10:21: And having an high priest over the house of God;

M'r:15:37: And Jesus cried with a loud voice, and gave up the ghost.

M'r:15:38: And **the veil of the temple** was rent in twain from the top to the bottom.

We see in Hebrews 10:20 that the veil is referred to as Christ's FLESH yet again making reference to scripture.

Jesus also reassured us not to be afraid to break through this cloak or veil by denouncing that God exists. He says that we should not worry that we have no cloak for our spiritual nakedness. His words about flowers finally make sense when read in connection to this veil.

Matthew;

> M't:6:28: **And why take ye thought for raiment**? Consider the lilies of the field, how they grow; they toil not, neither do they spin:
>
> M't:6:29: And yet I say unto you, That even Solomon in all his glory was not arrayed like one of these.

Luke;

> Lu:12:27: Consider the lilies how they grow: they toil not, they spin not; and yet I say unto you, that Solomon in all his glory was not arrayed like one of these.
>
> Lu:12:28: If then God so clothe the grass, which is to day in the field, and to morrow is cast into the oven; **how much more will he clothe you**, O ye of little faith?

By choosing methods to reveal the truth spoken of in the Old Testament, He was able to invent the New Testament, with all the instructions necessary to reveal that real truth, and abolish sin and guilt from the populace for ever. These methods included the use of 'parables' and also certain words with alternative or 'shadow' meanings (literary souls as it were) as will be described following.

With reference to parables Jesus said;

> *M't:13:10: And the disciples came, and said unto him,* **Why speakest thou unto them in parables?**
>
> *M't:13:11: He answered and said unto them,* **Because it is given unto you to know the mysteries of the kingdom of heaven, but to them it is not given**.

Jesus says outright "because it is given to you to know the mysteries of heaven but to them it is not given". Of course this indicates that only His disciples could be trusted with the secret that God does not actually exist.

This is the same entrustment that the High Priest had to enter the Holiest of Holies in the synagogue. It is a certain empowerment and knowledge that creates a viewpoint specific to one in authority. By this enlightenment the Disciples and Apostles were able to advise the common people who did not have this enlightenment on behaviour issues and other affairs of the soul. This made these apostles seem like very wise men indeed when in fact they were only let in on a secret that could have just as easily destroyed the whole movement.

Jesus could not come out and very well tell the populace this fact, although He does confess it to a few people as necessary in the course of His evangelising and healing which will soon be revealed.

In another place He says;

> M'r:4:11: *And he said unto them,* **Unto you it is given to know the mystery of the kingdom of God: but unto them that are without, all these things are done in parables:**

> M'r:4:12: *That seeing they may see, and not perceive; and hearing they may hear, and not understand; lest at any time they should be converted, and their sins should be forgiven them.*

Of course He admits that He is hiding something from the general populace or more importantly from the hierarchy of the day. He says He will tell these secrets but that these things are hidden.

His other method of encouraging insight is by the use of words that have particular and traditional meaning. Something should be mentioned here of their language at this point. Like the Arabic language, Hebrew is also a Semitic language. Words all have roots in tradition and history. Several meanings can be expressed by the same word simply by adding a prefix, a suffix or an extension of vowel, tense or verb. We'd like to explore this method of secrecy especially since it also exploits metaphors, similes, idioms and personification as devices to hide the truth but unfortunately it is beyond our means. Nevertheless an example of this has already been seen in the word Tsela according to Young's Concordance which can mean anything from Tsel = defence, shade, shadow to Tsela = beam, board, chamber, corner, halting, leaf, plank, rib, side, side chamber, another, one and adversity.

We must be very careful in making any claims at all. Who is to know what the actual translation really is anyway. There are a plethora of translations of the Holy Bible each claiming more perfection than its competitors. We are not just simply talking about translation from say Hebrew or Greek into English. The real dilemma is translating from ancient scripts into sensible renditions of the verse, which is called paraphrasing. Everybody holds a different argument as to what the original authors <u>meant</u> to say (not what was actually written). We will not get caught up with arguments about what original writers of the Bible MEANT to say but by some accident actually **wrote something that was completely heretical by mistake**. We wonder how such a thing could happen. We will not argue whether Jonah was swallowed by a whale or a great fish or for that matter a sea monster. Unless the interpreter knows the Heretical Truth and Blasphemous nature of the Ideal which we adopt as God or at least as the Holy Ghost, any translation is worthless. Without knowledge of the truth, all Biblical text will contradict itself. There is plenty of evidence of such contradiction and there are many examples of pious people becoming hypocrites in their zeal to demonstrate how very much they love god. We are bought into remembrance of such disasters as the Jonestown Massacre or the Texas Wacol incident which were bought about by some deluded person's interpretation of dogma. Believing that god exists leads to complete corruption of thought and human values. If one believes in god and in the glorious perfection of Heaven then it logically follows that a mortal life is rather worthless, tedious and futile. From such assumptions we get religious extremists and self-mutilating terrorists. Examples of this throughout history can be found in the terrible days of the Inquisition or in accusing innocent people of witchcraft. Even the best scientists of human history such as Galileo Galilei, were forced to disguise their discoveries for fear of death or incrimination.

The art of hiding a meaning through the use of grammatical devices such as metaphor simile and idiom, have long been the technique of poets, especially political poets who hid their meaning for fear of reprisals and persecution. Throughout the centuries such devices have been in use and are very familiar. However unless a writer says something explicitly, the author can usually get away with quite a bit of vague description and even accusation and heresy. These devices were put in use right from the beginning of the Bible, from Genesis to Revelations with its glamorous predictions, which is the most metaphoric of all biblical books. There are no such things as gods. This is the concept behind the Holy Ghost. God is just the personification of a set of ideals which Jesus Christ points out to us. Through these poetic devices in the gospels, the truth has been preserved albeit hidden from the eyes of the vain. So it is possible to discover a new (yet old) meaning to all the stories of the Bible both Old and New Testaments by understanding these literary devices.

So here we are with a new understanding of an ancient concept which has prevailed through the ages because of people's willingness to believe that something like a god exists. For two thousand years however Christians have been claiming the END IS NIGH. They use this threat in order to recruit more souls into their trap and nets of vanity because they view themselves as the very fishermen of Christ or missionaries of the word. The END has never happened however and the power of the religion continues to surge through mankind.

This time in our lifetime, something different is happening. This time the whole world seems to be in suspense awaiting some apocalyptic event. Perhaps the Maya got it right after all. Perhaps the Christians will get what they have been waiting for, namely the end of the Mystery of God.

> Re:10:7: But in the days of the voice of the seventh angel, when he shall begin to sound, **the mystery of God should be finished**, as he hath declared to his servants the prophets'

Maybe this book or similar writings will reveal that mystery of God and add to the already massive pressure of the Theory of Evolution and the immense pile of scientific data accumulating as testimony that we the people have outgrown childish concepts of god. Maybe the Internet will reveal a new enlightenment to the largest audience in history. Perhaps when more people get proper educations they will see the folly of worshipping gods in the 21st Century. God theory might be destined to be some outdated app on old mobile phones only accessed by a few die-hards. Perhaps if Christianity loses all its followers other religions might take notice also. Whatever is about to happen, it will be momentous.

CONCEPT FIVE

BAPTISM

We have already touched on the Baptism lightly but it is so important a concept that it needs complete explanation. It is fitting that I use the word concept here because the Baptism is likened to a birth or **conception** in woman. Everybody who has ever been baptised has been into the womb of Christianity and has been re-born. Baptism is a rebirth into new life.

> Joh:3:3: Jesus answered and said unto him, Verily, verily, I say unto thee, Except a man **be born again**, he cannot see the kingdom of God.
>
> Joh:3:4: Nicodemus saith unto him, How can a man be born when he is old? can he enter the second time into his mother's womb, and be born?
>
> Joh:3:5: Jesus answered, Verily, verily, I say unto thee, Except a man be born of water and of the Spirit, he cannot enter into the kingdom of God.
>
> Joh:3:6: That which is born of the flesh is flesh; and that which is born of the Spirit is spirit.

Holding a 'concept' and developing it into a full 'conception' or idea is the theory behind Baptism. The whole conception of Baptism is like giving birth to a child wherein the child is a new belief system about God. Before anyone can truly be Baptised and not just simply go through the motions blithely or unwittingly where no new knowledge is learned, the person needs to be informed that there are no such things as gods. This is termed slaying in the spirit and it is a spiritual DEATH and an education which is termed receiving the Holy Ghost (which is the Holy Atheism concept).

> M'r:1:8: I indeed have baptized you with water: but **he shall baptize you with the Holy Ghost**.

All this is necessary to purge the mind of misconceptions, prior to offering the new knowledge. If the neophyte is not informed that there are no such things as gods, (which is the confession of truth) then nothing is learned, no conception takes place, no spirit is born, no rebirth occurs and the person remains ignorant of the truth and this is called a mis-conception. To believe that god is an omnipotent being is a misconception.

> Ro:6:3: Know ye not, that so many of us **as were baptized into Jesus Christ were baptized into his death?**
>
> Ro:6:4: **Therefore we are buried with him by baptism into death: that like as Christ was raised up from the dead by the glory of the Father, even so we also should walk in newness of life.**
>
> Ro:6:5: For if we have been planted together in the likeness of his death, we shall be also in the likeness of his resurrection:
>
> Ro:6:9: Knowing that Christ being raised from the dead dieth no more; death hath no more dominion over him.
>
> Ro:14:11: For it is written, As I live, saith the Lord, every knee shall bow to me, and **every tongue shall confess to God**.
>
> Ro:15:9: And that the Gentiles might glorify God for his mercy; as it is written, For this cause **I will confess to thee among the Gentiles**, and sing unto thy name.

The confession is simply this that there are no such things as gods. Without this confession there can be no remission of sins. Jesus was called the Son of God because of the adoption of the spirit of god as an adopted Father figure and accordingly also the behaviour to promote a love of goodness abroad.

> M't:5:14: **Ye are the light of the world**. A city that is set on an hill cannot be hid.

When a person is informed with authority that there are no such things as gods, this should have the effect of purging their mind of all misconceptions about god, heaven and sin, thus leaving them with clean slate on which the new concept can be imprinted.

> M't:12:43: When the unclean spirit is gone out of a man, he walketh through dry places, seeking rest, and findeth none.

> M't:12:44: Then he saith, I will return into my house from whence I came out; and when he is come, **he findeth it empty, swept, and garnished**.

> M't:12:45: Then goeth he, and taketh with himself seven other spirits more wicked than himself, and they enter in and

When such a pure state is reached (we shall call this the Holy Atheism concept which is actually referred to in the New Testament as the Holy Ghost concept) it is only then that the person can truly appreciate that their sins and guilt have been removed.

> Ac:13:38: Be it known unto you therefore, men and brethren, that through this man is preached unto you the **forgiveness of sins**:

> M't:12:31: Wherefore I say unto you, **All manner of sin and blasphemy shall be forgiven** unto men: but the blasphemy against the **Holy Ghost** shall not be forgiven unto men.

> M't:12:32: And whosoever speaketh a word against the Son of man, it shall be forgiven him: but whosoever **speaketh against**

the Holy Ghost, it shall not be forgiven him, neither in this world, neither in the world to come.

There is no such thing as sin. We are all animals and animals do not sin. The Holy Ghost is the spirit that we need to adopt in order to accept an IDEAL such as godlessness as our Father Spirit. The word GHOST stands for a 'nothingness' or the 'shadow of something' and while we observe that god is also nothing physical, we confess that we have made an IDEAL into our god.

We believe there is no such thing as sin. All animal behaviour is simply animal behaviour that happens because that is the way animals have evolved. Evolution itself is without sin. Animals have no concept of morals or law or ethics or standards. We people, only have such concepts because our ideal (god) taught them to us. The ideal that we strive to live up to has abolished sin. The Baptism then breeds a new conception (birth) which is better than the previous misconception of god. The new conception is that there are no such things as Gods or Satan or Sin or Hell or Purgatory or any places or deities created by the mind of man. This is true and sound knowledge. Any anthropologist will confess that different cultures will have different laws and standards. So they will also have different gods. The person accepting true Baptism therefore feels reborn and new, with a new outlook and a new expectation of themselves, far less complicated than before. It should be added that their perception of Jesus is also made more pure, abolishing all the false opinions of miracles and magic and He being a god or a son of god. He is now seen as a normal human, full of the same weaknesses and failings as anyone of us, and from such an opinion can only come a more perfect understanding of the virtuous man He was.

> M't:9:2: And, behold, they brought to him a man sick of the palsy, lying on a bed: and Jesus seeing their faith said unto the sick of the palsy; Son, be of good cheer; thy sins be forgiven thee.

> M't:9:3: And, behold, certain of the scribes said within themselves, This man blasphemeth.

M't:9:4: And Jesus knowing their thoughts said, Wherefore think ye evil in your hearts?

M't:9:5: **For whether is easier, to say, Thy sins be forgiven thee; or to say, Arise, and walk?**

M't:9:6: But that ye may know that the Son of man hath power on earth to forgive sins, (then saith he to the sick of the palsy,) Arise, take up thy bed, and go unto thine house.

Forgiving sin is easy, it's a walk in the park for anyone who understands the concept of Baptism. When we go through DEATH (or are slain in the spirit this is represented by Jesus being crucified we are made into atheists which is the **first** concept of Baptism) we are then buried into the womb of Christianity. It is important that the Baptism immerses the person wholly under the waters. These waters are significant as the womb of Christianity and they also represent the tomb into which Jesus' body was placed after the crucifixion this is the **second** concept of Baptism. In Revelation we are told that the waters represent "Re:17:15: And he saith unto me, The waters which thou sawest, where the whore sitteth, **are peoples, and multitudes, and nations, and tongues**." So the water of Baptism represents Peoples and multitudes and nations and tongues this of course is HUMANITY which we pledge to serve also. "Joh:13:14: **If I then, your Lord and Master, have washed your feet; ye also ought to wash one another's feet**." Just as Jesus came to be the servant of many so too do we pledge to serve as many as we meet. When we arise from the Baptismal waters and are reborn, we are raised into new life and a new more perfect concept of the Ideal of God is formed within us. This represents the resurrection of Jesus after the third day in the den. This is the **third** concept of Baptism. Such a change is recorded by Peter who compares the old view of the Godhead to the new viewpoint after baptism.

In this following verse Peter indicates that the old flesh (scripture) which they once had, was filthy when compared to the 'Good Conscience toward god' which they now have.

> *1Pe:3:21: The like figure whereunto even **baptism** doth also now save us (not the putting away **of the filth of the flesh, but the answer of a good conscience toward God,**) by the resurrection of Jesus Christ:*

Once again the word 'Flesh' is used to indicate scripture or bread our daily bread which is scripture. This reference is saying that it was not scripture study that saved us but by the Baptism we became atheists and were reborn making a vow to serve all humanity which is our opinion of god. By this we found that we have a good conscience toward god.

The Baptism is the most crucial, most holy and most central demonstration of a pledge or vow that it is possible to make publicly, even more so than marriage. At the same time, in return, the individual is given the knowledge of the great and Holy Secret of Religion known as the mystery of god and also that which is also called the Holy Ghost or the Holy Atheism concept. They are inducted into the secret society of Christendom. They learn the mystery which was kept secret since time began and the only way that people can know that they are free from sin.

> *Ro:16:25: Now to him that is of power to stablish you according to my gospel, and the preaching of Jesus Christ, according **to the revelation of the mystery, which was kept secret since the world began,***

> *Ro:11:25: For I would not, brethren, **that ye should be ignorant of this mystery,** lest ye should be wise in your own conceits; that blindness in part is happened to Israel, until the fulness of the Gentiles be come in.*

> *Ro:11:26: And so all Israel shall be saved: as it is written, There shall come out of Sion the Deliverer, and shall turn away ungodliness from Jacob:*

> *Ro:11:27: For this is my covenant unto them, **when I shall take away their sins**.*

These are the sentiments expressed in Romans as in other places as well. A well-known quote is the one below referring to the wages of sin being death. This is telling us that if we remain in the corrupt church and doctrine of idolatry our delusion or sin will make us dead to the illumination of truth as well as the pleasures of life. This verse also acts as reinforcement that to be deluded by dogma is seen as being dead to the truth of atheism.

> *Ro:6:23:* **For the wages of sin is death**; *but the gift of God is eternal life through Jesus Christ our Lord.*

Therefore it is said that we should not attend churches in order to worship god.

> M't:6:6: **But thou, when thou prayest, enter into thy closet**, and when thou hast shut thy door, pray to thy Father which is in secret; and thy Father which seeth in secret shall reward thee openly.

We should not worship anything at all but take joy in the discovery of knowledge and the acquisition of wisdom. For this reason it is stated in Revelation to come away from the church which exploits us. We are invited to leave the grip of the church which has deceived us into believing in a delusion. To believe that gods actually exist in a physical way is the worst delusion known to humanity. Nothing but war and argument will ever be accredited to her achievements. In Revelations it is pointed out that this is the pinnacle of confusion and deceit. Leave her immediately according to Revelations 18:4.

> Re:18:2: And he cried mightily with a strong voice, saying, **Babylon** the great is fallen, is fallen, and is become the habitation of devils, and the hold of every foul spirit, and a cage of every unclean and hateful bird.

> Re:18:3: For all nations have drunk of the wine of the wrath of her fornication, and the kings of the earth have committed fornication with her, and the merchants of the earth are waxed rich through the abundance of her delicacies.

Re:18:4: And I heard another voice from heaven, saying, Come out of her, my people, that ye be not partakers of her sins, and that ye receive not of her plagues.

Re:18:5: For her sins have reached unto heaven, and God hath remembered her iniquities.

Re:18:6: Reward her even as she rewarded you, and double unto her double according to her works: in the cup which she hath filled fill to her double.

Re:18:7: How much she hath glorified herself, and lived deliciously, so much torment and sorrow give her: for she saith in her heart, I sit a queen, and am no widow, and shall see no sorrow.

Re:18:8: Therefore shall her plagues come in one day, death, and mourning, and famine; and she shall be utterly burned with fire: for strong is the Lord God who judgeth her.

Re:18:9: And the kings of the earth, who have committed fornication and lived deliciously with her, shall bewail her, and lament for her, when they shall see the smoke of her burning,

Re:18:10: Standing afar off for the fear of her torment, saying, Alas, alas, that great city Babylon, that mighty city! for in one hour is thy judgment come.

Babylon is referred to as a place where people are held captive just as in the Old Testament. The name means 'Confusion' and it is spiritual confusion that keeps people attached to the fantasy of God and Heaven. All the time that people are exploited by the promise of Heaven and everlasting life they will remain loyal to dogma and trapped by sin. The Tower of Babel is the story that introduces this world of religious confusion to us and this story is as old as the Bible itself. If you remember it was in building a tower to reach heaven (which is a religion) that the people were punished by scattering them throughout all the lands of Earth and confusing their language so that they could not understand each other. Even today, in

Christianity alone, there are so many denominations as to make a mockery of the oneness of Christ.

> 1Co:1:13: **Is Christ divided**? was Paul crucified for you? or were ye baptized in the name of Paul?

> Eph:4:5: **One Lord, one faith, one baptism,**

Of course we have to be baptised in the name of Christ in order to be informed of the Ideal of God. Christ is the only authority on this subject. He was the only person who understood Jewish Law so well that He gave us this new interpretation. To be baptised is to be shown all these literary tricks associated with understanding the Bible. How else can we know that gods do not exist? So it is only by His teaching that we understand atheism and His Ideal of God. It is only through Him that the veil of heaven is revealed and only through Him that the mystery of God is also exposed. It was His parables that disclosed the folly of dogma and freed us from being caught up in the infatuation of worship. There is no other teaching that can forgive sin. To just say 'your sins are forgiven' is not enough to allow people to know that they have no sin. It must be taught that God is an Ideal only, and that sin as with all aspects of dogma, is mere imagination. It takes a certain volume of evidence before people actually begin to believe these teachings but when they do they can never change their mind. Their conception becomes fast and frees them for the remainder of their life. Their thirst is finally quenched forever.

> Joh:4:14: But whosoever drinketh of the water that I shall give him **shall never thirst**; but the water that I shall give him shall be in him a well of water springing up into everlasting life.

Good spiritual life is considered to be contentment in the superior knowledge of truth and fact rather than a belief in imagined things. To live life to the fullest one needs to feel free of restrictions and obligations of worship.

> Lu:13:16: And ought not this woman (out of man - religion), being a daughter of Abraham, **whom Satan hath bound**, lo,

these eighteen (oppression) years, be loosed from this bond on
the sabbath day?

Being bound by Satan is to be forced into prayer and worship and other
commitments under a church. We have discussed where Satan's seat is and
that she teaches all the restraining ideas it can in order to bind us to the
delusion and ongoing commitment of doctrine.

The concept of Everlasting Life according to Jesus frees us from such
oppression. Nevertheless this discipline requires some recompense and
the nurturing of generosity was the repayment. Eternal life is a feeling of
safety and contentedness which soothes the spirit of a person to put them
at ease with the universe. Yet eternal life is something you must earn, even
though it is freely given and cannot be taken away

> *M'r:8:35: For whosoever will save his life shall lose it; but
> whosoever shall lose his **life for my sake and the gospel's**, the
> same shall save it.*

The explanations of those who try to save their life by worshipping gods
actually lose it because of the misconception and delusion they fall into.
They become dead to truthfulness as previously mentioned and fall into
perpetual dogma. Those who lose their life by giving up the comfort of
worship by becoming atheists, actually save their life and mentality by
finding purity, honesty and sincerity of thought. Some people never accept
the truth. Some prefer to harness thoughts of god and imaginations of
heaven and angels and all manner of supernatural things. Some people
even believe that they can communicate with the 'other world' and the
dead, which of course they can't. No-one can. Some people believe in
the supernatural world of spirits and séances and Tarot readings and all
manner of false notions. Such people have difficulty accepting the truth
because they have invested so much pride in their imagined worlds that
they are unable to back out and yet save face. Such people will always be
tormented by everything that challenges their view. They become hardened
to truthful exposure and will argue until the end of the world that they
are right. This torment follows them forever. This uncertainty is always
present with their thoughts.

Re:14:10: The same shall drink of the wine of the wrath of God, which is poured out without mixture into the cup of his indignation; and he shall be tormented **with fire and brimstone** in the presence of the holy angels, and in the presence of the Lamb:

Re:14:11: And the **smoke of their torment ascendeth up for ever and ever**: and they have no rest day nor night, who worship the beast and his image, and whosoever receiveth the mark of his name.

Re:14:12: Here is the patience of the saints: here are they that keep the commandments of God, and the faith of Jesus.

Re:14:13: And I heard a voice from heaven saying unto me, Write, **Blessed are the dead which die in the Lord from henceforth**: Yea, saith the Spirit, **that they may rest from their labours**; and their works do follow them.

All the tormented need to do in order to win freedom and contentment is confess that sin does not exist, and receive Christ's truthfulness. "Blessed are the dead which die in the Lord from henceforth". Then they can start to learn all the knowledge of the universe including evolution and astrophysics and quantum mechanics and Darwin's theory and palaeontology and well everything! Nothing is forbidden when there is no such thing as sin.

Jesus' idea was to continue the teaching of righteousness throughout the entire world. He realised that He would not achieve anything at all by simply railing at the synagogues. He knew the only way to change a doctrine is with a better doctrine. He knew that the process of establishing a new religion would be slow, but He felt sure that good people would grasp onto His knowledge of the truth, and perhaps continue His work.

*M'r:6:7: And he called unto him the twelve, and **began to send them forth** by two and two; and **gave them power over unclean spirits**;*

> *M'r:6:8: And commanded them that they should take nothing for their journey, save a staff only; no scrip, no bread, no money in their purse:*
>
> *M'r:6:9: But be shod with sandals; and not put on two coats.*
>
> *M'r:6:10: And he said unto them, In what place soever ye enter into an house, there abide till ye depart from that place.*
>
> *M'r:6:11: And whosoever shall not receive you, nor hear you, when ye depart thence, shake off the dust under your feet for a testimony against them. Verily I say unto you, It shall be more tolerable for Sodom and Gomorrha in the day of judgment, than for that city.*
>
> *M'r:6:12: And they went out, and preached that men should repent.*
>
> *M'r:6:13: And they cast out many devils, and anointed with oil many that were sick, and healed them.*

Now we see that the disciples by this time also had power to heal and cast out devils just as Jesus had shown them. Such healing and casting out unclean spirits is all cognitive work in nature. It is all by word of mouth. It is all by demonstration of truthful interpretation of scripture. So these men became the first psychologists. It was by way of enlightenment that the disciples were able to influence the populace. These were men speaking plain talk and sensible things, not berating the public with condemnation or with fire and brimstone sermons. They may not have been able to persuade some die-hard Israelites but they were effective with people open to learning new doctrine such as the Gentiles.

It is no wonder that Christianity took off the way it did. Its popularity was due to the fact that people were finally hearing the truth about religion and discovering how they had been exploited by their own hierarchy. The method of railing at the congregation with fire and brimstone sermons is only a modern adaptation; the early Christians had no need of such tactics. They had a message of Truth and a system of behaviour to commit to, such as Baptism, and the people who joined the movement were glad to be sensible, knowledgeable, people with true insight, and not just followers of misguided priests.

Not only did the disciples travel throughout the country to teach and raise people from their dead works, but so too did Jesus as follows.

> *M't:4:23:* **And Jesus went about all Galilee***, teaching in their synagogues, and preaching the gospel of the kingdom, and healing all manner of sickness and all manner of disease among the people.*

> *M't:9:35:* **And Jesus went about all the cities and villages***, teaching in their synagogues, and preaching the gospel of the kingdom, and healing every sickness and every disease among the people.*

Interestingly the two separate verses above are almost word for word describing Jesus' mission throughout the country. This shows that the disciples borrowed from each other a little when writing the gospels and simply repeated things as it pleased them. No harm done.

> *Lu:9:6: And they departed, and went through the towns, preaching the gospel, and healing every where.*

And the disciples did likewise after the fashion and example set by Jesus.

Although Jesus also travelled He must have taken some disciples with Him because the teaching was made through the Baptism. It is said however that Jesus did not baptise anybody.

> Joh:4:2: (**Though Jesus himself baptized not, but his disciples,**)

This is odd since it was promised that Jesus would baptize with Fire and the Holy Ghost.

> M't:3:11: I indeed baptize you with water unto repentance: but he that cometh after me is mightier than I, whose shoes I am not worthy to bear: **he shall baptize you with the Holy Ghost, and with fire:**

In order to baptise, one needs to baptise in the name of Jesus Christ. Jesus Himself could not very well do this. Jesus had to suffer the crucifixion first which represents the death and rebirth of baptism. This must be done in order for the Holy Ghost to be given.

> Joh:7:38: He that believeth on me, as the scripture hath said, out of his belly shall flow rivers of living water.

> Joh:7:39: (But this spake he of the Spirit, which they that believe on him should receive: **for the Holy Ghost was not yet given; because that Jesus was not yet glorified.**)

John may have believed that the Holy Ghost was not given until Jesus had resurrected but He would have been wrong. Mary the Mother of Jesus and Elizabeth Mother of John both received the Holy Ghost to their wombs. John and Jesus together received the Holy Ghost from the womb.

Mary mother of Jesus with Holy Ghost;

> M't:1:20: But while he thought on these things, behold, the angel of the Lord appeared unto him in a dream, saying, Joseph, thou son of David, fear not to take unto thee Mary thy wife: for **that which is conceived in her is of the Holy Ghost**.

John the Baptist promise of the Holy Ghost;

> Lu:1:15: For he shall be great in the sight of the Lord, and shall drink neither wine nor strong drink; **and he shall be filled with the Holy Ghost**, even from his mother's womb.

When Jesus was baptised however the Holy Ghost alighted on Him yet again.

> Lu:3:21: Now when all the people were baptized, it came to pass, that Jesus also being baptized, and praying, the heaven was opened,

Lu:3:22: **And the Holy Ghost descended in a bodily shape like a dove upon him**, and a voice came from heaven, which said, Thou art my beloved Son; in thee I am well pleased.

Poor old John the Baptist was never baptised at least there is no record of it in the Gospels.

This therefore becomes one of those New Testament dilemmas or inconsistencies that must drive some people nuts! We who are born of truth know the solution. We know what the Holy Ghost represents the truth and therefore have no issue with what other people make of it. The Holy Ghost is the concept, of the Holiness, of the knowledge, that there are no such things as gods. This Atheistic viewpoint or concept is called the Holy Atheism or the Holy Nothing or the Holy Ghost. It is the death of the notion that god exists, and with it so does Heaven and Hell and Satan and Sin, and all manner of devils and argument, and all the trappings of bigotry and dogma.

We are above such things because the notion of god was made clear to us that to worship a god is idolatry.

The Holy Ghost was definitely around before Jesus was born otherwise, how was it that He had this knowledge of the truth? The Holy Ghost also fell on Adam and Eve when they ate of the fruit of the tree of knowledge of good and evil, else how could they have died?

The Holy Ghost slays a person in the spirit. That is its job. Without slaying the spirit no new teaching could take place. Unless the old corrupt spirit is slain, there can be no new atheistic spirit to be re-born with. We see at least when Jesus was baptized that the Holy Ghost did arrive with John's baptism, even though the Gospel of John states that the Holy Ghost was not given until after Jesus was glorified (crucified). We also need to bear in mind that Jesus could not be reborn by this baptism. He could not be slain in the spirit as He already knew the truth.

> Lu:3:21: Now when all the people were baptized, it came to pass, that Jesus also being baptized, and praying, the heaven was opened,

> Lu:3:22: **And the Holy Ghost descended in a bodily shape like a dove upon him**, and a voice came from heaven, which said, Thou art my beloved Son; in thee I am well pleased.

It is understood that the baptism of Jesus was merely to follow protocol. It was merely a formality suffered for the purpose of fulfilling prophecy or the intricacies of the doctrine.

> M't:3:13: Then cometh Jesus from Galilee to Jordan unto John, to be baptized of him.

> M't:3:14: But John forbad him, saying, I have need to be baptized of thee, and comest thou to me?

> M't:3:15: And Jesus answering said unto him, **Suffer it to be so now: for thus it becometh us to fulfil all righteousness.** Then he suffered him.

So John did Baptize with fire (argument - words of power to reveal the mystery of god) without revealing the mystery of god to make the mind a clean slate or swept clean then sin cannot be forgiven. "M'r:1:4: John did baptize in the wilderness, and preach the baptism of repentance for **the remission of sins.**"

The sin of idolatry was everywhere but in these following verses we see that the disciples were not fazed by the thought of dealing with idols. They state that "we know that an idol is nothing in the world" however they go on to say in verse 7 that some people still view god as if an idol, and eat (read scripture) as a thing offered unto an idol. They point out also that their liberty of eating meat (saying prayers or worshipping the truth openly) may become a stumbling block for those people who do not share the same insights. So they 'take heed' not to insult the unenlightened.

*1Co:8:4: As concerning therefore the eating of those things that are offered in sacrifice unto idols, **we know that an idol is nothing in the world**, and that there is none other God but one.*

1Co:8:5: For though there be that are called gods, whether in heaven or in earth, (as there be gods many, and lords many,)

1Co:8:6: But to us there is but one God, the Father, of whom are all things, and we in him; and one Lord Jesus Christ, by whom are all things, and we by him.

*1Co:8:7: Howbeit there is not in every man that knowledge: for some with **conscience of the idol unto this hour eat it as a thing offered unto an idol; and their conscience being weak is defiled**.*

1Co:8:8: But meat commendeth us not to God: for neither, if we eat, are we the better; neither, if we eat not, are we the worse.

*1Co:8:9: But take heed lest by any means this liberty of yours become a **stumblingblock to them that are weak**.*

1Co:8:10: For if any man see thee which hast knowledge sit at meat in the idol's temple, shall not the conscience of him which is weak be emboldened to eat those things which are offered to idols;

The most common objection to the teaching of Jesus' viewpoint is that He also is deceitful. This deceitfulness could be seen as fraudulent. After all, He keeps this secret that there are no such things as gods, but since Jesus was honest and told the secret to whomever asked this opinion won't hold water either. Jesus always informs anyone prepared to listen of the 'Covering of Grace' in the "Word of God". No one is purposely left out of the 'Holy Ghost' as it were. Everybody is told as much as they seek after.

Every time Jesus healed some person of an ailment or raised them from the Dead he divulged this secret and entrusted them to it with the order "Tell no one!"

Matthew;

> M't:8:2: And, behold, there came a leper and worshipped him, saying, Lord, if thou wilt, thou canst make me clean.

> M't:8:3: And Jesus put forth his hand, and touched him, saying, I will; be thou clean. And immediately his leprosy was cleansed.

> M't:8:4: And Jesus saith unto him, **See thou tell no man**; but go thy way, shew thyself to the priest, and offer the gift that Moses commanded, for a testimony unto them.

Mark;

> M'r:7:34: And looking up to heaven, he sighed, and saith unto him, Ephphatha, that is, Be opened.

> M'r:7:35: And straightway his ears were opened, and the string of his tongue was loosed, and he spake plain.

> M'r:7:36: And he charged them that **they should tell no man**: but the more he charged them, so much the more a great deal they published it;

Luke;

> Lu:5:12: And it came to pass, when he was in a certain city, behold a man full of leprosy: who seeing Jesus fell on his face, and besought him, saying, Lord, if thou wilt, thou canst make me clean.

> Lu:5:13: And he put forth his hand, and touched him, saying, I will: be thou clean. And immediately the leprosy departed from him.

> Lu:5:14: **And he charged him to tell no man**: but go, and shew thyself to the priest, and offer for thy cleansing, according as Moses commanded, for a testimony unto them.

So we see that Jesus did inform the people of the secret mystery of God and immediately gives the instruction to "tell no man" otherwise it wouldn't be a secret. Jesus even confesses this fact to the Pharisees but they are none the wiser because they just don't know their own doctrine. Jesus needed to be popular in order for the whole concept to take root. He wanted to heal the hierarchy of their delusions and improve the behaviour of the layperson in the street. He wanted truth to be taught to the young rather than falsehoods which caused confusion and led behaviour astray. He wanted to heal the corruption that He felt had ruined Jewish Leadership. But in order to achieve all these goals he needed to be popular. Therefore He campaigned for this popularity and begged the people to make him popular.

> *Joh:3:14: **And as Moses lifted up the serpent in the wilderness, even so must the Son of man be lifted up**:*

In asking to be lifted up in this way Jesus is asking His followers to raise him up like a martyr or a hero of the people. He needed to be made famous in order to be recognised as the authority that He was. Albeit that His knowledge was enough to do this anyway. We are all taught that the serpent with a forked tongue represents deceit and it is true enough that there is a deceit at the core of all doctrine but more than this Jesus is alluding to an event in Numbers 21:6-9 Which also fits in nicely with the expected prophecy.

> *Nu:21:6: **And the LORD sent fiery serpents among the people, and they bit the people; and much people of Israel died.***

> *Nu:21:7: Therefore the people came to Moses, and said, We have sinned, for we have spoken against the LORD, and against thee; pray unto the LORD, that he take away the serpents from us. And Moses prayed for the people.*

> *Nu:21:8: And the LORD said unto Moses, Make thee a fiery serpent, and set it upon a pole: and it shall come to pass, that every one that is bitten, when he looketh upon it, shall live.*

> *Nu:21:9: And Moses made a serpent of brass, and put it upon a pole, and it came to pass, that if a serpent had bitten any man, when he beheld the serpent of brass, he lived.*

The explanation is simple and easily seen by people of the truth. The fiery serpents had a 'poisoned' bite. The poisonous words caused death to happen on their utterance. The serpent of brass was the ensign that allowed people to live if they had been bitten by the serpents that the Lord God had sent among them. Jesus was saying that if a person was bitten by a serpent sent by the traditional Lord God; (traditional doctrine) as we have seen, they died or were considered to be dead to truth, but by looking to Jesus and His explanation of the Honest Truth and mystery of God, then they lived again. This is yet another resurrection story and is themed with the promise of eternal life as well as asking the people to lift Jesus up.

The Serpent is one of the first metaphors used in the Bible appearing as it does in Genesis in the story of Eve and the fruit of knowledge. It is taken for granted that serpents have forked tongues and therefore are liars. Traditionally the serpent is recognised as being the tempter in Paradise. Throughout the entire Bible the Serpent or Leviathan is associated with death.

> *Ge:3:1: Now the serpent was more subtil than any beast of the field which the LORD God had made. And he said unto the woman, Yea, hath God said, Ye shall not eat of every tree of the garden?*
>
> *Ge:3:2: And the woman said unto the serpent, We may eat of the fruit of the trees of the garden:*
>
> *Ge:3:3: But of the fruit of the tree which is in the midst of the garden, God hath said, Ye shall not eat of it, neither shall ye touch it, lest ye die.*
>
> *Ge:3:4: And the serpent said unto the woman,* **Ye shall not surely die***:*

Ge:3:5: For God doth know that in the day ye eat thereof, then your eyes shall be opened, and ye shall be as gods, knowing good and evil.

Ge:3:6: And when the woman saw that the tree was good for food, and that it was pleasant to the eyes, and a tree to be desired to make one wise, she took of the fruit thereof, and did eat, and gave also unto her husband with her; and he did eat.

*Ge:3:7: **And the eyes of them both were opened, and they knew that they were naked; and they sewed fig leaves together, and made themselves aprons**.*

So in this story the Serpent actually is not the deceiver that he is made out to be. God it seems is the falsifier. God says don't eat the fruit or even touch it lest you die. But the Serpent says no you won't die go ahead and eat. They ate and just as the serpent described they did not die but instead their eyes were opened and they knew good and evil just as the fruit promised, and they became as gods themselves. So in all this; God seems to be the one who actually tells the lie, but wait! Before we are too hasty we must add that God's opinion of death was a spiritual death, which of course means that they became atheists. So in the end God did not lie either, and the Bible has it both ways.

The important part of this story is the fact that the fruit of the tree of knowledge of good and evil is TRUTH (there are no such things as gods). This describes the mystery of God as we have been outlining in this book also. This is the same truth that Jesus expounds.

Joh:8:44: **Ye are of your father the devil**, and the lusts of your father ye will do. He was a murderer from the beginning, **and abode not in the truth**, because there is no truth in him. When he speaketh a lie, he speaketh of his own: for he is a liar, and the father of it.

Joh:8:45: **And because I tell you the truth, ye believe me not**.

> Joh:8:46: Which of you convinceth me of sin? And if I say the truth, why do ye not believe me?

It is only the truth about the religion that there are no such things as gods, that can imbue one with knowledge of good and evil. No person under any delusion can know the truth while they yet give life to their delusion. All people are ruled by their belief system whether it is founded on God or worldliness. Some people's belief systems drag them into despair and depression while others are happy and contented. It is only ones belief system that induces good wholesome concepts or delusionary imaginations and paranoia. All people who are deluded by their incorrect worship will hate this little book as they hated Jesus before.

> Joh:15:18: **If the world hate you, ye know that it hated me before it hated you**.

Their thoughts have been poisoned by shamans of deceit who think it best to keep the congregation misinformed. Little do they realise that following the truth would open the whole world up to them and their followers. The public pledge of the baptism is a promise not only to serve god but to serve each other as well as the planet in general. What godly person do you know that speaks to save the eco systems of the planet? Are there any? Instead they all preach the rapture and that God will destroy the world! How absurd! The Earth is the 'Apple of His eye"

So Moses as does Jesus think of the analogy of religion as a great Serpent. In the Old Testament it is called Leviathan.

> Isa:27:1: In that day the LORD with his sore and great and strong sword shall punish **leviathan the piercing serpent, even leviathan that crooked serpent**; and he shall slay the dragon that is in the sea.

It must be remembered too that god created the Serpent in the first place.

> Job:26:13: **By his spirit he hath garnished the heavens; his hand hath formed the crooked serpent**.

This is why Moses chose to create the Brazen Serpent as an ensign of death as did Jesus.

> *Joh:3:14:* ***And as Moses lifted up the serpent in the wilderness,*** ***even so must the Son of man be lifted up****:*

This is also why serpents were used in the battle of Moses against Pharaoh. The analogy is that serpents contain poison in their bite and it is this poison that sends madness and death to its victims. This madness is used to describe the type of mentality that an over-zealous priest might display.

> *De:32:24: They shall be burnt with hunger, and devoured with burning heat, and with bitter destruction: I will also send the teeth of beasts upon them, with the* ***poison of serpents*** *of the dust.*

Perhaps the serpent's image is that given in Psalms "they have sharpened their tongues with poison" means they deceive by a clever use of words.

> *Psalms:140:3:* ***They have sharpened their tongues like a serpent; adders' poison is under their lips.*** *Selah.*

Of course there is always this meaning that our minds are corrupted by the sly speech of serpents like they beguiled Eve.

> *2Co:11:3: But I fear, lest by any means, as the serpent beguiled Eve through his subtilty,* ***so your minds should be corrupted from the simplicity that is in Christ****.*

Or perhaps it is the allusion to the poison of our lips as revealed in Romans;

> *Ro:3:13: Their throat is an open sepulchre; with their tongues they have used deceit;* ***the poison of asps is under their lips****:*

So serpents are seen as those people whose creed is to deceive others in order to exploit them. Their speech is full of poison, their tongue is also poisoned and they spread their poison by speaking evil of others or by spreading false information.

The Baptism is different, even though it too holds a secret so austere that it could easily destroy the entire doctrine that professes it. Yet the doctrine survives, because the enlightenment of truth is so impressive, that its proponents value it more highly than god itself. The secret is that 'truth' is God, "In the beginning was the Word, and the Word was with God, and the **Word was God**" and therefore becomes the Father of all knowledge. No knowledge can be said to be trustworthy without knowledge of the truth first.

So what is Baptism? Baptism is described as full immersion in water for the purpose of cleansing. The word 'Baptize' is supposedly translated from 'Baptizo' a first century word describing immersing a garment first into water then into dye hence cleansing and changing its appearance at the same time. The concept behind Baptism is similar in that one is fully immersed in water and is then raised up into new life as described above. There are however a number of things we can explore in order to find out more about the spiritual significance of Baptism.

> *Ro:6:4: Therefore we are **buried with him by baptism into death**: that like as Christ was raised up from the dead by the glory of the Father, even so we also should **walk in newness of life**.*

Jesus also said to Nicodemus that people must be born again in order to experience the kingdom of God.

> *Joh:3:3: Jesus answered and said unto him, Verily, verily, I say unto thee, **Except a man be born again, he cannot see the kingdom of God.***

> *Joh:3:4: Nicodemus saith unto him, How can a man be born when he is old? can he enter the second time into his mother's womb, and be born?*

> *Joh:3:5: Jesus answered, Verily, verily, I say unto thee, **Except a man be born of water and of the Spirit**, he cannot enter into the kingdom of God.*

Joh:3:6: That which is born of the flesh is flesh; and that which is born of the Spirit is spirit.

Joh:3:7: Marvel not that I said unto thee, Ye must be born again.

Jesus describes that one must be born of water and of spirit in order to be saved. So it is clear that spiritually it is water that holds the key to understanding Baptism. In order to understand the metaphor of water we should do some research in order to discover how the Bible both Old and New Testaments consider it.

The first mention of water is with the creation of Adam in Genesis.

*Ge:2:6: But there went up a **mist** from the earth, and watered the whole face of the ground.*

After this watering of the ground (Gods ground or population) Adam (Adam means 'Of the Ground') was created. So we see that the population was 'watered' prior to the creation of Adam whom we have already discussed was the first society of Hebrews.

We learn by this story that Adam or man (plural) became a living soul. So to be raised out of the waters is to be made a living soul or in other words to be resurrected to newness of life just as the Baptism dictates.

So here is the spiritual significance of water; it gives us "LIFE". Water holds the spirit of life. This is true for all water but especially so for fresh water (although some things can live in salt water such as fish which is a separate subject). Fresh water is the most valued commodity in the entire world. Nothing can live without fresh water to drink. No plants; no animals can survive without fresh water. Water is the very essence of life itself and so valued because all life depends on it. In Amos it is seen as 'Judgement' perhaps this is what is meant by its spirit?

*Am:5:24: But let **judgment run down as waters**, and righteousness as a mighty stream.*

Maybe Habakkuk has the right interpretation calling it the 'Knowledge of the Lord"

> *Hab:2:14: For the earth shall be filled with* **the knowledge of the glory of the LORD, as the waters cover the sea.**

Nevertheless Zechariah comes close to its real value referring to it as "Living Waters"

> *Zec:14:8: And it shall be in that day,* **that living waters shall go out from Jerusalem**; *half of them toward the former sea, and half of them toward the hinder sea: in summer and in winter shall it be.*

Jesus also alludes to this 'living water' in the story of the Samarian Woman (out of man – religion) at the well

> *Joh:4:10: Jesus answered and said unto her, If thou knewest the gift of God, and who it is that saith to thee, Give me to drink; thou wouldest have asked of him, and he would have given thee* **living water.**

> *Joh:4:11: The woman saith unto him, Sir, thou hast nothing to draw with, and the well is deep: from whence then hast thou that living water?*

> *Joh:4:12: Art thou greater than our father Jacob, which gave us the well, and drank thereof himself, and his children, and his cattle?*

> *Joh:4:13: Jesus answered and said unto her, Whosoever drinketh of this water shall thirst again:*

> *Joh:4:14: But whosoever drinketh of the water that I shall give him shall never thirst;* **but the water that I shall give him shall be in him a well of water springing up into everlasting life.**

We learn that it is not an actual woman but a wo-man (out of man or religion) that He is talking to in fact it is named as the Samarians. We can easily imagine Jesus talking to a synagogue full of Samarians and that He is talking about 'living water' from which we will **never thirst**

again. This is not actual water but a metaphor of water representing 'the truth' or 'everlasting life'. Now we know that 'everlasting life' is NOT meaning *agelessness*, but instead a contented and lively spirit that gives us 'life' or liveliness while we yet live. Everlasting means that it will last as long as we are alive. This conclusion can be made, because as we realise that if we commit idolatry, we become dead, so to speak, to all good works and opinions. If we are deluded in thought, we often become bigoted in opinion, and judgemental of others as well as numerous other behavioural misgivings. To live this way is not life at all. The only way to experience life to the fullest is to adopt the same spirit of freedom which comes with the realisation that sin is dead and irrelevant. This can only happen if one is baptised to Christ's truth of religion, that there are no such things as gods and no such thing as sin dictating how we should live. Jesus gives us exactly this freedom.

> *Joh:8:32:* **And ye shall know the truth, and the truth shall make you free.**

> *Ro:8:2:* **For the law of the Spirit of life in Christ Jesus hath made me free from the law of sin and death.**

The death that we have been referring to is not the final mortal death of the body either, but rather a spiritual death and discarding of misconception and false beliefs. The absolute death of the physical body is a different occurrence altogether. It is life extinct which is referred to in the Bible as the "Second Death"

> *Re:2:11:* He that hath an ear, let him hear what the Spirit saith unto the churches; He that overcometh **shall not be hurt of the second death**.

Revelations points to this 'Second Death" and promises that we shall not be hurt by it.

> *Re:20:6:* Blessed and holy is he that hath part **in the first resurrection: on such the second death hath no power,** but they shall be priests of God and of Christ, and shall reign with him a thousand years.

The first resurrection is with Baptism as already discussed. The second death is the final extinction of the physical body. The following verses tell of how some people will remain misguided all their life even until this final physical death of their body which is called the second death.

> *Re:20:14: And death and hell were cast into the lake of fire.* ***This is the second death.***

> *Re:21:8: But the fearful, and unbelieving, and the abominable, and murderers, and whoremongers, and sorcerers, and idolaters, and all liars, shall have their part in the lake which burneth with fire and brimstone:* ***which is the second death.***

Ecclesiastes however also points out that the second death is a final extinction of life and that there is no further "reward" or punishment after the end of life.

> *Ec:9:5: For the living know that they shall die:* ***but the dead know not any thing, neither have they any more a reward; for the memory of them is forgotten.***

Therefore the prophets all tell us to enjoy life while we can and to do what we like to do with all our might as there is no second chance at life.

> *Ec:9:10:* ***Whatsoever thy hand findeth to do, do it with thy might; for there is no work, nor device, nor knowledge, nor wisdom, in the grave, whither thou goest.***

This is basically the same teaching as Jesus Christ who sets us free to enjoy life not being dictated to by any religious dogma. His whole ministry was established in order to teach us about the true spirituality based on sane and knowledgeable principles and revealing too the mystery or secret vow at the core of the belief. Without this confession of faith there is only dogma. Christianity is the only religion in the world that confesses this skeleton in the cupboard.

> *Heb:9:3:* ***And after the second veil, the tabernacle which is called the Holiest of all;***

*1Jo:4:2: Hereby know ye the **Spirit of God**: Every spirit **that confesseth** that **Jesus Christ is come in the flesh (scripture)** is of God:*

*1Jo:4:3: And every spirit that **confesseth** not that Jesus Christ is come in the flesh is not of God: and this is that spirit of antichrist, whereof ye have heard that it should come; and even now already is it in the world.*

The indication of this verse taken from 1 John 4:2-3 says that Christ has come in the 'FLESH' and of course this word 'flesh' is a direct reference to that which Jesus Himself said, that unless a man eat of His 'Flesh' he cannot enter heaven. We also saw that Bread is Flesh and that these two metaphors both represented His Scripture. So to confess that He has come in the flesh is to admit that these metaphors also pronounce that god is an IDEAL just as Jesus describes. To come in the flesh then is to be revealed in the written form of the doctrine. This Ideal is revealed in His flesh or doctrine. Time and time again we see these teachings revealed in His Flesh or Doctrine or the New Testament.

Throughout the Bible the Holiest of all was the absolute realm of the High Priest alone. Inside the holiest of all was where the Ark of the Covenant stood, and this was prohibited to commoners. The Ark (Ark means 'coffin') of the covenant was the grave wherein was laid the laws for Israel but Jesus abandoned these traditions because they denied honesty to every person. Jesus preached truthfulness and therefore told us of the secret way, and gave us the knowledge that god was an adopted ideal, and not a creature living in a place called heaven. By this we discovered then, that we are also as gods just like Adam and Eve after they ate of the fruit of knowledge of good and evil.

Ge:3:5: For God doth know that in the day ye eat thereof, then your eyes shall be opened, **and ye shall be as gods**, knowing good and evil.

*Psalms:82:6: **I have said, Ye are gods; and all of you are children of the most High**.*

> *Isa:41:23: Shew the things that are to come hereafter,* **that we may know that ye are gods***: yea, do good, or do evil, that we may be dismayed, and behold it together.*

> *Joh:10:34:* **Jesus answered them, Is it not written in your law, I said, Ye are gods***?*

> *Joh:1:12: But as many as received him***, to them gave he power to become the sons of God***, even to them that believe on his name:*

> *Lu:17:21: Neither shall they say, Lo here! or, lo there! for, behold,* **the kingdom of God is within you.**

> 2Co:6:16: And what agreement hath the temple of God with idols? for **ye are the temple of the living God; as God hath said, I will dwell in them, and walk in them**; and I will be their God, and they shall be my people.

Isn't there enough evidence here to convince any and everybody, of the purity of Jesus Christ, in revealing the truth, and empowering everybody who reads the word of Truth? There is no freedom in being caught in the snare of doctrine or religion. There is only the trap of sin and the devaluing of the human spirit. As much as people seek out God in places of worship they never find the answers to their knowledge deficits. They are sold books and Bibles and concordances and hymn books and prayer books and icons and all paraphernalia but that which they actually seek, is free for the asking. This simple truth is that gods do not exist. Why seek gods when they don't exist? What stimulates a need to have a god look over your shoulder? Don't you know that you are gods according to the very Bible you sift through?

The snare of the church comes before us. The disciples were made "Fishers of Men" not because they were good at catching fish, but because they were good at catching men. The nets they used for catching men were nets of vanity.

> *Ec:7:26: And I find more bitter than death* **the woman(out of man)***, whose heart is snares and nets, and her hands as bands:*

*whoso pleaseth God shall escape from her; but the **sinner shall be taken by her.***

Of course we have already seen that woman ('doctrine' taken out of man) is a doctrine, and that the nets that she uses for beguiling, is vanity and promises of everlasting life, and other enticements of a hollow nature, and those whom are caught up by her spiel, are from then on classed as sinners.

*2Pe:2:18: For when **they speak great swelling words of vanity,** they **allure through the lusts of the flesh** (scripture), through much wantonness, those that were clean escaped from them who live in error.*

Those of a pure heart can see the truth and do not need it to be explained. They know in their soul that knowledge in truthfulness is superior to worshipping gods and idols and things that only exist under a misconception.

*1Tm:3:9: **Holding the mystery of the faith in a pure conscience.***

*Ti:1:15: **Unto the pure all things are pure:** but unto them that are defiled and unbelieving is nothing pure; but even their mind and conscience is defiled.*

*Ro:14:20: For meat destroy not the work of God. **All things indeed are pure**; but it is evil for that man who eateth with offence.*

*Jas:3:17: But the wisdom that is from above **is first pure,** then peaceable, gentle, and easy to be intreated, full of mercy and good fruits, without partiality, **and without hypocrisy.***

We know that anybody who believes that gods exist soon become hypocrites because it is impossible to live the way the Bible preaches, and not be so. One cannot have a clear mind and be deluded at the same time.

*M't:6:24: **No man can serve two masters:** for either he will hate the one, and love the other; or else he will hold to the one, and despise the other. **Ye cannot serve God and mammon.***

> Lu:16:13: **No servant can serve two masters**: for either he will hate the one, and love the other; or else he will hold to the one, and despise the other. **Ye cannot serve God and mammon.**

In fact the Bible itself is hypocritical for example Jesus was born of a virgin according to the New Testament, yet Matthew traces Joseph's (Jesus' stand-in Father) family-tree back to David and then to Adam, in order to prove Jesus' pure ancestry and right to be called King.

> *M't:1:16:* ***And Jacob begat Joseph the husband of Mary, of whom was born Jesus***, *who is called Christ.*

The Family-Tree cannot be traced using Joseph as father if Jesus was actually born of a virgin. Obviously Jesus was not born of a virgin or their meaning of what constitutes a virgin differs from ours.

> *M't:1:18: Now the birth of Jesus Christ was on this wise: When as his mother Mary was espoused to Joseph, **before they came together**, she was found with child of the Holy Ghost.*

> *M't:1:23: Behold, **a virgin shall be with child**, and shall bring forth a son, and they shall call his name Emmanuel, which being interpreted is, God with us.*

So was she a virgin? Obviously the Bible can't have it both ways. The disciples wrote about the virgin birth in order to satisfy a prediction, but Matthew also shows us that Jesus was born in the usual manner, as His genealogy through the line of Joseph suggests. This tells us that poetic license has been taken. We have just learned however that 'WOMAN' means 'Out of Man' because the doctrine (wo-man) was taken out of the society (Hebrews). Also that Eve (Foundation of Life was also doctrine) as was the 'WIFE' of Adam (Of the Ground – population) because they two were considered to be "ONE 'FLESH' or one religion. All these metaphors mean that the doctrine or scripture called the Bible was the WIFE of the people who believed in it. Therefore Mary (rebellious) The mother of Jesus was the wife of Israel (Ruling with God).

Now Jesus also called Himself the 'FLESH" or the Bible of the New Testament (because His word was made flesh) and also became 'WIFE' of Christianity as we see in Revelations.

> *Re:21:2: And I John saw the holy city, new Jerusalem, coming down from God out of heaven,* **prepared as a bride adorned for her husband.**

So then Mary (which means 'Rebellious') the mother of Jesus, was the wife of Israel and was indeed a virgin (a belief system) as she had no real husband or saviour prior to Jesus but was expecting either Immanuel or Elijah. The philosophy of Israel at the time was indeed fractured and rebellious, with many factions disputing the real meanings of verse just as they do today.

Mary (Rebellious – religion of Israel) was indeed a virgin (not having known a husband) and was a woman (taken out of man) and wife (flesh - Bible of Israel) which gave birth to Jesus (Saviour). In other words the belief system that Israel had at the time which gave birth to Jesus' philosophy was in fact a virgin belief system as it had no husband. This can be ratified another way too.

Jesus was Baptised by John.

> *M't:3:13:* ***Then cometh Jesus from Galilee to Jordan unto John, to be baptized of him.***

> *M't:3:14: But John forbad him, saying, I have need to be baptized of thee, and comest thou to me?*

> *M't:3:15: And Jesus answering said unto him, Suffer it to be so now: for thus it becometh us to fulfil all righteousness. Then he suffered him.*

Now to be Baptised is to be born again.

> *Joh:1:13: Which were born, not of blood, nor of the will of the flesh, nor of the will of man, but of God.*

> *Joh:3:3: Jesus answered and said unto him, Verily, verily, I say unto thee,* **Except a man be born again, he cannot see the kingdom of God.**

> *Joh:3:4: Nicodemus saith unto him, How can a man be born when he is old? can he enter the second time into his mother's womb, and be born?*

> *Joh:3:5: Jesus answered, Verily, verily, I say unto thee, Except a man be born of water and of the Spirit, he cannot enter into the kingdom of God.*

Baptism is therefore seen as a 'WOMAN' in whose womb one has been, in order to be Baptised, and are then, 'Born' again.

> *Re:12:1: And there appeared a great wonder in heaven;* **a woman (Baptism)** *clothed with the sun, and the moon under her feet, and upon her head a crown of twelve stars:*

> *Re:12:4: And his tail drew the third part of the stars of heaven, and did cast them to the earth:* **and the dragon stood before the woman which was ready to be delivered,** *for* **to devour her child as soon as it was born**.

Of course we remember that the Dragon (Serpent) represents the Church and here in Revelation it is said to be poised ready to devour the child as soon as it is born (or baptised). This means that as soon as anyone is baptised they are then straightaway indoctrinated into the Church which baptised them. In this way the Church devours its own offspring (*to devour her child as soon as it was born*).

This of course does not represent the original concept of baptism. The original concept of baptism was to teach the atheism and ideal of god (slay in the spirit) not perpetrate the dogma of controlled religion. A person baptised in the dogma of a church is not baptised at all. They are simply made wet and preached to once more, the vain repetitions of worship. True baptism is to be taught the Holy Atheism (this represents SPIRITUAL DEATH) and then to be buried into the life giving waters (buried in the amniotic fluid of religion, water) and then to be raised up again into newness of life (resurrected) into a new concept which is that we 'Love thy neighbour' wherein our sins have been demolished.

Christianity is the mother of Baptism. It is in the womb of Christianity where Baptism occurs. Her womb is the waters –peoples, and multitudes, and nations, and tongues that we are submerged. And when we are told the meaning to biblical metaphors we learn the truth that there are no such things as gods. This truth burns us to make us into a burnt offering to the Lord. But through it we realise that the news was indeed sweet in the mouth but after it was digested it became bitter. We therefore understood the Angel wormwood

> Re:12:3: And there appeared another wonder in heaven; and behold a great red dragon, having seven heads and ten horns, and seven crowns upon his heads.

> Re:12:4: And his tail drew the third part of the stars of heaven, and did cast them to the earth: and the dragon stood before **the woman which was ready to be delivered, for to devour her child as soon as it was born.**

> Re:12:5: And she brought forth a man child, who was to rule all nations with a rod of iron: and her child was caught up unto God, and to his throne.

We know that the woman described in revelations is Christianity and that she is with child which is of course the baptism – to be re born; and the red dragon is the church that does the baptism and is ready to devour or swallow up or indoctrinate the child as soon as it is born or baptised. But we know too that there was one child who realised the truth about god and thus was saved from the indoctrination and escaped to God in truth, Jesus.

We know that our sin is gone or forgiven by the fact that we have become atheistic; having confessed that sin does not exist; without god and without sin. We are then considered to be 'Fatherless and Widows' in our new desolation.

> Jas:1:27: Pure religion and undefiled before God and the Father
> is this, **To visit the fatherless and widows in their affliction**,
> and to keep himself unspotted from the world.

So by reason of such use of metaphors we learn that Jesus was also first born of the dead (those who believed in God).

> Col:1:18: *And he is the head of the body, the church: who is the
> beginning, the **firstborn from the dead**; that in all things he
> might have the preeminence.*

We have already learned that references to the dead apply to those who worship God and thereby commit idolatry. At the same time to be baptised of such a doctrine is to be reborn from the dead. Therefore Jesus was termed 'firstborn of the dead' and resurrected to new life.

> Ro:4:24: *But for us also, to whom it shall be imputed, if we believe
> on him that **raised up Jesus our Lord from the dead**;*

Jesus was therefore raised up from the dead just as it was promised (born again). Since John the Baptist baptised Jesus (and not any particular religion) He was born unto the Spirit of God and no other signified by a dove.

> Lu:3:22: And the **Holy Ghost descended in a bodily shape
> like a dove upon him**, and a voice came from heaven, which
> said, **Thou art my beloved Son; in thee I am well pleased.**

So in all of this we find out that the Bible does have it both ways concerning Jesus' birth because of the use of metaphor; two seeming contradictions are both permitted. The spiritual mother of Jesus was indeed a virgin but this metaphor spoke of a mother other than his worldly one. In fact Jesus disowns His worldly mother in public just for the purpose of showing this effect.

> M't:12:47: Then one said unto him, Behold, thy mother and thy
> brethren stand without, desiring to speak with thee.

M't:12:48: But he answered and said unto him that told him, **Who is my mother**? and who are my brethren?

M'r:3:32: And the multitude sat about him, and they said unto him, Behold, thy mother and thy brethren without seek for thee.

M'r:3:33: And he answered them, saying, **Who is my mother**, or my brethren?

M'r:3:34: And he looked round about on them which sat about him, and said, Behold my mother and my brethren!

M'r:3:35: **For whosoever shall do the will of God, the same is my brother, and my sister, and mother.**

Jesus discloses whom He now sees as His mother and His kin. It stands to reason that if His Father is a spiritual concept then so too is His Mother and kin.

There are many contradictions of this nature in the New Testament some internet sites boast having found hundreds of them. Mostly this amounts to nothing more than nit picking. Personally, it is felt that metaphor, simile or some other literary device can account for the majority of all contradictions. All who are familiar with the truth behind the Bible know that most if not all of these contradictions are meant to be. This flaw is intended to arouse a certain suspicion or spirit of search and discovery, of ancient texts, in order that scripture readers are led by their pure curiosity, into knowledge of truth. For this reason the Bible has been sitting in suspense awaiting a new enlightened one to find and fulfil the promise of end time prophecy. Alas however the only people that study the Bible with fervent effort are those who fall under the spell of their own imagination of what god is. Since their imagination of what god is, differs from the truth that there are no such thing as gods, they then fail to find the most simple of all the metaphors, numerology or truth in the meaning of names or words.

> Re:5:4: And I wept much, because **no man was found worthy to open and to read the book**, neither to look thereon.

This is how and why there are so many 'enlightened ones' these days sprouting their knowledge of the Bible and Fire and Brimstone with it. This is why television broadcasts religious shows so frequently. It is because some New Age denominations spare no effort or money in order to build ever widening regions of income, promising eternal life but not even understanding what that statement means. Do they even know what the mystery of god is? We whom are born of the truth know that there are no such things as gods. We also know that God is within us, and that God is an Ideal and we see this ideal as the Father of our beliefs and behaviour.

The Bible remains in suspense awaiting the great reveal to come. It will be made known to the world through the little book and others like it. Here then is a prediction. The religious leaders of the world will hate such publications as these and will stir up the law in an attempt to have such books removed. They will rail and shout and beat their breasts and utter all manner of slander in order to belittle such books but in all this they will remain ignorant that they themselves are part of the prophecy predicting this behaviour.

> Re:10:9: And I went unto the angel, and said unto him, **Give me the little book**. And he said unto me, Take it, and eat it up; and **it shall make thy belly bitter, but it shall be in thy mouth sweet as honey.**

> Re:10:10: And I took the little book out of the angel's hand, **and ate it up; and it was in my mouth sweet as honey: and as soon as I had eaten it, my belly was bitter**.

The truth is bitter. It is called the 'Bitter Truth' for a reason and that is because learning a truth means that we have to surrender a misconception. Every time a misconception is surrendered, a little bit of pride goes with it. It is this loss of pride that hurts. But we also heal and a healing of truth is indeed a strengthening of our beliefs and with that comes a reassertion of knowledge, strength and character.

The human race has improved its lot upon the planet, not because of religion but because of the accumulation of knowledge through Science. Religion has only divided us. We have made war because of religion and our differences of opinion. Had we known the truth about religions in the beginning, we might have avoided a multitude of sins.

Nevertheless it has come around to our present generation and the prophetic year in order to finally make this secret known. For this purpose ancient prophets wrote down the foundation of prophecy, and made the way clear for the truth to be uncovered. They imprinted a multitude of clues within scripture, along with open prophecies that begged to be fulfilled.

Over the millenniums many devotees have thought that they have found the secret of such prophecy, and have then campaigned to fulfil scripture under their own powers. Many even attracted a following but alas most of these charismatic movements ended in disaster. This is because many who pursue a career in religious studies see themselves as a healer of some kind. Their motives may be found in a good conscience, or kind heart, but without truth, spiritual concepts remain the same with or without studies. The unchanging opinion and concept held by the clergy and indeed all mankind, that god is an omnipotent being, remains. All people everywhere on earth that believe this are therefore doomed to live their life subservient to an illusion.

It is not surprising then that a loud shout of disdain will arise when it is shown that Christianity has a confession at its core that in truth there are no such things as gods. We confess this, not because it is a fashionable thing to do, but because we believe that Jesus Christ revealed the mystery of god, to the world already, thus purifying our thoughts and concepts.

CONCEPT SIX

METAPHORS

The Bible is full of metaphors, similes numbers and names which all have meanings. We have already explored some names and numbers but there are yet certain metaphors and similes that deserve a closer look.

VIRTUE

Jesus went about all Galilee working miracles but He did not want to do this at all. He knew that miracles sent the wrong message. People who waited for or boasted miracles had corrupt thinking. They were vain. How could Jesus sweep out people's minds and cleanse them from idolatry only to reinfest them with miracles.

> M't:12:44: Then he saith, I will return into my house from whence I came out; and when he is come, **he findeth it empty, swept, and garnished.**

> Lu:11:25: And when he cometh, **he findeth it swept and garnished.**

Jesus said that His generation of followers would not believe unless they saw miracles. In this He revealed how people's minds were already corrupted by the notion that gods and miracles exist.

> Joh:4:48: Then said Jesus unto him, Except ye see signs and wonders, ye will not believe.

Miracles were the embodiment of power but Jesus continued to say that it was not miracles that drew the crowds but His doctrine.

> Joh:6:26: Jesus answered them and said, Verily, verily, I say unto you, Ye seek me, not because ye saw the miracles, but because ye did eat of the loaves, and were filled.

Nevertheless Jesus was said to have worked miracles but doing so troubled Him because He knew that working miracles was vain. To exemplify this Jesus pointed out that when a miracle was worked He was lessened by it. He said that VIRTUE had gone out of Him. Virtue is 'moral goodness' and Jesus knew that propagating and perpetuating miracles had the result of reinforcing the vain attitudes of idolatry. This troubled Him deeply enough to point it out to the disciples.

> Lu:8:43: And a woman having an issue of blood twelve years, which had spent all her living upon physicians, neither could be healed of any,
>
> Lu:8:44: Came behind him, and touched the border of his garment: and immediately her issue of blood stanched.
>
> Lu:8:45: And Jesus said, Who touched me? When all denied, Peter and they that were with him said, Master, the multitude throng thee and press thee, and sayest thou, Who touched me?
>
> Lu:8:46: And Jesus said, Somebody hath touched me: **for I perceive that virtue is gone out of me.**
>
> Lu:8:47: And when the woman saw that she was not hid, she came trembling, and falling down before him, she declared unto him before all the people for what cause she had touched him, and how she was healed immediately.
>
> Lu:8:48: And he said unto her, Daughter, be of good comfort: thy faith hath made thee whole; go in peace.

M'r:5:25: And a certain woman, which had an issue of blood twelve years,

M'r:5:26: And had suffered many things of many physicians, and had spent all that she had, and was nothing bettered, but rather grew worse,

M'r:5:27: When she had heard of Jesus, came in the press behind, and touched his garment.

M'r:5:28: For she said, If I may touch but his clothes, I shall be whole.

M'r:5:29: And straightway the fountain of her blood was dried up; and she felt in her body that she was healed of that plague.

M'r:5:30: And Jesus, immediately knowing in himself that virtue had gone out of him, turned him about in the press, and said, Who touched my clothes?

Jesus knew that signs and wonders were the key to attracting the population but the real miracles lay in teaching the truth.

Joh:4:48: Then said Jesus unto him, Except ye see signs and wonders, ye will not believe.

His whole mission was to bring the Truth to the world.

Joh:18:37: Pilate therefore said unto him, Art thou a king then? Jesus answered, Thou sayest that I am a king. To this end was I born, and for this cause came I into the world, that I should bear witness unto the truth. Every one that is of the truth heareth my voice

It was through truth that people were cured and this was the true miracle that a person could be cured of the delusion that they were under and come to the knowledge of the truth.

> Joh:14:6: Jesus saith unto him, I am the way, the truth, and the life: no man cometh unto the Father, but by me.

But Jesus had the problem that the Jews were under the misconception of god. They believed god to be a real person and their delusion would not allow them to see the truth of Jesus' ideology.

> Joh:8:41: Ye do the deeds of your father. Then said they to him, We be not born of fornication; we have one Father, even God.

> Joh:8:42: Jesus said unto them, If God were your Father, ye would love me: for I proceeded forth and came from God; neither came I of myself, but he sent me.

> Joh:8:43: Why do ye not understand my speech? even because ye cannot hear my word.

> Joh:8:44: Ye are of your father the devil, and the lusts of your father ye will do. He was a murderer from the beginning, and abode not in the truth, because there is no truth in him. When he speaketh a lie, he speaketh of his own: for he is a liar, and the father of it.

> Joh:8:45: And because I tell you the truth, ye believe me not.

Nevertheless Jesus knew that the truth would come out one day. He visualised a world where knowledge and fact over-ruled dogma and He predicted this by saying that the spirit of truth would come.

> Joh:14:17: Even the **Spirit of truth**; whom the world cannot receive, because it seeth him not, neither knoweth him: but ye know him; for he dwelleth with you, and shall be in you.

> Joh:15:26: But when the Comforter is come, whom I will send unto you from the Father, even the Spirit of truth, which proceedeth from the Father, he shall testify of me:

Joh:16:7: Nevertheless I tell you the truth; It is expedient for you that I go away: for if I go not away, the Comforter will not come unto you; but if I depart, I will send him unto you.

Joh:16:13: Howbeit when he, the Spirit of truth, is come, he will guide you into all truth: for he shall not speak of himself; but whatsoever he shall hear, that shall he speak: and he will shew you things to come.

Claiming miracles caused people to perjure themselves in the name of god. This was a great sin and Jesus pointed out that to blaspheme the Holy Ghost was unforgivable.

M't:12:32: And whosoever speaketh a word against the Son of man, it shall be forgiven him: but whosoever speaketh against the Holy Ghost, it shall not be forgiven him, neither in this world, neither in the world to come.

Perjury is wilfully telling a lie or making misrepresentation while under oath. To say that miracles happen is to commit perjury against the Holy Ghost. To witness that a healing has taken place when in fact it hasn't, is to perjure against the Holy Ghost. This is the worst of all *sin* because it is against the Spirit of Truth. How can one be filled with the Spirit of Truth and claim miracles? The definition of miracle is an extraordinary and welcome event that is not explicable by natural or scientific laws, attributed to a divine agency. Since we are constantly under scrutiny of the Spirit of Truth we are therefore obliged to tell the truth especially truths about God and the Holy Ghost. To claim miracles happen, flies in the face of the Spirit of Truth. A lie cannot be sanctioned by God. We can't be believers in miracles and tellers of the truth at the same time. We cannot serve two masters.

M't:6:24: No man can serve two masters: for either he will hate the one, and love the other; or else he will hold to the one, and despise the other. Ye cannot serve God and mammon.

When someone lies they destroy their own credibility. How can they be taken seriously if they lie all the time? So it is with Christianity.

Liars destroy the credibility and the public image of the ideal. There is a responsibility associated with the Baptism and that is to not only serve mankind but to be honest. It is the Spirit of Truth that we adopt in order to prove our honesty.

Honesty has its own merit and brings with it a multitude of positive aspects not the least of which is trustworthiness. So it is the Spirit of Truth that blesses us with trustworthiness when we always tell the truth. Jesus hated liars and lies but He understood that people were themselves deceived and under a delusion. He therefore tolerated their lust for miracles but at the same time taught that the Spirit of Truth would come into the world. The problem with miracles is that people, who believe that God is real, claim that God can work miracles. There are two things wrong with this thought. The first is that god is only an ideal and is not a real entity in any physical form that can perform miracles and the second is that claims of this nature come not from the spirit of truthfulness but rather from infatuation with a spirit or charisma of evangelism. Such a spirit can infest people to believe they are healed when in fact nothing has happened at all and all that has happened is they have reinforced the false claims made while under such a spirit or spell. Common psychology can account for such witnessing and beliefs that are misconstrued. Jesus saw this as sickness also and he healed as many as He could using the spirit of truth to do so. The real miracle was in such a healing as He did, to turn someone to promote truthfulness rather than misconception. This was the true miracle. All things of a spiritual nature occur in the mind. Our very mental health depends on what we choose to believe. If we fall under a misconception then that will affect our lives in a great many ways even dictating who we choose as friends. Those who see the truth see a great light which is insight.

So we see that miracles are not anything that we should desire but rather shy away from because there is an inherent danger in accepting miracles; they get out of hand. They become more and more extreme as time and population increase. The telling of a small miracle leads to confirmation of larger ones until the truth is completely mocked. There are real miracles of course such as great scientific achievements like the discovery of penicillin or Anaesthesia or the discovery of how intravenous fluids work. There is a multitude of real miracles that bear truthful witness. Look to them for confidence. It should be taught that when we testify we should bear witness of the truth.

Virtue therefore left Jesus on each occasion when the misconception of what god was reinforced in place of the truth. It should be pointed out that Jesus performed many miracles that were truthful. He converted many to the truth which is the real miracle.

RAIN

Rain is an easy concept to grasp as it falls from heaven just as words fall onto our ears especially the words of sermons and preaching within the church.

Deuteronomy describes it as doctrine or the words of my mouth.

> De:32:1: Give ear, O ye heavens, and I will speak; and hear, O earth, **the words of my mouth.**

> De:32:2: **My doctrine shall drop as the rain**, my speech shall distil as the dew, as the small rain upon the tender herb, and as the showers upon the grass:

This same concept that waters or rain in particular is as doctrine falling on the ears of the listener appears in many places.

> Job:29:22: After my words they spake not again; and my speech dropped upon them.

> Job:29:23: And they waited for me as for the rain; and **they opened their mouth wide as for the latter rain.**

From these verses we see that rain is doctrine that falls on the ears of the listener. Rain is mentioned here in order to return to the prevailing condition prior to the creation of Adam.

> Gen. 2:5 For the Lord **God had not caused it to rain** upon the earth, and there was not a man to till them ground.

> Gen. 2:6 But there went up **a mist from the earth, and watered** the whole face of the ground.

This therefore is suggesting that there were not the teachings of righteousness from the Lord, that is to say RAIN from HEAVEN, and there was no person to sow the seeds of righteousness, 'Not a man to till the ground' in mankind. But then a mist went up and watered the whole face of the ground and the Lord God formed man from the dust of the ground or from a remnant of mankind; Adam emerged. We witness this emergence of man after the event of rain or preaching of God's word, throughout mankind. This rain of course brings to mind the 40 days of rain from Noah's Ark story. Was it really rain or was it also preaching?

It is RAIN (preaching) that is stopped in Revelation 11:6 as follows.

> Re:11:3: And I will give power unto my **two witnesses**, and they shall prophesy a thousand two hundred and threescore days, clothed in sackcloth.

> Re:11:4: These are the two olive trees, and the two candlesticks standing before the God of the earth.

> Re:11:5: And if any man will hurt them, fire (argument) proceedeth out of their mouth, and devoureth their enemies: and if any man will hurt them, he must in this manner be killed.

> Re:11:6: **These have power to shut heaven, that it rain not** in the days of their prophecy: and have power over waters to turn them to blood, and to smite the earth with all plagues, as often as they will.

It is through these metaphors that these miraculous things can be accomplished. This little book can cause the rain or preaching to cease if one becomes indoctrinated to the truth. This is the only way such miracles can occur. They happen in a spiritual way with a spiritual meaning and not in any carnal or worldly way. Nevertheless they are achieved and the prophecy is fulfilled.

FLESH

The story of Noah's Ark begins by explaining that all flesh was corrupt.

> Ge:6:12: And God looked upon the earth, and, behold, it was corrupt; **for all flesh had corrupted his way upon the earth.**

Here we need to examine what is meant by flesh. Does this 'Flesh' fit in with New Testament interpretation of 'Flesh' being scripture? To answer this we must first ask the question what is a religion? A religion is just doctrine. It is a belief system that people hold onto in order to make sense of the world around them. The belief system and the person holding it are one flesh. We see many references to the flesh especially in the New Testament where flesh is likened to doctrine. Adam's wife Eve was also doctrine just as Mary was doctrine to Joseph and Jesus is doctrine to Christianity. In John is recorded;

> Joh:1:14: And the **Word was made flesh**, and dwelt among us, and we beheld his glory, the glory as of the only begotten of the Father, full of grace and truth

Thus we see that the Word of God was made Flesh in the image of Jesus full of grace and truth. That is to say that Jesus' words were written down and these were seen as His flesh. It is His doctrine that is flesh.

In the next verse we see that the BREAD of the Pharisees was actually their DOCTRINE also as told by Jesus to the disciples. It is stated that bread is doctrine in the following verse as it is throughout the Bible.

> M't:16:11: How is it that ye do not understand **that I spake it not to you concerning bread, that ye should beware of the leaven of the Pharisees** and of the Sadducees?

> M't:16:12: Then understood they how that he bade them **not beware of the leaven of bread, but of the doctrine** of the Pharisees and of the Sadducees.

This is clear and precise. We learn that doctrine is bread. In another place Jesus tells us that His body is also Bread meaning of course that His doctrine is our daily bread just as it quotes in the Lord's Prayer.

> M't:26:26: And as they were eating, Jesus took **bread,** and blessed it, and brake it, and gave it to the disciples, and said, **Take, eat; this is my body**

Of course Jesus did not mean that his body was literally bread but that bread was a metaphor for His doctrine. This is reinforced in the Gospel of John.

> Joh:6:33: For the bread of God is he which cometh down from heaven, and giveth life unto the world.

> Joh:6:34: Then said they unto him, Lord, evermore give us this bread.

> Joh:6:35: And Jesus said unto them, **I am the bread of life**: he that cometh to me shall never hunger; and he that believeth on me shall never thirst.

Jesus states that He is the living BREAD and that His bread is His flesh. So we learn that Bread is Flesh is DOCTRINE.

> Joh:6:51: I am the living bread which came down from heaven: if any man eat of this bread, he shall live forever: and **the bread that I will give is my flesh,** which I will give for the life of the world.

We also see a reference to the Flesh in John chapter 1 whereupon he discusses Jesus who was sent by God.

> Joh:1:14: And **the Word was made flesh** (doctrine), and dwelt among us, (and we beheld his glory, the glory as of the only begotten of the Father,) full of grace and truth.

Even the Lord's Prayer mentions bread;

> M't:6:9: After this manner therefore pray ye: Our Father which art in heaven, Hallowed be thy name.

> M't:6:10: Thy kingdom come. Thy will be done in earth, as it is in heaven.

> M't:6:11: **Give us this day our daily bread**.

This bread is our daily bread or scripture which we eat and digest from our Bibles on a daily basis. The bread; Christ's flesh is scripture. Eve was also made of flesh; Adams flesh. She is flesh of his flesh.

> Ge:2:23: And Adam said, This is now **bone of my bones, and flesh** (doctrine) **of my flesh** (doctrine): she shall be called Woman (out of man- religion), because she was taken out of Man.

Let's have some amusement with this imagery of flesh. We have seen above that the Word was made flesh John 1:14. But it says in John 1:1 "In the beginning was the Word, and the Word was with God, and the Word was God". So if we replace "word" with "flesh" we now have "In the beginning was the FLESH and the FLESH was with God and the Flesh was God. Now we have also learned that Jesus' flesh is His BREAD as above John 6:51. So if we now replace FLESH for BREAD we now have "In the beginning was the BREAD and the BREAD was with God and the BREAD was God. We are not finished yet because now we realise that BREAD is DOCTRINE as it was also for the leaven of the Pharisees Matthew 16:11. Now by replacing BREAD with DOCTRINE John's statement goes like this "In the beginning was the DOCTRINE and the DOCTRINE was with God and the DOCTRINE was God. Now we know that DOCTINE is the WORD of GOD so by substituting DOCTRINE with WORD we have completed the circle "In the beginning was the WORD and the WORD was with God and the WORD was God".

But it is also stated that man does not live by bread alone.

> Lu:4:4: And Jesus answered him, saying, It is written, That **man shall not live by bread (doctrine) alone**, but by every word of God.

> M't:4:4: But he answered and said, It is written, **Man shall not live by bread alone**, but by every word that proceedeth out of the mouth of God.

So we learn that scripture alone is not enough to satisfy our thirst or hunger because we also hunger and thirst for knowledge and truth. If rain represents only preaching then we also need learning of other facets of life to complete us. If we try to achieve this entirely through preaching and the opinion of the piety then we are doomed to fail. Nevertheless there are doctrines and denominations that attempt exactly this. There are fundamentalist groups that grow into nothing more than cults some of which have large numbers others are smaller but all are deceived into thinking that they are special toward god.

The preaching of such doctrines is seen as **rain from heaven**. When there is too much of this influence on the congregation it begins to be dangerous as indoctrination without truth it is only brainwashing.

The rain of Noah's Ark was such a preaching. When we read the verse we find that it was doctrine (flesh) that was corrupt and not actual people.

> Ge:6:12: And God looked upon the earth, and, behold, it was corrupt; for all **flesh** (doctrine) had corrupted his way upon the earth.

> Ge:6:13: And God said unto Noah, The end of all **flesh** (doctrine) is come before me; for the earth is **filled with violence through them**; and, behold, I will destroy them with the earth.

It states that the earth was filled with violence through them (flesh-doctrine). It should be no surprise that the Hebrew word for Ark is 'Coffin" or that Noah's name means "Rest" which is what you do in a coffin and that the rain (preaching) went on for forty (this is the number for

conception in childbirth) days and forty nights. The Ark (coffin) also was
pitched with pitch (a black substance which is the colour used to signify
truth). Of animals they had two of each unclean beast and seven of every
clean beast. They were therefore in the belly of the Ark (coffin) out of sight
from God (Just as Jonah was in the belly of the whale) for the duration
of the raining (preaching). When the raining (preaching) was complete
they emerged to new life. We see by this that this story is about death and
resurrection. The fact that all flesh (doctrine) was corrupt gives us the clue
we need to investigate doctrine dealing with death and resurrection. It just
so happens that we can easily find such things in the New Testament. Even
the Baptism, a representation of being submerged in water (flood) carries
such imagery. This is the imagery of Noah's (rest) Ark (coffin).

> Ro:6:3: Know ye not, that so many of us as were baptized into
> Jesus Christ were **baptized into his death**?

> Ro:6:4: Therefore we are buried with him by baptism into
> death: that like as Christ was **raised up** from the dead by the
> glory of the Father, even so we also should walk in newness
> of life.

To be Baptized then is symbolic of death.

> 1Co:15:29: Else what shall they do which are **baptized for the
> dead**, if the dead rise not at all? why are they then baptized
> for the dead?

Rain therefore represents preaching the word of God but this is the corrupt
word of the delusion that gods are real. It is only such fundamentalist
worship that hunger for more and more sermons. They hunger or thirst for
water or rain and sermons and promises and prophecies and all manner of
false concepts that feed their egos and nourish their delusions.

Rain or water does not represent the truth that there are no such things
as gods.

> Joh:4:13: Jesus answered and said unto her, Whosoever
> drinketh of **this water shall thirst again:**

Joh:4:14: But whosoever drinketh of the water that I shall give him **shall never thirst**; but the water that I shall give him shall be in him a well of water springing up into everlasting life.

The 'water' that Jesus gives is living water or doctrine that springs into everlasting life, which finally quenches the thirst. The only thing that can quench this thirst of course is the truth that there are no such things as gods.

Joh:7:37: In the last day, that great day of the feast, Jesus stood and cried, saying, If **any man thirst, let him come unto me, and drink.**

In Revelation there is a reference to the two witnesses that are intended for the end time to proclaim the revelation of the mystery of God to the world. These are those who reveal this code of the Bible who show the metaphors and hidden meanings. With respect to the word 'RAIN' we see that it infers a preaching of the Gospels to the world. To say that it shall RAIN NOT in the days of their prophecy or the power to shut heaven means that they can make known the atheistic nature of the Bible. When they do this it renders all the words of all preachers everywhere worthless and meaningless. How can their sermons mean anything at all if there is no such thing as god?

Re:11:3: And I will give power unto my two witnesses, and they shall prophesy a thousand two hundred and threescore days, clothed in sackcloth.

Re:11:4: These are the two olive trees, and the two candlesticks standing before the God of the earth.

Re:11:5: And if any man will hurt them, fire (argument) proceedeth out of their mouth, and devoureth their enemies: and if any man will hurt them, he must in this manner be killed.

Re:11:6: **These have power to shut heaven, that it rain not** (No preaching) in the days of their prophecy: and have power over waters (spirit of life) to turn them to blood (spirit of worldliness), and to smite the earth with all plagues, as often as they will.

The purpose of all this is to make the expected prophecy happen at the allocated time. What else is there in the whole world that can put the fear of god into those people who make a living by selling god to the world and the souls of men and women with it? There is only the little book and others like it.

Re:18:12: **The merchandise of gold, and silver**, and precious stones, and of pearls, and fine linen, and purple, and silk, and scarlet, and all thyine wood, and all manner vessels of ivory, and all manner vessels of most precious wood, and of brass, and iron, and marble,

Re:18:13: And cinnamon, and odours, and ointments, and frankincense, and wine, and oil, and fine flour, and wheat, and beasts, and sheep, and horses, and chariots, and slaves, **and souls of men**.

Re:6:9: And when he had opened the fifth seal, I saw under the altar the souls of them that were slain for the word of God, and for the testimony which they held:

Re:6:10: And they cried with a loud voice, saying, **How long, O Lord, holy and true, dost thou not judge and avenge our blood on them that dwell on the earth**?

SALT AND BITTERNESS

Salt represents TRUTH wherever it appears in doctrine. The realisation that no person has ever seen God and therefore all evidence that God exists requires Faith. This is the beginning of insight.

> John 1:18 **No man hath seen God at any time;** the only begotten Son, which is in the bosom of the Father, he hath declared him.

All this is done to portray a side or aspect to the Bible that has never before been presented. The insight that God cannot be seen or comprehended, or the realization that God does not exist at all, can come as a terrible shock to some people, bearing both bitter and sweet implications. Revelations writes about how this realisation can affect a person. It predicts how the truth will be revealed by a little book and that we the people are to eat this little book. Naturally Revelations means that we read and digest the contents of the little book rather than actually eat it. Once we digest its contents we are turned into atheists and although it might be pleasant and insightful in the reading, the little book has an after taste. Some people might even resent the fact that the little book turns us into atheists. These would be people that are unable to appreciate the Ideal that God now represents. They feel offended by the fact that they had been fooled by the Bible, and even used by the church that beguiled them. Others feel robbed of their opinion that god was real. All in all Revelations sums it up nicely in the following verse.

> Re:10:8: And the voice which I heard from heaven spake unto me again, and said, Go and take the little book which is open in the hand of the angel which standeth upon the sea and upon the earth.

> Re:10:9: And I went unto the angel, and said unto him, Give me the little book. And he said unto me, **Take it, and eat it up; and it shall make thy belly bitter, but it shall be in thy mouth sweet as honey.**

> Re:10:10: And I took the little book out of the angel's hand, and ate it up; and it was in my mouth sweet as honey: and as soon as I had eaten it, my belly was bitter.

> Re:10:11: And he said unto me, Thou must prophesy again before many peoples, and nations, and tongues, and kings.

The little book mentioned in the Angels hand which makes one sweet and bitter is this same book about the mystery of God and the Truth of God. This is the only book that has the effect of being sweet in the mouth but bitter in the belly, because Truth is sweet when first heard but is often bitter as the realization of what it means takes hold.

And again this same knowledge that this truth is both sweet and bitter is mentioned in Revelations chapter 8;

> Re:8:10: And the third angel sounded, and there fell a **great star** (prophet) from heaven, burning as it were a lamp, and it fell upon the third (truth) part of the rivers, and upon the fountains of waters (spirit of life);

> Re:8:11: And the **name of the star (prophet) is called Wormwood**: and the third (truth) part of the **waters became wormwood; and many men died of the waters, because they were made bitter**.

Wormwood is frequently referred to in Biblical texts because of its bitterness but there is an ancient story related to wormwood. It is said that the plant wormwood sprang up in the tracks of the serpent as it writhed its way along the ground when it was cast out of paradise.

The truth about God (that there is no God) is bitter. It is also described as seasoning us with salt. This seasoning and bitterness is a reflection of this TRUTH. In small amounts salt symbolizes a healing of the mind and clarity of thought but in large amounts it signifies complete death and desolation. Just as the Dead Sea is so salty nothing can live there and as in Sodom and Gomorrah, total devastation overtook those who witnessed it. Salt represents knowledge of the truth about God, that God does not exist at all, that God is not an external power but is an internal influence. God is within us.

> Lu:17:21 Neither shall they say, Lo here! or, lo there! for, behold, **the kingdom of God is within you.**:

Salt is used for healing the spirit (or waters) as according to 2 Kings 19-22

> 2Ki:2:19: And the men of the city said unto Elisha, Behold, I pray thee, the situation of this city is pleasant, as my lord seeth: but the water is naught, and the ground barren.

> 2Ki:2:20: And he said, Bring me a new cruse, and put salt (truth) therein. And they brought it to him.

> 2Ki:2:21: **And he went forth unto the spring of the waters (spirit of life), and cast the salt (truth) in there, and said, Thus saith the LORD, I have healed these waters (spirit of life); there shall not be from thence any more death or barren land.**

> 2Ki:2:22: So the waters (spirit of life) were healed unto this day, according to the saying of Elisha which he spake.

This story about the healing of the waters reminds us that water is representing the 'spirit of life' but without truth there is no life. Therefore salt representing truth is used in order to heal the waters. By this method Death or barren land was revived, and this is remarkably similar to the Baptism which we have just studied.

In Matthew, Jesus says that we (His followers) are the SALT of the earth.

> M't:5:13: **Ye are the salt** (truth) **of the earth:** but if the salt (truth) have lost his savour, wherewith shall it be salted? it is thenceforth good for nothing, but to be cast out, and to be trodden under foot of men.

When we know that the metaphor of salt means 'truth' it is easy to comprehend the meaning of this statement. If we are the salt of the earth then we should know that we understand the truth and that we carry that truth with us wherever we go. Parents teach their salt to their children and so the earth (population) is gradually taught the ideal of God. Eventually after many generations the descendants do not take religion very seriously and this is because their ancestors were the salt of the earth.

Mark records another well-known instruction regarding salt this verse also mentions fire which in biblical terms represents argument.

> M'r:9:49: For every one shall be **salted** (made truthful) **with fire** (argument), and every sacrifice shall be **salted with salt (Truth).**

> M'r:9:50: Salt (Truth) is good: but if the salt (Truth) have lost his saltiness (Truthfulness), wherewith will ye season it? **Have salt** (truth) **in yourselves**, and have peace one with another

This is a repeat of the above verse with Mark. The encouragement to 'Have salt in yourselves' is a very appropriate notion even today is good advice. It means to treat each other with the respect of being truthful to each other. It goes on to say that if we do this then we will find peace with each other.

Luke of course repeats the verse because it is an important concept to grasp;

> Lu:14:34: **Salt** (truth) is good: but if the salt (truth) have lost his savour, wherewith shall it be seasoned?

> Lu:14:35 It is neither fit for the land, nor yet for the dunghill; but men cast it out. He that hath ears to hear, let him hear.

Job also finds that knowledge without truthfulness is as tasteless as the white of an egg.

> Job:6:6: Can that which is unsavoury be eaten without salt? or is there any taste in the white of an egg?

And in Colossians we see further instruction on how we should prepare our speech and this helps to reinforce what we already know about salt and truthfulness.

> Col:4:6: Let your speech be always with grace, **seasoned with salt (truth)**, that ye may know how ye ought to answer every man.

The knowledge of the truth about God is indeed a place of desolation. Where can our beliefs go if there is no God? Whom do we pray to? Who do we swear to? If we swear on a stack of Bibles does it even matter? What is there if there is no God?

Such a state of desolation is frequently described by the use of salt as the metaphor. Remember Lot's wife (Lot means 'concealed'). Lot's wife (Lot's flesh or doctrine) was his beliefs which looked back at the desolation of Sodom and Gomorrah and was turned into a pillar of salt.

> Ge:19:26: But his wife (i.e. religion) looked back from behind him, **and she became a pillar of salt** (truth and desolation of spirit).

Of course we know better than to take this verse at face value That Lot's wife actually turned into salt, but rather Lots wife (which represents his beliefs) saw the real truth about God and became "salted" by that knowledge. This is how Lot (concealed) lost his wife (or his belief system). To be a pillar of salt is to be held in esteem of the truth. For this reason Jesus called us the "salt of the earth" because we knew the truth and the secret mystery of God. Salt was frequently used by the Jews in their sacrifices representing truth.

> Nu:18:19: All the heave offerings of the holy things, which the children of Israel offer unto the LORD, have I given thee, and thy sons and thy daughters with thee, by a statute for ever: **it is a covenant of salt (truth) for ever** before the LORD unto thee and to thy seed with thee.

To be taken with a grain of salt, means that there is little substance of truth in a particular statement. All these metaphors related to salt are residual expressions of the truth that we once held but somehow lost.

The total desolation of spirit which can be felt when one goes from a worshipper to an atheist in one move is frightening. Without the resurrection of the spirit (from Baptism) this can be a lonely and desolate place and some people become atheists only to then turn their back on the illumination that blessed them so.

> Am:5:7: **Ye who turn judgment to wormwood**, and leave off righteousness in the earth,
>
> Am:5:8: Seek him that maketh the seven stars and Orion, and turneth the **shadow of death** into the morning, and maketh the day dark with night: that calleth for the waters of the sea, and poureth them out upon the face of the earth: The LORD is his name:

Deuteronomy describes the curse of God as a salty wasteland.

> De:29:19: And it come to pass, when he heareth the words of this **curse**, that he bless himself in his heart, saying, I shall have peace, though I walk in the imagination of mine heart, to add drunkenness to thirst:
>
> De:29:20: The LORD will not spare him, but then the anger of the LORD and his jealousy shall smoke against that man, and all the curses that are written in this book shall lie upon him, and the LORD shall blot out his name from under heaven.
>
> De:29:21: And the LORD shall separate him unto evil out of all the tribes of Israel, according to all the curses of the covenant that are written in this book of the law:
>
> De:29:22: So that the generation to come of your children that shall rise up after you, and the stranger that shall come from a far land, shall say, when they see the plagues of that land, and the sicknesses which the LORD hath laid upon it;

De:29:23: **And that the whole land thereof is brimstone, and salt, and burning, that it is not sown, nor beareth, nor any grass groweth therein, like the overthrow of Sodom, and Gomorrah, Admah, and Zeboim, which the LORD overthrew in his anger, and in his wrath**:

This curse applies to those people who having been educated that there are no such things as gods, then set out to live an undisciplined life. They have disrespect for the law knowing there is no sin unto death. Their conscience is also empty and unmindful of other's needs.

We see salt describing this desolation and bitterness but there is another agent also used for this purpose, wormwood. Proverbs describe religion as having sweet words but that her end is bitterness;

Proverb:5:3: For the lips of a strange woman (out of man-religion) drop as an honeycomb, and her mouth is smoother than oil:

Proverb:5:4: But her end is **bitter as wormwood** (bitter), sharp as a **twoedged sword** (word of God).

Deuteronomy explains that the only end that can come from worshiping idols is that of bitterness.

De:29:17: And ye have seen their abominations, and their idols, wood and stone, silver and gold, which were among them:)

De:29:18: Lest there should be among you man, or woman, or family, or tribe, whose heart turneth away this day from the LORD our God, to go and serve the gods of these nations; **lest there should be among you a root that beareth gall and wormwood;**

Jeremiah reinforces these opinions. A life with no respect for others or indeed no respect for the earth can only end in disappointment and bitterness. If a person sows discord while they live, then they shall reap discord later in life. If we don't respect our children, they will not respect us, and their life will also be full of bitterness.

> Jer:9:15: Therefore thus saith the LORD of hosts, the God of Israel; Behold, I will feed them, even this people, with **wormwood** (bitterness), and give them water of gall to drink.

> Am:5:6: Seek the LORD, and ye shall live; lest he break out like fire (argument) in the house of Joseph, and devour it, and there be none to quench it in Bethel.

> Am:5:7: Ye who turn judgment to **wormwood (bitterness)**, and leave off righteousness in the earth,

Finally in Revelations we have this account of what will happen as planned when all these things are revealed. These revelations do not hit the whole world at once although it might seem like it does, with news reporting media being what it is. These revelations take place one person at a time. When you think about it, only the person reading the little book can be set free, or cursed by what they read. However this occurs to so many people in such a short time that it seems to affect the whole world all at once.

> Rev:8:10: And the third angel sounded, and there fell a great star (prophet) from heaven, burning as it were a lamp, and it fell upon the third (truth) part of the rivers, and upon the fountains of waters (spirit of life);

> Re:8:11: And the name of **the star is called Wormwood** (bitterness): and the third (truth) part of the waters (spirit of life) became wormwood (bitterness); and many men died of the waters, because they were made bitter.

The revelation of the truth of God salts us and leaves us bitter. That revelation is sweat to some people but bitterness to others. The fact that god does not actually exist but that we only have an Ideal in place of God, is hard to accept especially to the proud. But the act of being taught the truth is a burning purging that our souls must confront.

Ezekiel explains how to prepare **a burnt offering** for the Lord.

> Eze:43:23: When thou hast made an end of cleansing it, thou shalt offer a young bullock without blemish, and a ram out of the flock without blemish.

> Eze:43:24: And thou shalt offer them before the LORD, **and the priests shall cast salt (truth) upon them, and they shall offer them up for a burnt offering unto the LORD.**

It is delegated to the priest to cast salt (truth) upon the offering. This means that the priest should inform the person that god is not real. This is truth as it is documented as part of the process of baptism but in reality this never happens. It is supposed that knowing the truth symbolizes what it means to be a burnt offering for the Lord. It is clear that the bitterness of knowing the Truth about God, and the thought that there is no God, has the effect of making one bitter, because of the loss of the fantasy usually associated with the imagined god. This is how one is burned. Atheists have been burned by the truth. The water or charismatic spirit of worship has been driven out of them.

FISH

Christians saw themselves as fish. Fish live in water and water represents the Spirit of Life. They often painted the sign of a fish over doorways denoting their secret meetings so that other likeminded Christians could attend. This imagery is consistent with the Apostles being "fishers of men" and catching men as fish.

> M't:4:19: And he saith unto them, Follow me, and I will make **you fishers of men**.

Also in Mark;

> M'r:1:17: And Jesus said unto them, Come ye after me, and I will make you to **become fishers of men**.

The notion that the apostles were fishers of men meant that **men were fish** as depicted in Ecclesiastes.

> Ec:9:12: For man also knoweth not his time: **as the fishes that are taken in an evil net**, and as the birds that are caught in the snare; **so are the sons of men snared in an evil time**, when it falleth suddenly upon them.

The metaphor of people being fish which live in the water (spirit of life) is basically a simple one. Firstly the water is assumed to be the 'Spirit of Life" already discussed. People who are spirit filled are then said to be of the water and hence classed as fish. This simile also gives us the notion that fish are caught in a net and people also are caught in the net of the religion.

Jesus also said this describing the kingdom of heaven;

> M't:13:47: Again, the **kingdom of heaven** (religion) **is like unto a net**, that was cast into the sea, and gathered of every kind:

> M't:13:48: Which, when it was full, they drew to shore, and sat down, and gathered the good into vessels, but cast the bad away.

The imagery that fish are people as we saw above, being caught in the net is also consistent with Jesus seeking to pay his taxes and asking for a coin from the fish's mouth.

> M't:17:27: Notwithstanding, lest we should offend them, go thou to the sea, and cast an hook, and take up **the fish** (person) **that first cometh up**; and when thou **hast opened his mouth**, thou shalt find a piece of money: that take, and give unto them for me and thee.

It is clear that Christ is referring to another person possibly someone within the circle of associates willing to pay tribute for them. It is clear that the metaphor of people being fish was common. There were the drawings of fish over doorways everywhere in the ancient world.

In Job we find this reference to fish that are able to speak;

> Job:12:8: Or speak to the earth, and it shall teach thee: **and the fishes (people) of the sea (humanity) shall declare unto thee.**

Ezekiel also uses fish as a metaphor of fishermen and nets;

> Eze:47:10: And it shall come to pass, that the **fishers** shall stand upon it from En-gedi (fountain of the seer) even unto En-eglaim (fountain of two calves); they shall be a place to spread forth **nets**; their **fish** (people) shall be according to their kinds, **as the fish** (people) **of the great sea** (humanity), exceeding many.

And in Ezekiel we see that this imagery is not just confined to the New Testament.

> Eze:32:3: Thus saith the Lord GOD; I will therefore **spread out my net** over thee with a company of many people; **and they shall bring thee up in my net.**

So the concept of fishermen catching fish or people in their nets is ancient. This was carried over into the New Testament and why not since Jesus was a Jew He would have been very fluent with these pictures. The concept in the New Testament seems to disclose that a fish represents a spirit filled person but a serpent represents someone who knows the truth. There is a difference. The spirit filled may be people of the dogma who believe that there is a god. Such people are infatuated with the notion that god is real and therefore they believe in such things as miracles among others. The truth filled people (serpents) do not have the luxury of believing in god as a real person because they know this to be idolatry. Therefore the following statement of Christ, is saying that a parent would not give their child a serpent instead of a fish. However if this is indeed the case what good parent would prefer to deceive their children rather than tell them the truth? It must be confessed that we do exactly this and repeat it with Santa Clause and the Easter Bunny and the Tooth Fairy and all the other deceptions we feed our offspring.

> M't:7:10: Or if he ask a **fish, will he give him a serpent**?

> Lu:11:11: If a son shall ask bread of any of you that is a father, will he give him a stone? or if he **ask a fish, will he for a fish give him a serpent**?

Now Fishermen use nets of cord to catch fish but to catch men they use nets of vanity; as we read in Ecclesiastes

> Ec:7:26: And I find more bitter than death the woman (out of man- religion), **whose heart is snares and nets,** and her hands as bands: whoso pleaseth God shall escape from her; but the **sinner shall be taken by her.**

Of course the SINNER is taken by the religion which uses nets and snares in order to catch people. It is only religious people who call themselves sinners. But is there any other way of building up a diocese? The nets and snares are promises of heavenly treasure including eternal life. Many denominations in the world today are primarily concerned with growth, only for the purpose of enriching their own coffers. There is an obvious absence of mindedness and responsibility to the congregation and in fact to the needs of the planet and ecology as a whole, and all the things that should be a concern to a society based group of people, who claim to be carers.

Ecclesiastes also tells us that these nets are evil of course the writer is alluding to the worship of miracles and God as a Supreme Omnipotent Being and other idolatry.

> Ec:9:12: For man also knoweth not his time: **as the fishes that are taken in an evil net,** and as the birds that are caught in the snare; **so are the sons of men snared in an evil time, when it falleth suddenly upon them.**

In Psalms another allusion to nets and one that we can find some solace and hope that divine justice will prevail.

> Psalms:141:10 Let **the wicked fall into their own nets,** whilst that I withal escape.

And Matthew again;

> M't:13:47: Again, the **kingdom of heaven** (religion) **is like unto a net,** that was cast into the sea, and gathered of every kind:

So now we are getting down to the tin tacks of it all. The kingdom of heaven exists only in our minds. Jesus says that the imagined kingdom of heaven is like a net that is cast into a sea of people and people are caught up into the doctrine of the church that casts it. This is confirmed by Habakkuk where it is seen that the hierarchy catch people in their nets;

> Hab:1:15: They take up all of them with the angle, they catch them in their **net,** and gather them in their drag: therefore they rejoice and are glad.

Hab:1:16: **Therefore they sacrifice unto their net**, and **burn incense unto their drag**; because by them their portion is fat, and their meat plenteous.

Hab:1:17: Shall they therefore empty their net, and not spare continually to slay the nations?

Here is a perfect analogy of the 'Fishers of men' (disciples) who continually slay nations by catching men (people) in their nets (of doctrine). Habakkuk is saying that traditional churches (represented by the fishers of men) cast their nets (of doctrine) into the sea of people (Mankind) and then they 'sacrifice to their net and burn incense to their drag' (catch congregation).

The sea of people is also alluded to in Revelations. If people are fish they live in water and Revelations speaks of just such an image.

Re:17:15: And he saith unto me, **The waters which thou sawest, where the whore sitteth, are peoples, and multitudes, and nations, and tongues**.

It cannot be any clearer that humanity is seen as a sea of people. Do not get confused here with Adam who was also taken from a population. With Adam the population was not 'spirit filled' but here in Revelation the sea of people are the 'spirit filled'. In order to be part of humanity one must first be humane. One can only become humane if one is born of the 'Spirit of Goodness'. We do not say one has to have the spirit of god, because there is no such thing as god. God is just an Ideal. One therefore has to be in the spirit of this Ideal in order to be humane.

It is even better if one is both humane and baptised. All people that are truly baptised are humane by virtue of their understanding of belonging to the baptism. However not everyone who is humane is baptised. Some people may not have even heard of God or Jesus but are by nature humane. So it is in many countries. If people cherish goodness they are by default born of the spirit of life regardless of what their knowledge of God or Jesus is.

In these examples we see that men (people) are taken or caught up in the nets which are cast by the fishers of men (priests and evangelists). Many ancient terms survive to this day that personify fish. A common saying is "There's plenty more fish in the sea" meaning there are more persons one could catch. Another saying "he is like a fish out of water" meaning he is floundering in his attempts to do a particular task. There are many more but this is enough to show how the term fish is still applied to represent people even today without a knowledge of god.

FIRE

Fire is used as a tool to describe argument. It is another metaphor that is used frequently but in all its uses we can still see the meaning below the surface. The best of course is that fire represents the words we speak usually in anger. In James 3:6 it is immediately identified as the tongue but what is meant is argument usually over the word of God.

> Jas:3:6: And the **tongue is a fire** (argument), a world of iniquity: so is the tongue among our members, that it defileth the whole body, and setteth on fire (argument) the course of nature; and it is set **on fire of hell**.

To be set on fire of Hell designates it as religious in nature. Only godly preaching is termed 'fire and brimstone' and this is because In Hebrews is this statement about what God is.

> Heb:12:29: For our **God is a consuming fire** (argument).

In 1 Peter we witness another allusion to fire. Here it is the 'trial of your faith' which must by nature be tested in due course by the 'fire' of people's opinion.

> 1Pe:1:7: That the **trial of your faith**, being much more precious **than of gold** (pure words) that perisheth, though it be tried with **fire** (argument), might be found unto praise and honour and glory at the appearing of Jesus Christ:

And of course in Revelations the fire comes out of the **mouth** which is very explicit. The following excerpts from Revelation all assert that fire comes out of the mouth which means that fire is like argument.

> Re:11:4: These are the two olive trees, and the two candlesticks standing before the God of the earth.
>
> Re:11:5: And if any man will hurt them, **fire** (argument) proceedeth **out of their mouth**, and devoureth their enemies: and if any man will hurt them, he must in this manner be killed.

Re:14:18: And another angel came out from the altar, which had power over **fire** (argument); and cried with **a loud cry** to him that had the sharp sickle, saying, Thrust in thy sharp sickle, and gather the clusters of the vine of the earth; for her grapes are fully ripe.

Re:16:8: And the fourth angel poured out his vial upon the sun (god worship); and power was given unto him to scorch men with **fire** (argument).

Re:16:9: And men were scorched with great heat, and **blasphemed the name of God**, which hath power over these plagues: and they repented not to give him glory.

Proverbs says that 'fire' resides in the lips of an ungodly man

Prop. 16:27 An ungodly man diggeth up evil: and **in his lips** there is **a burning fire** (argument).

If argument is the fire of our mouths, can a man of god withstand the 'Fire and Brimstone' arguments of those who are caught up in idolatry? Shadrach, Meshach, and Abednego, in the book of Daniel were cast into the fire (argument) because they would not worship the golden images (idolatry). The fire (argument) had no effect on them! This demonstrates the power of truth over falsehood. In truth is confidence and strength. These men could not worship any idols even Baal (The Lord) because they knew the Truth.

Da:3:24: Then Nebuchadnezzar the king was astonied, and rose up in haste, and spake, and said unto his counsellers, **Did not we cast three men bound into the midst of the fire**? They answered and said unto the king, True, O king.

Da:3:25: He answered and said, Lo, I see four men loose, walking in the midst of the fire, and they have no hurt; and the form of the **fourth is like the Son of God.**

The fire of Nebuchadnezzar was argument over which god should be worshipped. It's a lengthy story especially if the interpretation is to be explained but put simply is this. The three best orators of the King argued with Shadrach, Meshach, and Abednego. Hence it is said that they were bound and thrown into the fiery furnace. But the three best orators of the King were themselves destroyed by the fire (argument) and not Shadrach, Meshach, and Abednego.

> Da:3:16: Shadrach, Meshach, and Abed-nego, answered and said to the king, O Nebuchadnezzar, we are not careful to answer thee in this matter.

> Da:3:17: If it be so, our God whom we serve is able to deliver us from the burning fiery furnace, and he will deliver us out of thine hand, O king.

> Da:3:18: But if not, be it known unto thee, O king, that we will not serve thy gods, nor worship the golden image which thou hast set up.

> Da:3:19: Then was Nebuchadnezzar full of fury, and the form of his visage was changed against Shadrach, Meshach, and Abed-nego: therefore he spake, and commanded that they should heat the furnace one **seven times** more than it was wont to be heated.

> Da:3:20: And he commanded the most mighty men that were in his army to bind Shadrach, Meshach, and Abed-nego, and to cast them into the burning fiery furnace.

> Da:3:21: Then these men were bound in their coats, their hosen, and their hats, and their other garments, and were cast into the midst of the burning fiery furnace.

> Da:3:22: Therefore because the king's commandment was urgent, and the furnace exceeding hot, **the flame of the fire slew those men that took up Shadrach, Meshach, and Abed-nego.**

Jesus also speaks about fire and imparts insight as to what it means as a reference.

> Luke 12:49-51 **I am come to send fire** (argument) on the earth
> and what will I if it be already kindled.

This fire which Christ says he will send onto the earth is perpetual argument over the word of god. When he spoke of the tares being cast into the **fire** (argument) or of the trees (places of worship) being cast into everlasting fire (argument), this is what he meant.

> Matt. 7:19 Every **tree** (place of worship) that bringeth not forth
> good fruit is hewn down, and cast into the **fire** (argument).

The notion that trees and bushes are burned with fire is seen for example in the parable of the tares.

> M't:13:40: As therefore **the tares are gathered and burned
> in the fire (argument)**; so shall it be in the end of this world.

We see that they are burned with fire (argument) but this is not a new concept. In Exodus 3:2 Moses hears the word of god emanating from a bush that is on fire (argument) yet is not consumed.

> Ex:3:2: And the angel of the LORD appeared unto him in a
> **flame of fire (argument) out of the** midst of a bush: and he
> looked, and, behold, the bush burned with fire (argument), and
> the bush was not consumed.

The special nature of god's fire is that it burns but does not consume.

> Ac:2:3: And there appeared unto them **cloven tongues like as
> of fire (argument)**, and it sat upon each of them.

> Ac:2:4: And they were all filled with **the Holy Ghost (Holy
> Atheism)**, and began to speak with other tongues, as the Spirit
> gave them utterance.

This is also witnessed in Acts 2:3 where the apostles were crowned with tongues of fire (argument) above their heads and immediately they began 'talking in tongues'.

This is perpetual argument over the word of god which is kept alive by the preachers who berate the Bible. There will always be a remnant of people who will follow the various idolatrous doctrines for their own reasons. Such groups will always argue against science and truth, because their delusion inhibits reasoning. Therefore this fire (argument), once kindled will go on forever. This also is described as fire (argument) of the altar, in Revelations.

> Re:8:5: And the angel took the censer, and filled it with **fire (argument) of the altar**, and cast it into the earth: and there were **voices**, and thunderings (yelling), and lightnings (insights), and an earthquake (people trembling).

This fire of the altar of god is referred to in several places but in Chapter 3:18 it is identified as the spirit of God.

> Re:3:18: I counsel thee to **buy of me gold tried in the fire**,(argument) that thou mayest be rich; and white (pure) raiment (veil), that thou mayest be clothed, and that the **shame of thy nakedness** do not appear; and anoint thine eyes with eyesalve, that thou mayest see.

> Re:4:5: And out of the throne proceeded lightnings (insights) and thunderings (yelling) and voices: and there **were seven lamps of fire (argument) burning before the throne, which are the seven Spirits of God.**

If fire (argument) before the altar is the spirit of God we must try to visualise what type of arguing this is. Chapter 8 of Revelations describes how the third (truth) part of all things is destroyed by this fire of the altar mixed with hail stones.

> Re:9:18: By these three was the third (truth) part of men killed, by the **fire (argument)**, and by the **smoke**, and by the **brimstone, which issued out of their mouths.**

So we see that the third (truth) part of men was destroyed by the fire (argument) smoke and brimstone that issued out of their mouths. We know that if it issued out of their mouths then it definitely refers to 'argument' as a fire. Godly or Priestly argument is exactly what it says "Fire and Brimstone" preaching. Enough description has been given to this type of worship in the little book for it to be quite clear what is meant. There seems to be two main types of preaching these days. The first is the traditional staid and reserved kind of sermon delivery given at the same place at the same time on the same subject matter as it has been for thousands of years. The general public are familiar with these sermons and such are usually accepted as harmless teaching of the same lessons of the Gospels.

The other type of evangelising is associated with New Age Evangelising. This is usually delivered as "Fire and Brimstone" preaching and condemnation of the spirit, if you don't believe in God. Such vehement campaigning is broadcast on television, and the Internet to maximise its audience. These doctrines usually claim certain powers, which are not powers at all. They baptize in the name of Christ, but their baptisms do not teach the death of misconceptions, or the rebirth in atheism, although they claim 'slaying in the spirit' as one of their signs. They practice 'speaking in tongues' inspired by Acts 2:4 but unlike in the New Testament where it is claimed the Apostles spoke in particular languages, these New Age devotees merely mumble in gibberish in a spontaneous manner. This makes a mockery of language and God as well. Some New Age practices even take live snakes along to handle in the course of their ministry inspired by Mark 16:18.

> M'r:16:17: And these signs shall follow them that believe; In my name shall they cast out devils; they shall speak with new tongues;

> M'r:16:18: **They shall take up serpents**; and if they drink any deadly thing, it shall not hurt them; they shall lay hands on the sick, and they shall recover.

Such people believe that they prove their own worship as true believers if they do this and survive. It must be pointed out that several people have indeed been bitten and have passed away because of this practice.

Other New Age practices include the 'laying on of hands' in healing the sick. This one is very popular as many people really do have ailments.

Nevertheless merely claiming in the name of God that they have been healed is actually perjury and false witness. If such testimony is given in the name of God it must by definition be identified as the worst of all sins. We don't recommend it, even if there are no such things as gods, to be offended by it. The general impression of all these shallow practices is that they are performed to enthral the public, and seduce them into joining their ranks. This is not really done in order to "save their souls" as it is clamed but it is done simply to enlarge their diocese.

When they claim that they are saving their souls they do not say what they are saving them from or what they are saving them for. Some claim everlasting life but do not describe what everlasting life actually means.

However we of the atheistic view do know that our souls are saved from being corrupted by dogma for ever. We appreciate that this belief also sets us free to pursue any occupation or entertainment we desire knowing that there is no such thing as sin. This freedom however comes with the responsibility of promoting good works. This is our burden, to promote goodness instead of hedonism. Our concept of God namely that God is an Ideal, needs us to live as God would have us live, if God was real. Why should we do this when there is absolutely no punishment for being selfish? We follow Good (God) because we understand the incentive of promoting all good works for the benefit of our children's future and for the well-being of the planet. With dogma there was no concern shown either for our own kind or for the planet, because of the selfish view that in the midst of the apocalypse, we would be instantly translated by the Rapture and that God would intervene on our behalf. This was the incorrect idea that we would be saved while the Earth was being totally destroyed by God's enemies.

The fact is this. God has no enemies. The Earth is not going to be destroyed. God is the Ideal of Good behaviour and responsibilities. It is a Concept which gives birth to a multitude of benefits even while we live. Our reward is already with us.

> Re:16:8: And the fourth angel poured out his vial upon the sun (god worship); and power was given unto him **to scorch men with fire** (argument).

> Re:16:9: And men were scorched with great heat, and **blasphemed the name of God**, which hath power over these plagues: and they repented not to give him glory.

Finally in Revelation we see that the fourth angel poured his vial upon the sun (god worship). This act obviously sets all who are indoctrinated to god worship (idolatry) against the very angel with the fire (argument). This causes great public argument and debate over whether god is real or not. Books such as these are at the heart of this turmoil and even as the reader reads these words they can see this happening. It is a simple vision not too difficult to imagine. For all of us who are visionaries and hold a pleasant vision of the future, know that we need to follow goodness, and the Ideal of God, in order to fulfil these expectations.

Jesus will reveal all the metaphors and literary tricks that hitherto hid this truth from the world, to the reader as they read it. This unfolding on such a personal note, that only the reader can see, will surely add weight to the accuracy of these predictions. Nobody can make you think things against your will. Your mind will conjure images that only you will see. If you understand the messages contained in this book you will surely be aware that the end time is promised, as a revealing of the secret mystery of god.

When all these things are visualised by the reader then the mystery of god is truly complete.

> Re:10:7: But in the days of the voice of the seventh angel, when he shall begin to sound, **the mystery of God should be finished**, as he hath declared to his servants the prophets.

Now of course it may seem presumptuous to make such claims as these prophecy claims but the fact of the matter is this that experiencing these revelations is what the New Testament actually predicts. If it was not true we would not be able to describe it, but the vision is true and the reader of these things in this book, will experience them as they read along. What more substantiation is necessary? The reader will experience it as they read and will be filled with wonder for the Lord.

POTTERS VESSELS AND WATERPOTS

People are seen as sheep and fish so why not pots? God is seen as the Master Potter and we as the pots. We are supposed to be as malleable clay that God can fashion into the ideal followers of God. But what the Master Potter makes however, he can also break.

> Psalms:2:9: Thou shalt break them with a rod of iron; thou shalt dash them in pieces like a **potter's vessel**.

People therefore are seen as these vessels, either molded into new vessels or broken into shards depending on their behavior.

> Psalm 32:12 I am forgotten as a dead man out of mind: I am like a **broken vessel.**

Revelations also uses this analogy. It is claimed in Revelation 2:26 in the letter to Thyatira that the one who overcomes the blasphemy and idolatry and practices of the church, shall be given power over nations and he shall rule them with a rod of iron and as the vessels of a potter they shall be broken.

> Re:2:18: And unto the angel of the church in Thyatira write; These things saith the Son of God, who hath his eyes like unto a flame of fire, and his feet are like fine brass;

> Re:2:19: I know thy works, and charity, and service, and faith, and thy patience, and thy works; and the last to be more than the first.

> Re:2:20: Notwithstanding I have a few things against thee, because thou sufferest that woman Jezebel, which calleth herself a prophetess, to teach and to **seduce my servants to commit fornication, and to eat things sacrificed unto idols.**

> Re:2:21: And I gave her space to repent of her fornication; and she repented not.

Re:2:22: Behold, I will cast her into a bed, and them that commit adultery with her into great tribulation, except they repent of their deeds.

Re:2:23: And I will kill her children with death; **and all the churches shall know that I am he which searcheth the reins and hearts:** and I will give unto every one of you according to your works.

Re:2:26: And he that overcometh, and keepeth my works unto the end, to him will I give power over the nations:

Re:2:27: And he shall rule them with a rod of iron; **as the vessels of a potter** shall they be broken to shivers: even as I received of my Father.

This is portraying how a single person can obtain real power over the word of God. It is through the metaphors and by understanding the purity of thought behind the parables. All interpretation that worships god as an idol or as a real person denies the truth that God is an Ideal. All church attendance that seeks out heavenly reward even life everlasting will fall on its face because there is no reward for dogma. Only those people who understand the truth that god does not exist, yet continue to behave in such a way that God would be proud to name Himself by, shall surname themselves by God. They surname themselves as children of God through the process of adoption. When they marry Christ they take His surname and become Christians.

Here then we see how and where Jesus received his power. It was through this metaphoric language that confessed the truth. The breaking of the people is achieved by revealing the mystery of god through uncovering the truth. This was the redeemer of the Jews. This is also the apocalypse of the Christians. By taking the mystery out of God, the spirit of the vessels is broken. This constitutes the harvesting of the Lord or as becoming a burnt offering as previously stated.

> Re:10:7: But in the days of the voice of the seventh angel, when he shall begin to sound, **the mystery of God should be finished**, as he hath declared to his servants the prophets.

So we witness that the mystery of God is revealed and completed by the revelation of the secret which has been held since the beginning. This whole process has a name and it is called the Apocalypse, a Greek word which simply means the uncovering or the revealing of the secret which refers to the unveiling of the mystery of god as stated above.

The idea that people are vessels made from clay or dry earth mixed with water, is consistent with that of Adam being 'of the dust of the ground' and requiring a 'mist' to rise and 'water' the whole face of the ground to bring about his creation. Also the concept of the Baptism is in line with this imagery. However if this clay is dried out again, it returns to dust or dry earth.

> Job:10:9: Remember, I beseech thee, **that thou hast made me as the clay**; and wilt thou bring **me into dust again**?

> Gen 2:7 And the Lord God formed man **of the dust** of the ground.

> Gen. 3:19 For **dust thou art and unto dust thou shalt return**

We learn that we are dust. Being the dust of humanity makes us just a small portion of all the population. Even so if water (spirit of life) is added to dust we can manufacture clay. When Jesus spat on the dust He made clay with His fingers with which He anointed the blind man's eyes in order to make the blind man see the truth.

> Joh:9:6: **When he had thus spoken, he spat on the ground, and made clay** of the spittle, and he anointed the eyes of the blind man with the clay,

This miracle of anointing the blind man is once again written in code. The concept that Jesus spat (water - spirit of life; spoken from the mouth of Jesus) made clay (made the man malleable as clay) and anointed his eyes so that the blind could see (told the man the truth about god so that the man could understand truth).

In Romans the allusion to the potter is made clear.

> Ro:9:20: Nay but, O man, who art thou that repliest against God? Shall the thing formed say to him that formed it, Why hast thou made me thus?

> Ro:9:21: **Hath not the potter power over the clay**, of the same lump to make one vessel unto honour, and another unto dishonour?

We are once again reminded that we are the clay and that God is the Master Potter. This idea that as clay we are to be malleable to god's tuition is seen in every aspect of Christian teaching. The whole purpose of Christian Teaching is not to make us perfect before God, that's impossible, but to improve our behavior so that as a community we improve each other's lives.

The step from clay to pottery requires a firing. Above we have just discussed what FIRE is representative of. Fire is argument over the word of God. This argument or discussion is the teaching process that turns us into something known as vessels of God.

Water-pots made of clay, once fired, can now hold water (spirit of life) themselves. They can hold their own water (spirit of life) or be filled with other substances. Many precious things can be stored in earthenware pots. The Scripture scrolls themselves were preserved in earthenware pots. It is interesting to note that the Dead Sea Scrolls were found in such earthenware containers, perfectly preserved after two thousand years.

This sets up the imagery that people, like these vessels or earthenware pots or water pots as they were called, could contain the knowledge of God. God's laws could be written on the hearts of the people, the prophet tells us, and Jesus confirms this by saying that God is within you.

People therefore are seen not only as sheep or fish but also as vessels for the word of god.

Jesus filled such vessels (water pots) with water (spirit of life) but when it was drawn out it became wine! This happened at Cana (which means to take a surname) in Galilee (circle) at a wedding. Note the name meanings here - Cana means to take a surname which is exactly what the bride does at a wedding. She takes on the surname of the bridegroom. Christianity is the bride to Jesus Christ hence the surname in Christianity (belonging to Christ).

Galilee means 'circle' and this refers to Jesus' circle of associates which include the disciples, His family and a few Hebrews such as Joseph of Arimathaea, and one called Nicodemus these two were Levites who conspired with Jesus in order to ensure the prophecy was completed as it was meant to be.

Water, as we have seen, represents the Spirit of Life and salt water also the Spirit of Truthfulness and is imbued in us as the teachings of righteousness. It is a life giving substance which keeps one sober but also quenches the thirst for knowledge. Wine on the other hand is intoxicating, it may be a comforter of souls but it does not quench the desire to know the truth and in fact increases spiritual thirst and confusion. Salt water (spirit of truthfulness) represents the thirst quenching truth but wine the ongoing doctrine of comfort (and intoxication) as given by the church.

In the following verse we see an example of the behavior induced by new wine. We know by the fact that it was the third (truth) hour of the day that what was happening here was a revelation of the truth.

> Ac:2:13: Others mocking said, These men are full of **new wine**.

> Ac:2:14: But Peter, standing up with the eleven, lifted up his voice, and said unto them, Ye men of Judaea (praise), and all ye that dwell at Jerusalem (possession of peace), be this known unto you, and hearken to my words:

> Ac:2:15: For these are not drunken, as ye suppose, seeing it is but the third (truth) hour of the day.
>
> Ac:2:16: But this is that which was spoken by the prophet Joel (Lord is god);
>
> Ac:2:17: And it shall come to pass in the last days, saith God, I will pour out of my Spirit upon all **flesh** (doctrine): and your sons and your daughters shall prophesy, and your young men shall see visions, and your old men shall dream dreams:

Salt water however, representing correct interpretation of Scripture and truth, is that which Jesus spoke of as Living Water which is the only Water (truth) that can actually quench the thirst for truth.

> John 4:14 Whosoever drinketh **of the water** (truth) that I shall give shall never thirst.

When wine is used as a metaphor, it represents the **comforter** that which gladdens our hearts and lifts our spirits. It also represents idolatry in some places because of its red colour and its intoxicating effect. Water never fills this role. Truth is not something which has to be re-given or delivered each week to bolster the spirit. Truth is a once only application. Once you know it; that is the end of the matter. It quenches the thirst! We have said that there is no need to keep returning to doctrine once the truth is known and this is so, but remember that the Baptism is a pledge to serve humanity. Therefore it is necessary to set up a way of ministering this service. The role of the church therefore is as an organizer of this labour. The congregation should meet regularly in order to help each other and their environment and not necessarily to drink old wine (repetitive sermons and idolatry) only. That is, not just to receive the same old sermons as such things are dead works which achieve nothing.

Now we begin to understand the miracle of turning water into wine. The Waterpots of stone (spiritual house) were six (idolatry) servants who had been indoctrinated to Jesus' teaching about the misconception about what God is, and this knowledge had quenched their thirst with the spirit of atheism (truth) so that wine (sermons miracle worship and idolatry) are then delivered to us in a new light (a new insight) to comfort us and reassure us that our reward is with us. This all serves to remind us to remain righteous and not self-righteous, a teaching on humility. Our reward is the direct result of the work of our hands. Good works produce good reward, but no works produce no reward at all, hence God's presence is reflected through our own demeanor.

The Apostles speak of different kinds of wine - new wine and old wine. Old wine therefore is the traditional sermons and miracle worship; the same old themes preached week after week, year after year, until they lose all their meaning and value - these are the leaves of the fig!

New wine only follows the revelation of truth! It has not had time to ferment into intoxicating liquor (delusion). It is a refreshing of spirit and its doctrine (truths) differ from old wine in that they very seldom refer to old concepts of Scripture or fire and brimstone type preaching. New wine is, sermons given in the light of Truth - God is an Ideal - which has wiped away the misconception of godhead, idols, and supernatural powers from their minds.

The New Testament was the new wine of Jesus whereas the Old Testament was the old wine and comfort of the Jews, at the time of Christ. Nowadays our wine has become the old wine because of the way it is traditionally taught.

So the wedding at Cana (to take a surname) in Galilee (the circle) represents the revealing of a new spiritual identity by turning the 'water' (spirit of life) into 'wine' (sermons with truth) and surnaming themselves as belonging to Christ. By this it is shown that Christianity is destined to be the Bride of Christ as prophesied in Revelations. Therefore just as Eve (Foundation of life) was the wife of Adam (of the ground) Mary (Rebellious) became the wife of Israel (Ruling with God) and Christianity (belonging to Christ) becomes the wife of Christ (Saviour). All this is signified by this wedding parable.

Why is all this necessary? It has already been pointed out that Jesus' Judaism had turned the truth of god into a lie and had continually committed idolatry through worshipping Baal (the Lord) or God as an idol. The hierarchy was therefore considered to be an adulterous woman (out of man-religion), a rebellious nation. This idea of rebellion falls neatly into prophetic language when one considers Mary, the Mother of Christ and consequently the Mother of Christianity. The name Mary means 'Rebellious' and the imagery is easy to see when reading the old prophetic books.

> Joh:2:10: And saith unto him, Every man at the beginning doth set forth good wine; and when men have well drunk, then that which is worse: but thou hast kept the **good wine until now**.

The marriage at Cana is a rehearsal predicting how we shall become the wife of Christ. It probably did not actually take place as a real wedding since it is not mentioned anywhere else in the New Testament. We know too that the Gospel of John is far more ethereal than the worldliness of other disciples. He has a far superior spiritual understanding than any other writers of the time. It is easy to see why Jesus called him the beloved disciple.

Other uses of the imagery of pottery can be easily discovered. One of the most concise is that of Isaiah.

> Isa:64:8: But now, O LORD, **thou art our father; we are the clay, and thou our potter**; and we all are the work of thy hand.

The imagery is plain to see that we are clay which can be fashioned into vessels by the master potter. God however is not the only potter, for as we have seen in Revelations that the one who overcomes the seven trials, as set out in the seven letters to the seven churches, is also given the power to break these churches by word of mouth. The teachings of truth are strong enough to put the fear of God into all those who commit idolatry by worshipping God as an omnipotent being.

> Re:2:26: And he that overcometh, and keepeth my works unto the end, **to him will I give power over the nations:**

> Re:2:27: And he shall rule them with a rod of iron; as the vessels of a potter shall they be broken to shivers: **even as I received of my Father**.

This promise is made sure by the statement "even as I received of my Father". Of course this is referring to Jesus Christ and how Jesus came by His own power. It is through earnest study and the purging of vanity that truth is uncovered little by little until a full understanding is gained. We are sure that the readers of this book will appreciate this same disclosure of this truthful secret of Christ.

> Re:10:1: And I saw another mighty angel come down from heaven, clothed with a cloud: and a rainbow was upon his head, and his face was as it were the sun, and his feet as pillars of fire:

> Re:10:2: And he had in his **hand a little book open**: and he set his right foot upon the sea, and his left foot on the earth,

> Re:10:3: And cried with a loud voice, as when a lion roareth: and when he had cried, seven thunders uttered their voices.

> Re:10:4: And when the seven thunders had uttered their voices, I was about to write: and I heard a voice from heaven saying unto me, Seal up those things which the seven thunders uttered, and write them not.

> Re:10:5: And the angel which I saw stand upon the sea and upon the earth lifted up his hand to heaven,

> Re:10:6: And sware by him that liveth for ever and ever, who created heaven, and the things that therein are, and the earth, and the things that therein are, and the sea, and the things which are therein, that **there should be time no longer:**

Re:10:7: But in the days of the voice of the seventh angel, when he shall begin to sound, **the mystery of God should be finished**, as he hath declared to his servants the prophets.

Re:10:8: And the voice which I heard from heaven spake unto me again, and said, Go and **take the little book** which is open in the hand of the angel which standeth upon the sea and upon the earth.

Re:10:9: And I went unto the angel, and said unto him, **Give me the little book. And he said unto me, Take it, and eat it up; and it shall make thy belly bitter, but it shall be in thy mouth sweet as honey.**

Re:10:10: And I took the little book out of the angel's hand, **and ate it up; and it was in my mouth sweet as honey: and as soon as I had eaten it, my belly was bitter.**

Re:10:11: And he said unto me, Thou must prophesy again before many peoples, and nations, and tongues, and kings.

Above are the verses of Revelation that decide when it is an appropriate time to reveal these mysterious things about god. That time turns out to be when someone has broken the code and is able to show it to others; in other words to write that same little book. The little book needs to be written when its contents can be advertised without those who read it being put to death. It's bad enough that they have to suffer the spiritual death of the wormwood doctrine of the absence of god, without suffering bigots and chauvinists as well.

We are told to eat the little book "And he said unto me, Take it, and eat it up; and it shall make thy belly bitter, but it shall be in thy mouth sweet as honey". We eat this little book by reading it and digesting its contents. This is the same instruction Jesus gave of His Flesh - to eat it. This is His Daily Bread or Scripture of the New Testament. We now have the little book which reveals the mysterious code of the truth that there is no such thing as god.

Hence we are also made bitter because of the lesson of the Wormwood or bitterness after knowing the truth. We also know the name of the one who writes this little book as it is stated that the name of that star or prophet is called Wormwood.

> Re:8:11: And the name of the star (prophet) is **called Wormwood**: and the third part of the waters became wormwood; and many men died of the waters, because they were made bitter.

REAPING THE HARVEST OF GOD

Jesus explains the teaching of truth, this giving of living waters slays people in their idolatrous spirit. This idolatrous worship is what Jesus refers to as the First Death as such a person afflicted is dead to the truth. Revealing this to them is called 'reaping the harvest of god'.

> Joh:4:35: Say not ye, There are yet four months, and then cometh harvest? behold, I say unto you, Lift up your eyes, and look on the fields; for they are white already to harvest.

> Joh:4:36: **And he that reapeth receiveth** wages, and gathereth fruit unto life eternal: that both he that soweth and he that reapeth may rejoice together.

> Joh:4:37: And herein is that saying true, One soweth, and another reapeth.

> Joh:4:38: I sent you to reap that whereon ye bestowed no labour: other men laboured, and ye are entered into their labours.

Also Revelations has instructions to whomever the visionary is at the end of time, to reap the harvest of God;

> Re:14:15: And another angel came out of the temple, crying with a loud voice to him that sat on the cloud, Thrust in thy sickle, and **reap**: for the time is come for thee to reap; for **the harvest of the earth is ripe**.

In Job we see the use of reaping as taking away their clothing and thus leaving them naked. The reaping which is affected by revealing the heretical truth has the potential to turn many people into atheists and by doing so it is claimed they therefore become a burnt offering to the Lord. Such people no longer have a covering for their spirituality.

> Job:24:6: **They reap** every one his corn in the field: and they gather the vintage of the wicked.

Job:24:7: **They cause the naked to lodge without clothing**, that they have no covering in the cold.

This state of mind of being atheist is to be without spiritual clothing. This is also termed being naked or swept clean and Jesus told a story about just such a state. This story is related in both Matthew and Luke as follows.

M't:12:43: When the unclean spirit is gone out of a man, he walketh through dry places, seeking rest, and findeth none.

M't:12:44: Then he saith, I will return into my house from whence I came out; and when he is come, he **findeth it empty, swept, and garnished**.

Lu:11:24: When the unclean spirit is gone out of a man, he walketh through dry places, seeking rest; and finding none, he saith, I will return unto my house whence I came out.

Lu:11:25: And when he cometh, **he findeth it swept and garnished**.

Reaping the field of God is exactly this; to slay worshippers of god in the spirit. This is to cut them down with the truth. There is no other way to purge their mind of vanity but that they should be harvested. It is said that one sows and another reaps.

Joh:4:37: And herein is that saying true, **One soweth, and another reapeth**.

Joh:4:38: **I sent you to reap** that whereon ye bestowed no labour: other men laboured, and ye are entered into their labours.

We did not sow what Christ sowed but we reap the harvest of His labours. This is all of Christendom waiting for the time of the **revealing of the mystery of god** which is the truth of atheism. This is that truth that there is no such thing as god. What other truth is there that can reap the followers?

Re:14:15: And another angel came out of the temple, crying with a loud voice to him that sat on the cloud, **Thrust in thy sickle, and reap: for the time is come for thee to reap; for the harvest of the earth is ripe.**

Re:14:16: And he that sat on the cloud thrust in his sickle on the earth; and the earth was reaped.

People sow their own seed in the course of their life. Their spiritual seed is not their children but rather their opinions and behavior. If one sows discord then one will reap discord, if one sows righteousness one will reap righteousness.

Ga:6:7: Be not deceived; God is not mocked: **for whatsoever a man soweth, that shall he also reap.**

Now we reap the field of god which is all Christendom. We divulge the truth that there is no such thing as god. All god worship is idolatry and the following verses promise to give the reader the hidden manna which is the secret to the mystery of god and so it is done by the little book.

Re:2:17: He that hath an ear, let him hear what the Spirit saith unto the churches; To him that overcometh **will I give to eat of the hidden manna, and will give him a white stone, and in the stone a new name written, which no man knoweth saving he that receiveth** it.

LIGHTNING INSPIRATION

As with all metaphors they are often difficult to see at first. The word lightning does not easily conjure images of what it means but when it is known, we wonder how we did not see it in the first instance. Lightning which refers to inspiration is one of those.

> M't:24:27: For **as the lightning** (inspiration) cometh out of the east, and shineth even unto the west; **so shall also the coming of the Son of man be**.

In this verse Matthew is telling us how the Son of Man will return. We know that God is within us which gives us the insight to also realize that the coming of the Son of Man will be from within us also. This is inspiration which is spoken of.

The same verse in Luke tells us the same story.

> Lu:17:20: And when he was demanded of the Pharisees, when the kingdom of God should come, he answered them and said, The kingdom of God cometh not with observation:
>
> Lu:17:21: Neither shall they say, Lo here! or, lo there! for, behold, the kingdom of **God is within you**.
>
> Lu:17:22: And he said unto the disciples, The days will come, when ye shall desire to see one of the days of the Son of man, and ye shall not see it.
>
> Lu:17:23: And they shall say to you, See here; or, see there: go not after them, nor follow them.
>
> Lu:17:24: **For as the lightning, that lighteneth out of the one part under heaven, shineth unto the other part under heaven; so shall also the Son of man be in his day.**
>
> Lu:17:30: Even thus shall it be in the day **when the Son of man is revealed**.

> Lu:21:27: And then shall they **see the Son of man coming in a cloud** with power and great glory
>
> M'r:13:26: And then **shall they see the Son of man coming in the clouds** with great power and glory.
>
> M't:24:30: And then shall appear **the sign of the Son of man** in heaven: and then shall all the **tribes of the earth mourn**, and they shall **see the Son of man coming in the clouds** of heaven with power and great glory.

In these verses Luke describes the sudden illumination or inspiration that Christ will appear in the veils or clouds of heaven as it was promised but not in the widely accepted opinion of a physical body dropping out of the skies like an aircraft. To say or even think that god will drop out of the skies in some chariot is too naïve for words. God is within us so does this mean that He must come out of us first before He can appear on the Earth? Of course such a thing is ridicule. There is no actual person called god. God is an ideal as Jesus taught us. As such, both God and Jesus can only appear in our minds eye, or in our thoughts which is inspiration. For Jesus to return He must appear in our thoughts as inspired by whatever medium is presenting Him. However the actual scripture calls for the Son of Man to be seen in the clouds (covering) of heaven but for everybody to see Him at once, He must first be described to everybody at once. Of course this can't happen without todays mass publications. This book will be one of the first publications to announce that Jesus can only be seen in the FLESH. That is to say according to His own description. Joh:6:56: He that eateth my flesh, and drinketh my blood, dwelleth in me, and I in him. His flesh is our daily bread of course, this is His doctrine and our scripture, which we have in the form of the New Testament. The lightning therefore is inspiration and a sudden vision that forms in our mind, as we read about the metaphors and literary devices He used to camouflage the truth.

In Matthew 24:30 it states that all the "tribes of the earth mourn, and they shall see the Son of man coming in the clouds of heaven". Of course they will mourn because the realization that god is an ideal is an anti-climax to the fantasy that has been expected for so long. Nevertheless we do know

175

the truth and even when we hear it for the first time it gels within us and we recognize the value of insight.

Timothy writes about inspiration. We don't know where inspiration comes from. Even scientists studying the brain are amazed that we humans can create thought and invent things out of nothing. Where does such creativity come from? Where does inspiration come from? What is it in the biology of the brain that can cause a completely new thought to arise? We don't know.

> II Timothy 3:16 **All scripture** is given **by inspiration of God**, and is profitable **for doctrine**, for reproof for correction, for instruction in righteousness:

Slowly we begin to see that this indicates that Lightning is a metaphor for inspiration? Again we see it in other associations for example we know that rain from heaven is teachings of righteousness, so when we see verses such as this in Psalm 135

> Psalm 135:7 He causeth the vapours to ascend from the ends of the earth; he maketh **lightning's (inspiration) for the rain (preaching)**; he bringeth the wind out of the treasuries.

We can loosely tie rain (preaching) with lightning (inspiration) remembering what Timothy wrote about all scripture being given **by inspiration** of God (an Ideal).

Another verse from Luke states.

> Luke 10:18 And he said unto them, I beheld Satan (Deception) **as lightning** fall from heaven.

This verse also indicates that our thoughts which create heaven are within the mind and to imagine Satan fall from heaven indicates that this happens within the realms of our own imagination or inspiration. Satan of course does not actually exist either just like god. For that matter neither does Heaven. So in order for any of these imaginary things to be seen at all means that they must be visualized in our own mind. For this reason we see the very careful wording of the New Testament as it states that the Son of Man will be REVEALED and not simply seen. To be revealed implies that someone or something has to do the revealing. This of course applies to the Apocalypse (a Greek word meaning 'to reveal'). So if this is the case then the little book is announcing the apocalypse just as predicted in Revelations.

> Re:10:10: And I took the little book out of the angel's hand, and ate it up; and it was in my mouth sweet as honey: and as soon as I had eaten it, my belly was bitter.

To be revealed in scripture means that the metaphor is fully understood and the hidden meaning is exposed. It is through the hidden meaning that we learn about the secret life and teachings of Jesus. Indeed even the Holy Ghost which is the knowledge that there are no such things as gods is enlightenment. Jesus brought all this knowledge to us but the deeper message was lost for millennia. By revealing this deeper layer of meaning we see Jesus' own mortality and through this we can appreciate a new respect for what He suffered for the salvation of the Truth.

VEIL & COVERING

The whole of Jesus' teachings proclaim the issue that the truth was covered by a veil or covering. The notion that the truth is hidden by this covering is consistent from Genesis to Revelation. It is central to understanding the message against idolatry. Believing in the covering, (which covers our spiritual nakedness), and not the fruit or truth, is the misconception which is also the deceit of the church. This is the veil Matthew spoke of when Jesus was on the cross.

> M't:27:50: Jesus, when he had cried again with a loud voice, yielded up the ghost.

> M't:27:51: And, behold, **the veil of the temple** was rent in twain from the top to the bottom; and the earth did quake, and the rocks rent;

This thought, that the veil was torn in two, was also expressed by Mark and Luke.

> M'r:15:37: And Jesus cried with a loud voice, and gave up the ghost

> M'r:15:38: And the **veil of the temple** was rent in twain from the top to the bottom.

> Lu:23:45: And the sun (god worship) was darkened, and the **veil of the temple** was rent in the midst.

Luke also tells us that the Sun (god worship) was also darkened meaning that the truth was exposed at this time. The veil is referring to the covering of the truth by fables and stories and as we read through Acts and other books of the New Testament we gradually become aware that the teachings are always leaning toward removing or uncovering this veil.

We see such explanation or attempt at revealing these things in 2Corinthians 3:13-17

2Co:3:13: And not as Moses, which put a **vail over his face**, that the children of Israel could not stedfastly look to the end of that which is abolished:

2Co:3:14: But their minds were blinded: for until this day remaineth the same vail untaken away in the reading of the old testament; which vail is done away in Christ.

2Co:3:15: But even unto this day, when Moses is read, the vail is upon their heart.

2Co:3:16: **Nevertheless when it shall turn to the Lord, the vail shall be taken away.**

2Co:3:17: Now the Lord is that Spirit: and where the Spirit of the Lord is, there is liberty.

And the same thoughts in Hebrews

Heb:10:16: This is the covenant that I will make with them after those days, saith the Lord, I will put my laws into their hearts, and in their minds will I write them;

Heb:10:17: And their sins and iniquities will I remember no more.

Heb:10:18: Now where remission of these is, there is no more offering for sin.

Heb:10:19: Having therefore, brethren, boldness **to enter into the holiest** by the blood of Jesus,

Heb:10:20: By a new and living way, which he hath consecrated for us, **through the veil, that is to say, his flesh**;

The veil which they call His flesh, tells us that His doctrine actually forms the veil. Every word of Jesus' testament is dedicated to exposing this veil or covering which is cast over the wording of both Old and New Testaments. This code is easily recognized once a person is shown the trick. In order to be considered inspired writing, all doctrine must comply with this code. Doctrine that does not comply with this code is easily recognized as fraud. Therefore many recently accredited books of modern and ancient writings are not considered to belong to the same authorship as the existing Holy Bible. The Dead Sea Scrolls for example, do not show signs of this code (except for the known book of Isaiah). There are other recently discovered gospels which also do not conform to this code just as there are particular Bibles of certain denominations that also stand apart.

The code of the mystery of god is established in Genesis. Moses wrote these first books of the Torah with the code already written into them. All the writers after Him have also observed the same practice concluding with the writers of the New Testament. Therefore we do know that this code is indeed the fingerprint of authority. Without this code there is no evidence of the same insight.

By revealing this code of the mystery of god, it can be shown that TRUTH is most highly regarded. Some say that the truth reveals that the Bible is a fraud. If there is no such thing as god why then refer to God so much. Why in our Court of Law do we swear on the Bible to tell the Truth, if the Bible is not truthful about what god is?

The fact is that the Bible does confess what god is. That is what the little book is all about. It must be published before the authors pass away and deny this knowledge to the World. The little book has only one agenda and that is to reveal this code. It turns out that the Bible is TRUTHFUL it does confess what god really is. However it is not the Bible that preaches 'Fire and Brimstone'. It is not the Bible that is at fault when people form misconceptions. It is not the Bible that cause people to follow delusions.

3Jo:1:4: **I have no greater joy than to hear that my children walk in truth**.

MOUNTAINS

Without the symbolism of mountains there would probably not have been a Bible at all. It was on a mountain that Noah's Ark came to rest, it was on a Mountain that Moses received his commandment to free Israel and also received the Ten Commandments and it was on a mountain that Abraham went to sacrifice his son Isaac. There are many events associated with mountains, too many to list but we will explore a different use of the metaphor of mountains. **Mountains** represent **Religions**. They are lofty, often shrouded in clouds of mystery and seem to last throughout the ages. This is the notion that great institutions outlive the people that invent them. Kingdoms or civilisations for example move on through the ages whilst their occupants, the people are transient, the institution seems to last for ever. Civilisations and religions too, give the effect of permanency whilst people are replaced by others. Therefore these institutions are likened to great mountains which give the same feeling of eternity.

Mountains are separated by one other feature of enormous importance. God dwells in the heights of the Mountains just as God dwells in religions.

> Psalms:125:1 **They that trust in the LORD shall be as mount** (religion) **Zion** (fortress), which cannot be removed, but **abideth for ever**.

> Psalms:125:2: As the **mountains** (religions) are round about Jerusalem**, so the LORD is round about his people** from henceforth even for ever.

> Ho:4:13: They sacrifice upon the tops of **the mountains** (religions), and **burn incense** upon the hills, under oaks and poplars and elms, because the shadow thereof is good: therefore your daughters shall commit whoredom, and your spouse's shall commit adultery.

> Ho:10:8:The high places also of Aven (vanity), **the sin of Israel** (ruling with god), shall be destroyed: the thorn and the thistle shall come up on their altars; and they shall say to the **mountains** (religions)**, Cover us; and to the hills, Fall on us**.

The SIN of ISRAEL is idolatry. It is the one continual sin that the Jews never rid them-selves of. The high places of Aven (vanity) represents their religion which commits the sin of Israel and for that they will say to the mountains cover us and to the hills fall on us. This is exactly what is recorded in Revelations when the revealing of the mystery of god takes place.

> Re:6:15: And the kings of the earth, and the great men, and the rich men, and the chief captains, and the mighty men, and every bondman, and every free man, **hid themselves in the dens and in the rocks** (churches) **of the mountains** (religions);

> Re:6:16: And said to **the mountains** (religions) **and rocks** (churches), **Fall on us, and hide us from the face of him that sitteth on the throne**, and from the wrath of the Lamb:

> Re:6:17: For the great day of his wrath is come; and who shall be able to stand?

> Re:17:9: And here is the mind which hath wisdom. The seven heads **are seven (word of god) mountains** (religions), on which the woman (out of man -religion) sitteth.

> Re:17:10: And there are seven kings: five are fallen, and one is, and the other is not yet come; and when he cometh, he must continue a short space.

Isaiah also writes about the Lords religion as a mountain;

> Isa:2:2: And it shall come to pass in the last days, **that the mountain of the LORD's house shall be established in the top of the mountains**, and shall be exalted above the hills; and all nations shall flow unto it.

> Isa:2:3: And many people shall go and say, **Come ye, and let us go up to the mountain (religion) of the LORD**, to the house of the God of Jacob; and he will teach us of his ways, and we will walk in his paths: for out of Zion shall go forth the law, and the word of the LORD from Jerusalem.

And Joel observes that God dwells in His Holy Mountain;

> Joe:3:17: So shall ye know that I am the LORD your God **dwelling in Zion** (Fortress)**, my holy mountain** (religion): then shall Jerusalem be holy, and there shall no strangers pass through her any more.

Micah reports that all nations shall know God in His Holy Mountain;

> Mic:4:2: And many nations shall come, and say, Come, and let us go up to the **mountain** (religion) of the LORD, and to the house of the God of Jacob (supplanter); and he will teach us of his ways, and we will walk in his paths: for the law shall go forth of Zion (Fortress), and the word of the LORD from Jerusalem (Possession of Peace).

These mountains are not physical mountains but are metaphors for Religions. It is at the pinnacle of the religion where god dwells. If mountains therefore represent religion, this then throws a new light on interpreting Revelations;

> Re:6:12: And I beheld when he had opened the sixth (idolatry) seal, and, lo, there was a great earthquake (people quake); and the sun (miracle worship) became black as sackcloth of hair, and the moon (truth) became as blood;

> Re:6:13: And the stars (prophets) of heaven fell unto the earth, even as a fig tree casteth her untimely figs (worshippers), when she is shaken of a mighty wind.

> Re:6:14: And the heaven departed as a scroll when it is rolled together; and every mountain (religion) and island were moved out of their places.

> Re:6:15: And the kings of the earth, and the great men, and the rich men, and the chief captains, and the mighty men, and every bondman, and every free man, hid themselves in the dens and in the rocks (churches) of the mountains (religions);

> Re:6:16: **And said to the mountains (religions) and rocks (churches), Fall on us, and hide us from the face of him that sitteth on the throne, and from the wrath of the Lamb:**
>
> Re:6:17: **For the great day of his wrath is come; and who shall be able to stand?**

Mountains therefore represent the very religions that own them. Jesus was tempted on such a mountain

> M't:4:8: Again, the devil (deceiver) taketh him up into an exceeding high **mountain** (religion), and sheweth him all the kingdoms of the world, and the glory of them;
>
> Lu:4:5: And the devil (deceiver), taking him up into an high **mountain** (religion), shewed unto him all the kingdoms of the world in a moment of time.
>
> Lu:4:6: And the devil (deceiver) said unto him, All this power will I give thee, and the glory of them: for that is delivered unto me; and to whomsoever I will I give it.
>
> Lu:4:7: If thou therefore wilt worship me, all shall be thine.
>
> Lu:4:8: And Jesus answered and said unto him, **Get thee behind me, Satan**: for it is written, Thou shalt worship the Lord thy God, and him only shalt thou serve.

In Corinthians we see that Paul writes that with his knowledge of the mystery of god he could remove mountains (religions).

> 1Co:13:2: And though I have the gift of prophecy, and understand **all mysteries**, and all knowledge; and though I have all faith, so that **I could remove mountains** (religions), and have not charity, I am nothing.

This is reminiscent of the power of the little book that its disclosure will reveal that all worship of god is vain. Even though people run to their respective religions, they will be unable to hide from the gossip and reports of there not being such a thing as god.

> Re:6:16: And said to the **mountains** (religion) and **rocks** (churches), Fall on us, and **hide us from the face of him that sitteth on the throne**, and from the wrath of the Lamb:

Another well-known prophecy of the end times is that of Daniel who states that a certain person (stone) was cast out of the mountain (religion) without hands i.e. under his own power. This person is responsible for the revealing of the mystery

> Da:2:34: Thou sawest till that **a stone** (persons spiritual house - Jesus) was cut out without hands (no help), which smote the image (Israel religion) upon his feet that were of iron and clay, and brake them to pieces.

> Da:2:35: Then was the iron, the clay, the brass, the silver, and the gold, broken to pieces together, and became like the chaff of the summer threshingfloors; and the wind carried them away, that no place was found for them: and the stone that smote the image became a **great mountain** (religion – Christianity), and filled the whole earth.

> Da:2:36: This is the dream; and we will tell the interpretation thereof before the king.

In hindsight it is easy to see the meanings of past prophecy but it is not always that simple with prediction. It certainly helps if we know the meaning of the symbolism and metaphors before-hand. Daniel predicted the coming of one person (we now assume to be Jesus) who broke away from the mother religion (mountain) in order to correct the delusional thinking of those who controlled the reins. This prediction was not unique however as there were other prophets saying the same things.

Hosea:

> Ho:10:8: The high places also of Aven (vanity), the sin of Israel (ruling with god), shall be destroyed: the thorn and the thistle shall come up on their altars; and they shall say to the mountains (religions), Cover us; and to the hills (place of worship), Fall on us.

Zephaniah:

> Zep:3:11: In that day shalt thou not be ashamed for all thy doings, wherein thou hast transgressed against me: for then I will take away out of the midst of thee them that rejoice in thy pride, and thou shalt no more be haughty because of my holy mountain (religion).

Of course there are too many references to mountains to reprint here, suffice it to say that all references to 'mountains' reflect the notion that the religion was a mighty institution, that seemed to be eternal just as mountains are eternal.

ROCKS

If Mountains are religions then it follows that Rocks are churches. In the following verse we see how Moses drew water from a rock. The story only makes sense if the rock represents the church or synagogue from which the spirit (water) flows freely.

> Nu:20:8: Take the rod, and gather thou the assembly together, thou, and Aaron (enlightened) thy brother, and speak ye unto the **rock** (church) before their eyes; and it shall give forth his water (preaching), and thou shalt bring forth to them water (preaching) out of the **rock** (church): so thou shalt give the **congregation** and their beasts drink.

> Nu:20:9: And Moses took the rod from before the LORD, as he commanded him.

> Nu:20:10: And Moses and Aaron gathered the **congregation** together **before the rock (Church)**, and he said unto them, Hear now, ye rebels; must we fetch you **water out of this rock (Church)?**

> Nu:20:11: And Moses lifted up his hand, and with his rod he smote **the rock** (church) twice (those who struggle together): and the water (spirit of life) came out abundantly, and the **congregation** drank, and their beasts also.

> Nu:20:12: And the LORD spake unto Moses and Aaron, Because ye believed me not, to sanctify me in the eyes of the children of Israel, therefore ye shall not bring this congregation into the land which I have given them.

> Nu:20:13: This is the water of Meribah (means 'contention or quarrelling'); because the children of Israel strove with the LORD, and he was sanctified in them.

The imagery of the rock continues with King David describing it as;

2Sa:22:2: And he said, **The LORD is my rock** (church), and my fortress, and my deliverer;

2Sa:22:3: The God of **my rock** (church); in him will I trust: he is my shield, and the horn of my salvation, my high tower, and my refuge, my saviour; thou savest me from violence.

In psalms there are also references to the church being a rock;

Psalms:18:1: I will love thee, O LORD, my strength.

Psalms:18:2: **The LORD is my rock** (church), and my fortress, and my deliverer; my God, my strength, in whom I will trust; my buckler, and the horn of my salvation, and my high tower.

And in another Psalms;

Psalms:31:1: In thee, O LORD, do I put my trust; let me never be ashamed: deliver me in thy righteousness.

Psalms:31:2: Bow down thine ear to me; deliver me speedily: **be thou my strong rock** (church), for an house of defence to save me.

Psalms:31:3: **For thou art my rock** (church) and my fortress; therefore for thy name's sake lead me, and guide me.

Psalms:31:4: Pull me out of the net that they have laid privily for me: for thou art my strength.

Psalms:31:5: Into thine hand I commit my spirit: thou hast redeemed me, O LORD God of truth.

The New Testament continues this imagery of the church as a rock; Here is a verse from Matthew.

M't:16:18: And I say also unto thee, That thou art Peter, and **upon this rock I will build my church**; and the gates of hell shall not prevail against it.

Luke also writes about the rock and the church in this way the following parable portrays the solid foundation of that of the rock;

> Lu:6:47: Whosoever cometh to me, and heareth my sayings, and doeth them, I will shew you to whom he is like:

> Lu:6:48: He is like a man which built an house, and digged deep, and laid the foundation on a **rock** (church): and when the flood (preaching) arose, the stream beat vehemently upon that house, and could not shake it: for it **was founded upon a rock** (church).

In 1 Corinthians they talk of the spiritual drink which comes from the rock or church.

> 1Co:10:4:And did all drink the same **spiritual drink**: for they drank of that spiritual **Rock** (church) that followed them: **and that Rock (church) was Christ.**

And finally in Revelations we see the imagery used to describe the end time

> Re:6:14: And the heaven departed as a scroll when it is rolled together; and every mountain (religion) and island were moved out of their places.

> Re:6:15: And the kings of the earth, and the great men, and the rich men, and the chief captains, and the mighty men, and every bondman, and every free man, **hid themselves in the dens and in the rocks (churches) of the mountains (religions);**

> **Re:6:16: And said to the mountains (religions) and rocks (churches)**, Fall on us, and hide us from the face of him that sitteth on the throne, and from the wrath of the Lamb:

> Re:6:17: For the great day of his wrath is come; and who shall be able to stand?

In 1 Corinthians 10:4 there is this reference to Jesus being our rock or church.

> 1Co:10:4: And did all drink the same spiritual drink: for they drank of that spiritual Rock (church) that followed them: and that Rock (church) was Christ.

And in Luke also Jesus tells the parable of the sower referring to the seed (word of god) that fell on a rock (church).

> Lu:8:13: They on the **rock** (church) are they, which, when they hear, receive the word (of god) with joy; and these have no root, which for a while believe, and in time of temptation fall away.

There are enough references here to show that the idea of a rock representing a church is well established. The Old Testament is full of such relationships.

> Ex:17:6: Behold, I will stand before thee there **upon the rock** (church) in Horeb (waste); and thou shalt smite the rock (church), and there shall come water (spirit of life) out of it, that the people may drink. And Moses (drawn out of the water) did so in the sight of the elders of Israel (ruling with god).

One of the first mentions of this metaphor is found in Exodus cited below;

> Ex:33:20: And he said, **Thou canst not see my face**: for there shall **no man see me, and live**. (to see the truth causes death)

> Ex:33:21: And the LORD said, Behold, there is a place by me, and thou shalt stand upon a **rock**: (church)

> Ex:33:22: And it shall come to pass, while my glory passeth by, that I will put thee **in a clift of the rock**, (hide in the church) and will cover (veil of the mystery of god) thee with my hand while I pass by:

> Ex:33:23: And I will take away mine hand, and thou shalt see my back parts: but my face shall not be seen.

The above story explains the reason for the establishment of the veil or covering of the mystery of god. To see the truth (in this case gods face) means certain death (atheism). This is a well discussed notion and by now should be easily recognisable.

STONES

Mountains are Religions, Rocks are Churches and Stones are people. To be more precise a stone represents a person's heart or spiritual house. There is a saying "Heart of Stone" meaning that a person is hard-hearted and such a saying referring to the heart may be true but not all people are hard hearted. Many people have a soft and malleable heart which of course is the more desirable state, when it comes to religion. Most religions want people that are compliant, and not questioners or troublemakers, pointing out every false opinion or contradiction, of which the pastors are unable to find a suitable answer. There are many such contradictions in the New Testament even in Bibles that have been heavily edited. Even such specific Bibles don't answer every inconsistency and people who question the book are an embarrassment and interruption to sermons. Such people are usually ostracised anyway and lucky if that's all that happens to them.

The custom of "stoning" a wrongdoer is probably a misrepresentation of the law also. According to the King James Bible to stone somebody was to change their heart from evil to good or from carnal to enlightenment. It can sometimes refer to a particular person or it might be more general in its application. Below we see how Jacob became known as the **stone** of Israel.

> Ge:49:24: But his bow abode in strength, and the arms of his hands were made strong by the hands of the mighty God of Jacob; **from thence is the shepherd, the stone of Israel**:

In Matthew we have Jesus describing himself as that Stone;

> M't:21:42: Jesus saith unto them, Did ye never read in the scriptures, The **stone** (a person's spiritual house in this case Christ) which the builders rejected, the same is become the head of the corner: this is the Lord's doing, and it is marvellous in our eyes?

> M't:21:43: Therefore say I unto you, The kingdom of God shall be taken from you, and given to a nation bringing forth the fruits thereof.

M't:21:44: And whosoever shall fall on this **stone** (a person's spiritual house in this case Christ) shall be broken: but on whomsoever it shall fall, it will grind him to powder.

The same concept is repeated in Mark

M'r:12:10: And have ye not read this scripture; The **stone** (a person's spiritual house in this case Christ) which the builders rejected is become the head of the corner:

Luke writes likewise;

Lu:20:17:And he beheld them, and said, What is this then that is written, The **stone** (a person's spiritual house in this case Christ) which the builders rejected, the same is become the head of the corner?

Lu:20:18: Whosoever shall fall upon that **stone** (a person's spiritual house in this case Christ) shall be broken; but on whomsoever it shall fall, it will grind him to powder.

And in Acts it is repeated yet again;

Ac:4:10: Be it known unto you all, and to all the people of Israel, that by the name of Jesus Christ of Nazareth, whom ye crucified, whom God raised from the dead, even by him doth this man stand here before you whole.

Ac:4:11: **This is the stone** (a person's spiritual house in this case Christ) which was set at nought of you builders, which is become the head of the corner.

The other associations are more general and use stones to point to ordinary people.

In Matthew this view is clear;

M't:3:9: And think not to say within yourselves, we have Abraham to our father: for I say unto you, that **God is able of**

these stones (a person's spiritual house in this case people) to raise up children unto Abraham.

And Luke repeats the notion that people are stones.

> Lu:3:8: Bring forth therefore fruits worthy of repentance, and begin not to say within yourselves, We have Abraham to our father: for I say unto you, **That God is able of these stones** (a person's spiritual house in this case people) to raise up children unto Abraham.

Also in Luke is found this allusion referring to people as stones.

> Lu:19:39: And some of the Pharisees from among the multitude said unto him, Master, rebuke thy disciples.

> Lu:19:40: And he answered and said unto them, I tell you that, if these should hold their peace, **the stones** (a person's spiritual house in this case people) would immediately cry out.

In 1 Peter 2:4 the association that stones represent people is very clear where it states that **Ye as lively stones** are built up a spiritual house.

> 1Pe:2:4: To whom coming, as unto **a living stone** (a person's spiritual house in this case Christ), disallowed indeed of men, but chosen of God, and precious,

> 1Pe:2:5: **Ye also, as lively stones** (a person's spiritual house in this case people), **are built up a spiritual house**, an holy priesthood, to offer up spiritual sacrifices, acceptable to God by Jesus Christ.

Daniel interprets the dream of king Nebuchadnezzar using the image of a stone to represent the prophet at the last day to smite the image of religious confusion in Nebuchadnezzar's dream.

> Da:2:31: Thou, O king, sawest, and behold a great image. This great image, whose brightness was excellent, stood before thee; and the form thereof was terrible.

Da:2:32: This image's head was of fine gold, his breast and his arms of silver, his belly and his thighs of brass,

Da:2:33: His legs of iron, his feet part of iron and part of clay.

Da:2:34: Thou sawest till that **a stone** (a person's spiritual house - Jesus) was cut out without hands, which smote the image upon his feet that were of iron and clay, and brake them to pieces.

Da:2:35: Then was the iron, the clay, the brass, the silver, and the gold, broken to pieces together, and became like the chaff of the summer threshing floors; and the wind carried them away, that no place was found for them: **and the stone** (a person's spiritual house) **that smote the image became a great mountain** (religion), and filled the whole earth.

This account is a well-documented prediction of the "end time". The **stone** (a person's spiritual house) was cut out of the **mountain** (religion) without hands (without help). It is a prediction of the end times and how it will be brought about by a single person whose spiritual house is based in truth.

In the prophecy of Revelation this stone also appears as a gift to "he who overcomes" from the church at Pergamos.

Re:2:17: He that hath an ear, let him hear what the Spirit saith unto the churches; To him that overcometh will I give to eat of the hidden manna, and will give him **a white stone** (a new heart or spiritual house), and in the **stone** (a person's spiritual house) **a new name written**, which no man knoweth saving he that receiveth it.

This white stone is to replace our hardened heart with a new heart. This thought is also expressed by Job talking about Leviathan.

Job 41:24 **His heart (Leviathan) is as thin as a stone** (a person's spiritual house); yea, **as hard as a piece nether millstone**

Millstones are used to grind the wheat into flour so that bread (scripture) can be made. This bread (Scripture) is what Jesus called the bread of life. We see then that our stone (a person's spiritual house) is really our interpretations of that bread. Our own opinions or our ego is our stone (spiritual house). Jesus asks.

> Lu:11:11: **If a son shall ask bread** (Scripture) of any of you that is a father, **will he give him a stone**? (a spiritual house) or if he ask a fish (worshipper), will he for a fish give him a serpent (truth)?

There is another reference to stones being people virtually repeating the above verses in I Peter 2:4

> 1Pe:2:3: If so be ye have tasted that the Lord is gracious.

> 1Pe:2:4: To whom coming, as unto **a living stone** (a person's spiritual house in this case Christ), disallowed indeed of men, but chosen of God, and precious,

> 1Pe:2:5: **Ye also, as lively stones** (a person's spiritual house in this case people), **are built up a spiritual house**, an holy priesthood, to offer up spiritual sacrifices, acceptable to God by Jesus Christ.

> 1Pe:2:6: Wherefore also it is contained in the scripture, Behold, I lay in Sion a chief **corner stone** (a person's spiritual house in this case Christ), elect, precious: and he that believeth on him shall not be confounded.

> 1Pe:2:7: Unto you therefore which believe he is precious: but unto them which be disobedient, the **stone** (a person's spiritual house in this case Christ) which the builders disallowed, the same is made the head of the corner,

> 1Pe:2:8: **And a stone (a person's spiritual house) of stumbling**, and a rock (church) of offence, even to them which stumble at the word, being disobedient: whereunto also they

were appointed. 1Pe:2:3: If so be ye have tasted that the Lord is gracious.

Peter's verse makes it very clear that **we as lively stones** are built up a **Spiritual House**. Even today we have a remnant of this concept in our language. If then stones represent people as spiritual houses what then is really meant by a stoning? A stoning is the breakdown of one spiritual house and it being replaced by another more perfect attitude. It is not meant to be a physical murdering of a person. It is in fact a rehabilitation program designed to change a person's attitude. This is what happens with the Baptism. We are told the mystery of god (that there is no such thing as gods) and we therefore die a spiritual death (atheism). Immediately following this however we are counseled in our vow to serve humanity in the name of truth and god or resurrected. This then effectively replaces our old idolatry (worship stone) with a new state of mind called truthful knowledge (truthful stone). So by the Baptism we are effectively 'stoned to death'.

Jesus' views on stoning are as follows.

> Joh:8:4: They say unto him, Master, this woman (out of man – religion) was taken in adultery, in the very act.
>
> Joh:8:5: Now Moses (drawn out of the water) in the law commanded us, that such should be stoned (change her spiritual house): but what sayest thou?
>
> Joh:8:6: This they said, tempting him that they might have to accuse him. But Jesus stooped down, and with his finger wrote on the ground (on their hearts), as though he heard them not.
>
> Joh:8:7: So when they continued asking him, he lifted up himself, and said unto them, **He that is without sin among you, let him first cast a stone** (spiritual house) at her.

In this verse Jesus stooped down and with his finger wrote on the ground (on their hearts). This indicates that there is more to the story than merely Jesus' indifference. Could it be that Jesus revealed to them the true metaphor of 'stoning' thus embarrassing them with their hypocrisy? It is also pertinent to note his response "He that is without sin" would know the truth that there is no such thing as god, and therefore would be pure in thought and be the only one qualified to understand what the true meaning of stone was.

The best person to begin to teach the woman (out of man - religion) a new spiritual identity would be the one who is without sin. The Pharisees and Sadducees all worshipped God and consequently always thought of themselves as sinners. Worship dictates this oppression. Jesus on the other hand could never be convinced of sin.

> Joh:8:46: **Which of you convinceth me of sin**? And if I say
> the truth, why do ye not believe me?

THIEF

Having read about the bread of life, we suddenly become aware that another meaning is indicated by the verse concerning Christ's return in the flesh. Just as the hypocrite Pharisees expected their Messiah to fly in on the clouds like an aircraft, so too do many Christians expect Jesus to fly in like some glorious space craft. This is ludicrous and the folly of it is seen when we accept the Truth of Jesus' own words - that Scripture is His Flesh or doctrine which we have had with us all along. The revealing therefore is when the people of earth become aware of this fact and finally put an end to the misconception of deluded idolatry!

> 2Th:2:6: And now ye know what withholdeth that he might be **revealed** in his time.

> 2Th:2:7: For the **mystery of iniquity doth already work**: only he who now letteth will let, until he be taken out of the way.

> 2Th:2:8: And then shall that **Wicked be revealed**, whom the Lord shall consume with the spirit of his mouth, and shall destroy with the brightness of his coming:

> 2Th:2:9: Even him, **whose coming is after the working of Satan** (deceiver) with all power and signs and lying wonders,

> 2Th:2:10: And with all deceivableness of unrighteousness in them that perish; **because they received not the love of the truth**, that they might be saved.

> 2Th:2:11: And for this cause **God shall send them strong delusion**, that they should believe a lie:

The clouds with which He will return become obvious as the covering or veil of the truth that He represented as being revealed by the apocalypse. It is by this revealing of what the covering or veil is, that destroys the concept of God and Heaven. This destruction is likened to one being robbed of their delusion and fairytale notions about heaven.

Re:16:15: Behold, I come as a **thief**. Blessed is he that watcheth, and keepeth his garments, lest he walk **naked**, (know the truth) and they see his shame.

This THIEF analogy is repeated in many places;

1Th:5:2: For yourselves know perfectly that the day of the Lord so cometh as a **thief** in the night.

1Th:5:3: For when they shall say, Peace and safety**; then sudden destruction cometh** upon them, as travail upon a woman (out of man - religion) with child (Baptism); and they shall not escape.

It comes as a thief because the idolaters will feel robbed. They placed their trust in an idol and now there is no reward. Peter gives the same warning and reminds us that Heaven will come to an end one day.

2Pe:3:10: But the day of the Lord will come as a **thief** in the night; in the which the **heavens shall pass away** with a great noise, and the elements shall melt with fervent heat, the earth also and the works that are therein shall be burned up.

But Peter goes on in just two more verses to say.

2Pe:3:13: Nevertheless we, **according to his promise, look for new heavens** and a new earth, wherein dwelleth righteousness.

This new heaven is a new hope that is not based on any fanciful notion or delusion but rather a firm knowledge based in truth.

M't:21:42: Jesus saith unto them, Did ye never read in the scriptures, The stone (spiritual house) which the builders rejected, the same is become the head of the corner: this is the Lord's doing, and it is marvellous in our eyes?

M't:21:43: Therefore say I unto you, **The kingdom of God shall be taken from you**, and given to a nation bringing forth the fruits thereof.

Jesus spoke of himself as being the cornerstone of the religion. Yet in other places it is referred to as a stone of stumbling and a rock of offence.

> 1Pe:2:7: Unto you therefore which believe he is precious: but unto them which be disobedient, the **stone** (spiritual house) which the builders disallowed, the same is made the head of the corner,

> 1 Peter 2:8 And a **stone** (a person's spiritual house) of stumbling and a **rock** (church) of offence, even to them which **stumble at the word**, being disobedient: whereunto also they were appointed.

Of course the stumbling is produced by believing in miracles which are not real, by being deluded or by committing idolatry through worshiping an imagined god. Stumbling at the word means that those who fervently study the word of god (Bible) continually come across verses that are contradiction or heretical or blasphemous and the student has no idea why. There is only one viewpoint that offers peace of mind when it comes to the Bible and that is the truth that there are no such things as gods. Jesus said this right from the beginning and throughout all His testimony as did John the Baptist and all the disciples who were taught the truth.

Yet there are other warnings about the Thief analogy.

In Revelations John writes,

> Re:3:3: Remember therefore how thou hast received and heard, and hold fast, and repent. If therefore thou shalt not watch, **I will come on thee as a thief**, and thou shalt not know what hour I will come upon thee.

But the best and most precise statement of all is foretold again in Revelations.

> Rev. 16:15 **Behold, I come as a thief** Blessed is he that watcheth, and keepeth his garments, lest he walk **naked**, and they see his shame.

From these verses we understand that the idea of the thief is one who robs us of our treasures and raiment and hence leaves us naked. This is consistent with all that has gone before in the little book. The nakedness is a spiritual nakedness which we are familiar with already. Those under the veil or under grace who believe in god shall be robbed of their beliefs by the revealing of the code to scripture.

FIRST DEATH

People who worship God are under the covering or veil of scripture and are not aware of the truth that God does not exist at all. These are said to be dead to the truth. The revealing of this truth to them is termed the first death. There are several occurrences where this death is referred to in the scriptures as it is a fairly common state for the general public to be in. One such example is found in Matthew 8:21 as follows.

> M't:8:21: And another of his disciples said unto him, Lord, suffer me first to go and bury my father.

> M't:8:22: But **Jesus said unto him, Follow me; and let the dead bury their dead**.

By Jesus saying "let the dead bury their dead" we are given an insight into what being dead means. In truth dead people can't bury other dead people so we know that something else is indicated by this statement. The dead who do the burying are those who believe in the covering or veil of miracles and all manner of god worship and not the truth.

Jesus himself was counted as dead even whilst he was living. We see this in the verse from Revelations 1:5 below in which we learn that Jesus is the first born of the dead.

> Re:1:5: And from Jesus Christ, who is the faithful witness, and the **first begotten of the dead**, and the prince of the kings of the earth. Unto him that loved us, and washed us from our sins in his own blood,

And the same thoughts are expressed in Colossians as follows.

> Col:1:18: And he is the head of the body, the church: who is the beginning, the **firstborn from the dead**; that in all things he might have the preeminence.

Now we also see these insinuations when Jesus is preaching to the populous as in John 5:25

> Joh:5:25: Verily, verily, I say unto you, The hour is coming, and now is, **when the dead shall hear the voice of the Son of God**: and they that hear shall live.

This verse is referring to the common people who were under the Jewish religion at the time. Only living people can hear of course and the reference to the dead hearing is calling on this spiritual metaphor to describe people who are dead to the truth. Other indicators can be found to support this notion. We cite verses from 1Peter 4:5

> 1Pe:4:5: Who shall give account to him that is ready to judge the quick and the dead.

> 1Pe:4:6: For for this cause was **the gospel preached also to them that are dead**, that they might be judged according to men in the flesh, but live according to God in the spirit.

Having the Gospel preached also to the DEAD can only mean one thing that is that they are not dead at all but very much alive and hearing the words of the preaching. Being dead to the truth, (that there is not any such thing as god), means that they believed there actually was a god and as a result were unable to reason. It is not just a denial of the truth which is at stake here. The inability to understand worldly issues comes into play as well. If our minds are controlled by worship or more specifically a delusion then we are not free to make informed decisions and all our decisions are coloured by what we believe.

Now there are also references to the Baptism as being the death that people go through in order to be cleansed of sin.

> Ro:6:3: Know ye not, that so many of us as were baptized into Jesus Christ **were baptized into his death?**

> Ro:6:4: Therefore we are **buried with him by baptism into death**: that like **as Christ was raised up from the dead** by the glory of the Father, even so we also should walk in newness of life.

> Ro:6:5: For if we have been **planted together in the likeness of his death**, we shall be also in the likeness of his resurrection:

And we also have Jesus' own words to complete this metaphor.

> Joh:5:24: Verily, verily, I say unto you, He that heareth my word, and believeth on him that sent me, hath everlasting life, and shall not come into condemnation; but **is passed from death unto life**.

This verse says that whoever hears His words are passed from death into life. It is quite clear that this death is spiritual death which comes about by not knowing truth. In Romans 8:10 we see another statement that says the body is dead even while we are yet alive.

> Ro:8:10: And if Christ be in you, **the body is dead because of sin**; but the Spirit is life because of righteousness.

And concerning death and resurrection Jesus had this to say.

> M't:22:31: But as touching the **resurrection of the dead**, have ye not read that which was spoken unto you by God, saying,

> M't:22:32: I am the God of Abraham, and the God of Isaac, and the God of Jacob? **God is not the God of the dead, but of the living**.

In this verse Jesus says God is not a God of the dead but of the living indicating that the resurrection of the dead is actually referring to the living. It is a living resurrection.

And finally we have in 1 John 3:14 the statement that we have passed from death into life.

> 1Jo:3:14: We know that we have passed from **death unto life**, because we love the brethren. He that loveth not his brother abideth in death.

So we learn that the First Death is to believe that gods exist. It is to be oblivious to the presence of the veil. It is to be naive in spirit and trusting of everything one is told about god. The first death is a cocoon of sanctuary in which the person is isolated from the harsh reality of the truth, that there are no such things as gods. This is because those people who are devout or zealous about god, have no idea that god and religion was actually invented by society, and are therefore ignorant of the truth. Having their minds filled with holy thoughts and worship there is no room left for real enlightenment such as knowledge. These days science is the main opponent to religion. The little book may have something to say but in reality it is science that challenges ones intellect. Naturally it will be offensive to some people that the little book states that all god worshippers commit idolatry. We did not say this but Jesus Christ did. He said all these things before and was duly crucified for the offence. Nevertheless the truth will be known eventually and the little book is not the first inkling that the population has had of it. Many attempts throughout history have been made by the same effort. All were squashed by the powerful people in control and so the veil of the mystery remains.

> 1Pe:1:3: Blessed be the God and Father of our Lord Jesus Christ, which according to his abundant mercy hath begotten us again unto a lively hope **by the resurrection of Jesus Christ from the dead,**

> 1Pe:1:4: To an inheritance incorruptible, and undefiled, and that fadeth not away, reserved in heaven for you,

> 1Pe:1:5: Who are kept by the power of God through faith unto salvation **ready to be revealed in the last time.**

> 1Co:3:13: Every man's work shall be made manifest: for the day shall declare it, **because it shall be revealed by fire (argument); and the fire (argument) shall try every man's work** of what sort it is.

THE SWORD

As we have seen the Bible is twofold in nature. On the surface there is the literal meaning, the stories and fables read literally, but underlying this is a spiritual message. This twofold style is represented as the Bible being a SWORD with two edges. The SWORD of God is described as being the WORD of God. The coincidental spelling of WORD – SWORD is fascinating. The WORD of God is scripture. As we have seen, the word of God has dual meanings and this is reflected by the Sword of God being a two edged sword. The Word of God is the Holy Bible and this sword is often said to come out of the mouth just as words do.

> Re:1:16: And he had in his right hand seven stars: and out **of his mouth went a sharp two edged sword** (word): and his countenance was as the sun shineth in his strength.

The symbolism of the sword coming out of the mouth is easy to understand since it refers to the Word of God. It is repeated in Revelation 2:12

> Re:2:12: And to the angel of the church in Pergamos write; These things saith he which hath the **sharp sword** (word) **with two edges**;

And again in the following verse the sword comes out of the mouth just as words do;

> Re:2:16: Repent; or else I will come unto thee quickly, and will fight against them **with the sword** (word) **of my mouth.**

Now in Revelation there is the following account also describing that the Word of God is the Sword of God and that it comes out of the mouth;

> Re:19:13: And he was clothed with a vesture dipped in blood: and his name is called **The Word of God**.

> Re:19:14: And the armies which were in heaven followed him upon white horses, clothed in fine linen, white and clean.

> Re:19:15: And **out of his mouth goeth a sharp sword** (word
> with double meaning), that with it he should smite the nations:
> and he shall rule them with a rod of iron: and he treadeth the
> winepress of the fierceness and wrath of Almighty God.

Now in Ephesians we read that the "sword of the spirit is the word of God". This is a clear indication that the sword represents the word of God.

> Eph:6:17: And take the helmet of salvation, and the **sword of
> the Spirit, which is the word of God**:

And a likewise verse in Hebrews

> Heb:4:12: For the **word of God** is quick, and powerful, and
> sharper than any **twoedged sword**, piercing even to the dividing
> asunder of soul and spirit, and of the joints and marrow, and is
> a discerner of the thoughts and intents of the heart.

These writings reveal the twin nature of Biblical texts the two meanings stem from the two viewpoints of belief in God. One viewpoint is that God exists this is the idolatrous view and one opinion which is considered to be dead to the truth. The other and more honest is that "there is no such thing as god" this is the heretical view which slays people in the spirit, given enough evidence, and enables the rebirth of baptism.

Understanding the sword of God therefore gives us the power we need in order to reveal the mystery of the Bible. Without knowledge of the Sword of God it would be impossible to interpret even basic coding. This is because the imagery of the sword of god is embedded throughout all the texts. It permeates all stories and is the backbone to all the literature of the Bible. Because it is so widespread in its presence it gives us the tool we need to prove or disprove biblical quotations. Here is power. Revealing the heretical view of god can be devastating to believers and their faith. It becomes possible to cut them down with their own words and to visit on them the same browbeating they pour onto the world at large.

The Sword of God (Bible or Word of God) is used as a sickle to reap the population of the world.

Re:14:15: And another angel came out of the temple, crying with a loud voice to him that sat on the cloud, **Thrust in thy sickle, and reap: for the time is come for thee to reap; for the harvest of the earth is ripe.**

Re:14:16: And he that sat on the cloud **thrust in his sickle on the earth; and the earth was reaped.**

CONCEPT SEVEN

THE LIFE OF JESUS

Before Christ was born there was the prophecy of His birth. The Levites were one of the twelve tribes of Israel. They were the one tribe given an understanding of the mystery of god by Moses. By this covenant they were never to be numbered or associated with the rest of the tribes of Israel but instead were held apart because of the secret and mystery of god which they kept.

> Nu:1:47: But the Levites after the tribe of their fathers **were not numbered among them.**

> Nu:1:48: For the LORD had spoken unto Moses, saying,

> Nu:1:49: Only thou shalt not number the tribe of Levi, neither take the sum of them among the children of Israel:

> Nu:1:50: But **thou shalt appoint the Levites over the tabernacle of testimony,** and over all the vessels thereof, and over all things that belong to it: they shall bear the tabernacle, and all the vessels thereof; and they shall minister unto it, and shall encamp round about the tabernacle.

> Nu:1:51: And when the tabernacle setteth forward, the Levites shall take it down: and when the tabernacle is to be pitched,

> the Levites shall set it up: and the stranger that cometh nigh
> shall be put to death.

The expectation of a saviour to come was broadly accepted throughout all Israel but only the Levites knew who, when and where. Since the Levites were entrusted with the Ark of the Covenant and in fact all paraphernalia of the Tabernacle of Testimony they also held positions of power in controlling planned prophecy. We call it planned prophecy because most of it was contrived. There is some prophecy that can be predicted because of frequency of occurrence such as earthquakes and huge storms. Other natural disasters that are cyclic in nature such as astronomical events like an eclipse are also easily prophesied. Some events that are behavioural in nature repeat or are likely to happen because of human nature. For example predicting that religion will lose sight of the fact that god does not exist and hence all worshippers commit idolatry is also easily achieved. Then there is prophecy of a personally fulfilled role. Now there are two ways that a personally fulfilled role can be accomplished. One is by waiting long enough for a fervent believer who after much Bible study believes that he or she is the Messiah. The occurrence of this type of self-fulfilling prophecy is remarkably frequent. There is always someone ready to suffer all indignities in order to be seen as the long awaited messiah. Most of these people and their attempts usually fall into a small cult groups or peter out altogether as another failed mission.

The other more impressive way to ensure that a prophecy will be fulfilled exactly the way it is predicted is to groom someone for the role. This assignment fell to the Levites. It was their task to firstly make the prediction and secondly ensure that at the expected time it would be satisfactorily fulfilled.

In the case of the prophecy of Jesus, it is well known that there were many prophecies made about him in the Old Testament. Nevertheless it is not widely known that the grooming for this prophecy was a great deal more difficult than the few prophecies indicated. Before Jesus could emerge there had to be John the Baptist to prepare the way. Not many people give a lot of thought as to how complex this mission was to prove. The Levites had to groom two people John and Jesus. Their roles were vastly different but Jesus' Testament depended entirely on the success of Johns. Without John there would be no Jesus. Not only that but they were introducing a whole new concept into religion; the Baptism. Both these men and their friends and family had to have a sound working understanding of what the Baptism represented. As we have seen the Baptism is far more complex than just getting wet. The entire concept of Death; Rebirth and Resurrection had to be firstly thought of, then all the intricacies such as its allusion to conception in women established and finally it had to be worked in with the established belief system then finally taught to Jesus and John as children until they were fluent with all its variances.

The risk here is that one never knows if the children preserved for this education, will actually be strong enough to make the concept succeed. What if the children or one of the children refused, or met with an accident and died, or had chronic health issues, or simply had the wrong type of temperament? The gamble was high but then we don't know how many attempts the Levites had made over the last 400 years BC.

By the time John and Jesus were due to be born the theory of Baptism was well understood by all the Levites given the task of their education. We know that Levites were involved because Matthew writes of them being sent to verify the saviour. Note that the word CHRIST is actually a version of the Greek 'Christos' meaning 'Messiah" or 'Saviour'.

> Joh:1:15: John bare witness of him, and cried, saying, This was he of whom I spake, He that cometh after me is preferred before me: for he was before me.

> Joh:1:16: And of his fulness have all we received, and grace for grace.

> Joh:1:17: For the law was given by Moses, but grace and truth came by Jesus Christ.

> Joh:1:18: **No man hath seen God at any time**; the only begotten Son, which is in the bosom of the Father, he hath declared him.

Joh:1:19: **And this is the record of John, when the Jews sent priests and Levites from Jerusalem to ask him, Who art thou?**

Joh:1:20: **And he confessed, and denied not; but confessed, I am not the Christ (Saviour).**

Joh:1:21: And they asked him, What then? Art thou Elias? And he saith, I am not. Art thou that prophet? And he answered, No.

Joh:1:22: Then said they unto him, Who art thou? that we may give an answer to them that sent us. What sayest thou of thyself?

Joh:1:23: He said, I am the voice of one crying in the wilderness, Make straight the way of the Lord, as said the prophet Esaias.

Joh:1:24: And they which were sent were of the Pharisees.

Joh:1:25: And they asked him, and said unto him, Why baptizest thou then, if thou be not that Christ, nor Elias, neither that prophet?

Joh:1:26: John answered them, saying, I baptize with water: but there standeth one among you, whom ye know not;

Joh:1:27: He it is, who coming after me is preferred before me, whose shoe's latchet I am not worthy to unloose.

So we learn that Priests and more importantly Levites (keepers of the secret) were sent to affirm that this John the Baptist was indeed setting up the expected return of the Saviour. John and Jesus alike needed to have trustworthy witnesses to add credibility to their mission. Without this recognition they would not have been taken seriously. There was always someone on the inside to verify their cause and indeed help with designing their impression on the rulers of the day.

Jesus didn't just happen along He was prepared to be the Messiah from birth as was John the Baptist. Jesus and John were cousins. Their families were not only related by a bloodline but they were probably Levites as well with associations at least with people in power to have been selected for this auspicious title. Mary Mother of Jesus was found to be with child of the Holy Ghost! The Holy Ghost is the Holy Nothing! The Holy Ghost as we have seen and devoted many words to, relate to the void left behind when god is missing. In place of God all we have is an IDEA. This idea formed the covering or mystery of god which is as old as the history of Israel itself. The Levites would have needed to train both John and Jesus with this knowledge as well as their new solution to the idolatry which Israel fell under.

So Mary was found to be with this idea. Mary is a woman (out of man - religion) and as a religious concept taken out of man, she represents the 'wife' (flesh or doctrine) of Israel (Ruling with God). She is therefore seen as a woman with no husband (saviour) because Israel was awaiting a messiah. The expected messiah had a task to provide Israel with this husband (saviour). In the Gospel of John we witness Jesus talking on His own to a woman (out of man - religion) or church group, the Samarians. The apostles had gone away to buy meat (doctrine). Jesus relates a story that the Samarians (those who watch for god) have had five husbands in the past but that the sixth one was not here yet. This story is remarkably the same as Israel who at that time also had a history of five husbands but was awaiting the next saviour.

> Joh:4:1: When therefore the Lord knew how the Pharisees had heard that Jesus made and baptized more disciples than John,
>
> Joh:4:2: (**Though Jesus himself baptized not, but his disciples,**)
>
> Joh:4:3: He left Judaea, (Praise) and departed again into Galilee (Of the Circle or conspiracy).
>
> Joh:4:4: And he must needs go through Samaria (those who watch for god).
>
> Joh:4:5: Then cometh he to a city of Samaria (those who watch for god), which is called Sychar (liar), near to the parcel of

ground that Jacob (supplanter) gave to his son Joseph (he will increase).

Joh:4:6: Now Jacob's (supplanter) well was there. Jesus therefore, being wearied with his journey, sat thus on the well: and it was about the sixth (idolatry) hour.

Joh:4:7: There cometh a woman of Samaria to draw water: Jesus saith unto her, Give me to drink.

Joh:4:8: (For his disciples were gone away unto the city to buy meat (doctrine).)

Joh:4:9: Then saith the woman of Samaria unto him, How is it that thou, being a Jew, askest drink of me, which am a woman (out of man) of Samaria? (those who watch for god) for the Jews have no dealings with the Samaritans (those who watch for god).

Joh:4:10: Jesus answered and said unto her, If thou knewest the gift of God, and who it is that saith to thee, Give me to drink; thou wouldest have asked of him, and he would have given thee living water (spirit of life).

Joh:4:11: The woman (out of man) saith unto him, Sir, thou hast nothing to draw with, and the well is deep: from whence then hast thou that living water? (spirit of life)

Joh:4:12: Art thou greater than our father Jacob, which gave us the well, and drank thereof himself, and his children, and his cattle?

Joh:4:13: Jesus answered and said unto her, Whosoever drinketh of this water shall thirst again:

Joh:4:14: But whosoever drinketh of the water that I shall give him shall never thirst; but the water that I shall give him shall be in him a well of water springing up into everlasting life.

Joh:4:15: The woman (out of man) saith unto him, Sir, give me this water,(spirit of life) that I thirst not, neither come hither to draw.

Joh:4:16: Jesus saith unto her, **Go, call thy husband (saviour), and come hither**.

Joh:4:17: The woman (out of man) answered and said, I have no husband (saviour). Jesus said unto her, Thou hast well said, I have no husband (saviour):

Joh:4:18: **For thou hast had five husbands (saviours); and he whom thou now hast is not thy husband (saviour): in that saidst thou truly**.

Joh:4:19: The woman(out of man) saith unto him, Sir, I perceive that thou art a prophet.

Joh:4:20: Our fathers worshipped in this mountain (religion); and ye say, that in Jerusalem (possession of peace) is the place where men ought to worship.

Joh:4:21: Jesus saith unto her, Woman (out of man), believe me, the hour cometh, when ye shall neither in this mountain (religion), nor yet at Jerusalem (possession of peace), worship the Father.

Joh:4:22: Ye worship ye know not what: we know what we worship: for salvation is of the Jews.

Joh:4:23: But the hour cometh, and now is, when the true worshippers shall worship the Father in **spirit and in truth**: for the Father seeketh such to worship him.

Joh:4:24: **God is a Spirit: and they that worship him must worship him in spirit and in truth**.

Joh:4:25: The woman saith unto him, I know that Messias cometh, which is called Christ: when he is come, he will tell us all things.

> Joh:4:26: Jesus saith unto her, **I that speak unto thee am he.**

Jesus then states that neither in this religion (Samarians) nor in Jerusalem (Possession of Peace) or Israel (Ruling with God), will people worship god (commit idolatry by worshipping a god). He says that God is a Spirit (which is an enthusiasm for helping each other) and that God must be worshipped in Spirit and in Truth. This statement means that in order to worship God people needed to adopt the Spirit of helping their neighbour as well as knowing the truth (that god does not actually exist and that god worship is therefore idolatry).

We see therefore that this intercourse with the group of Samarian parishioners Jesus actually outlines His own mission and the state of Israel as well. Israel did have five husbands prior to Jesus, these were;

1/ Noah
2/ Abraham
3/ Moses
4/ David
5/ Elijah

Jesus saw Himself as the sixth but He doesn't count Himself in because He says in Joh:4:18: For thou hast had five husbands (saviours); and he whom thou now hast is not thy husband (saviour): in that saidst thou truly. So He says that He is not to be the sixth because by His own doctrine He was to put an end to idolatry (god worship) by revealing the truth.

However this opinion of Jesus of there being only five husbands is revisited in Revelation 17;

> Re:17:1: And there came one of the seven (word of god) angels (messengers) which had the seven (word of god) vials, and talked with me, saying unto me, Come hither; I will shew unto thee the judgment of the great whore that sitteth upon many waters (spirit of life):

Re:17:2: With whom the kings of the earth have committed fornication, and the inhabitants of the earth have been made drunk with the wine of her fornication.

Re:17:3: So he carried me away in the spirit into the wilderness: and I saw a woman (out of man-religion) sit upon a scarlet coloured beast, full of names of **blasphemy**, having seven (word of god) heads and ten (proven) horns.

Re:17:4: And the woman (out of man – religion) was arrayed in purple and scarlet colour, and decked with gold and precious stones (spiritual house) and pearls, having a golden cup in her hand full of **abominations and filthiness of her fornication:**

Re:17:5: And upon her forehead was a name written, MYSTERY, BABYLON (religious confusion) THE GREAT, THE MOTHER OF HARLOTS AND ABOMINATIONS OF THE EARTH.

Re:17:6: And I saw the woman (out of man – religion) drunken with the blood of the saints, and with the blood of the martyrs of Jesus: and when I saw her, I wondered with great admiration.

Re:17:7: And the angel said unto me, Wherefore didst thou marvel? I will tell thee the mystery of the woman (out of man – religion), and of the beast that carrieth her, which hath the seven (word of god) heads and ten horns

Re:17:8: The beast that thou sawest **was, and is not; and shall ascend out of the bottomless pit, and go into perdition**: and they that dwell on the earth shall wonder, **whose names were not written in the book of life** from the foundation of the world, when they behold the beast that **was, and is not, and yet is.**

Re:17:9: And here is the mind which hath wisdom. The seven heads are seven (word of god) mountains (religions), on which the woman (out of man-religion) sitteth.

Re:17:10: **And there are seven kings: five are fallen, and one is, and the other is not yet come; and when he cometh, he must continue a short space.**

Re:17:11: **And the beast that was, and is not, even he is the eighth, and is of the seven, and goeth into perdition.**

Now it is reported that there are Seven Kings or saviours of the earth. There are the first five listed above but now we can add Jesus as the sixth much to His dismay that Christianity is now worshipping god as a god and therefore committing idolatry. We know this through the story told in Revelation above.

1/ Noah
2/ Abraham
3/ Moses
4/ David
5/ Elijah
6/ Jesus Christ
7/ the one whom brings the little book (written about the angel wormwood)
8/ The Holy Ghost; that thing which **was, and is not, and yet is**.

It is said that the eighth 'is and yet is not' because it is only a concept in which case it has no physical attributes yet it exists as an idea. In fact this is the exact description of God. He was and is not (doesn't exist) yet is (because it is an Ideal).

So we understand the notion of 'Husbands' and religiously speaking of 'wife's' which are 'flesh' or doctrine to each of these husbands.

Mary therefore represented such a wife. In the Gospel of Matthew the disciple first outlines Jesus' genealogy through the line of His Father Joseph, in order to prove His ancestry not only from Adam but also from King David. Thus he establishes His right to be called King of the Jews.

M't:1:1: **The book of the generation of Jesus Christ**, the son of David, the son of Abraham.

M't:1:2: Abraham begat Isaac; and Isaac begat Jacob; and Jacob begat Judas and his brethren;

M't:1:3: And Judas begat Phares and Zara of Thamar; and Phares begat Esrom; and Esrom begat Aram;

M't:1:4: And Aram begat Aminadab; and Aminadab begat Naasson; and Naasson begat Salmon;

M't:1:5: And Salmon begat Booz of Rachab; and Booz begat Obed of Ruth; and Obed begat Jesse;

M't:1:6: And Jesse begat David the king; and David the king begat Solomon of her that had been the wife of Urias;

M't:1:7: And Solomon begat Roboam; and Roboam begat Abia; and Abia begat Asa;

M't:1:8: And Asa begat Josaphat; and Josaphat begat Joram; and Joram begat Ozias;

M't:1:9: And Ozias begat Joatham; and Joatham begat Achaz; and Achaz begat Ezekias;

M't:1:10: And Ezekias begat Manasses; and Manasses begat Amon; and Amon begat Josias;

M't:1:11: And Josias begat Jechonias and his brethren, about the time they were carried away to Babylon:

M't:1:12: And after they were brought to Babylon, Jechonias begat Salathiel; and Salathiel begat Zorobabel;

M't:1:13: And Zorobabel begat Abiud; and Abiud begat Eliakim; and Eliakim begat Azor;

M't:1:14: And Azor begat Sadoc; and Sadoc begat Achim; and Achim begat Eliud;

M't:1:15: And Eliud begat Eleazar; and Eleazar begat Matthan; and Matthan begat Jacob;

M't:1:16: **And Jacob begat Joseph the husband of Mary, of whom was born Jesus, who is called Christ.**

M't:1:17: So all the generations from Abraham to David are fourteen generations; and from David until the carrying away into Babylon are fourteen generations; and from the carrying away into Babylon unto Christ are fourteen generations.

However if Jesus was truly born of a virgin Mother this genealogy is meaningless. Anybody could have stood in as a father.

We note also that throughout Jesus testimony He never refers to Joseph as His father but rather to the Ideal of God as His adopted Father. Also when it comes to recognising His Mother He also never refers to Mary as His Mother but rather to His brethren.

M't:12:46: While he yet talked to the people, behold, his mother and his brethren stood without, desiring to speak with him.

M't:12:47: Then one said unto him, Behold, thy mother and thy brethren stand without, desiring to speak with thee.

M't:12:48: But he answered and said unto him that told him, **Who is my mother? and who are my brethren?**

M't:12:49: **And he stretched forth his hand toward his disciples, and said, Behold my mother and my brethren!**

M't:12:50: For whosoever shall do the will of my Father which is in heaven, the same is my brother, and sister, and mother.

Here is the birth of Jesus according to Matthew as a virgin birth.

M't:1:18: Now the birth of Jesus Christ was on this wise: When as his mother Mary was espoused to Joseph, before they came together, **she was found with child of the Holy Ghost.**

M't:1:19: Then Joseph her husband, being a just man, and not willing to make her a publick example, was minded to put her away privily.

M't:1:20: But while he thought on these things, behold, the angel (messenger) of the Lord appeared unto him in a dream, saying, Joseph, thou son of David, fear not to take unto thee Mary thy wife: **for that which is conceived in her is of the Holy Ghost**.

M't:1:21: And she shall bring forth a son, and thou shalt call his name JESUS: for he shall save his people from their sins.

M't:1:22: Now all this was done, that it might be fulfilled which was spoken of the Lord by the prophet, saying,

M't:1:23: Behold, a virgin shall be with child, and shall bring forth a son, and they shall call his name Emmanuel, which being interpreted is, God with us.

M't:1:24: Then Joseph being raised from sleep did as the angel (messenger) of the Lord had bidden him, and took unto him his wife:

M't:1:25: And knew her not till she had brought forth her firstborn son: and he called his name JESUS.

Note: there is a great deal of argument surrounding the meaning of the name 'Jesus' as it seems that the name is a phonetic rendition of the Greek name Iesous and as such is a made up word. We personally like to think of it as Je-suis which is French and means 'I am' but this is also made up and meaningless.

Returning to the Virgin account of Jesus' birth; it is recorded by Matthew that Jesus was conceived of the Holy Ghost 'for that which is conceived in her is of the Holy Ghost". We know that this is not accurate because Jesus had to wait for the Baptism of John in order to be "Born of the Holy Ghost" but the Holy Ghost was not given to the world until Christ was crucified.

> Lu:3:21: Now when all the people were baptized, it came to pass, **that Jesus also being baptized, and praying, the heaven was opened,**
>
> **Lu:3:22: And the Holy Ghost descended in a bodily shape like a dove upon him, and a voice came from heaven, which said, Thou art my beloved Son; in thee I am well pleased.**

The fact is that only the Baptism can impart the Holy Ghost. Being given the Holy Ghost or Holy Atheism is understood as being 'Slain in the Spirit" or to be made dead by the knowledge that there are no such things as gods. Jesus already knew this as he and John the Baptist were groomed for their task. It can be argued that because Jesus already knew this that the earlier conception of Mary was his receiving the Holy Ghost but this is not so. Only Mary and Joseph knew the Holy Ghost as Jesus was not yet born of anything. So to say that He and John were of the Holy Ghost before they were conceived is inaccurate. An unborn baby cannot conceive an idea which is what the Baptism is. They could not be baptised while in the actual womb and therefore had to wait until they were grown in order to be baptised. Jesus knew and understood this and it is for this reason that he explains to John that He must first be Baptised before He could commence His ministry.

> M't:3:11: I indeed baptize you with water unto repentance: but he that cometh after me is mightier than I, whose shoes I am not worthy to bear: **he shall baptize you with the Holy Ghost, and with fire:**
>
> M't:3:12: Whose fan is in his hand, and he will throughly purge his floor, and gather his wheat into the garner; but he will burn up the chaff with unquenchable fire.

M't:3:13: **Then cometh Jesus from Galilee to Jordan unto John, to be baptized of him.**

M't:3:14: **But John forbad him, saying, I have need to be baptized of thee, and comest thou to me?**

M't:3:15: **And Jesus answering said unto him, Suffer it to be so now: for thus it becometh us to fulfil all righteousness. Then he suffered him.**

M't:3:16: And Jesus, when he was baptized, went up straightway out of the water: and, lo, the heavens were opened unto him, and he saw the Spirit of God descending like a dove, and lighting upon him:

M't:3:17: And lo a voice from heaven, saying, This is my beloved Son, in whom I am well pleased.

In this encounter we see that John the Baptist has never been baptised himself and in fact seeks Jesus to Baptise him.

M't:3:14: **But John forbad him, saying, I have need to be baptized of thee, and comest thou to me?**

Jesus however disagrees and is instead baptised by John. Jesus says that in order to fulfil a certain prophecy it must be so.

M't:3:15: **And Jesus answering said unto him, Suffer it to be so now: for thus it becometh us to fulfil all righteousness. Then he suffered him.**

So we see that right from the onset Jesus and John both conspired in order to fulfil prophecy. In fact this is what they had been raised and educated to do. They knew before-hand everything that was destined to take place as it had been carefully choreographed.

John's birth was not very different to that of Jesus.

Lu:1:5: There was in the days of Herod, the king of Judaea (Praise), a certain priest named Zacharias (God is renowned), of the course of Abia (God is Father): and his wife (doctrine) was of the daughters of Aaron (Enlightened), and her name was Elisabeth (God is Swearer).

Lu:1:6: And they were both righteous before God, walking in all the commandments and ordinances of the Lord blameless.

Lu:1:7: And they had no child, because that Elisabeth (God is swearer) was barren, and they both were now well stricken in years.

Lu:1:8: And it came to pass, that while he executed the priest's office before God in the order of his course,

Lu:1:9: According to the custom of the priest's office, his lot was to burn incense when he went into the temple of the Lord.

Lu:1:10: And the whole multitude of the people were praying without at the time of incense.

Lu:1:11: And there appeared unto him an angel (messenger) of the Lord standing on the right side of the altar of incense.

Lu:1:12: And when Zacharias (God is renowned) saw him, he was troubled, and fear fell upon him.

Lu:1:13: But the angel (messenger) said unto him, Fear not, Zacharias (God is renowned) : for thy prayer is heard; and thy wife Elisabeth (God is swearer) shall bear thee a son, and thou shalt call his name John (Grace)

Lu:1:14: And thou shalt have joy and gladness; and many shall rejoice at his birth.

Lu:1:15: For he shall be great in the sight of the Lord, and shall drink neither wine nor strong drink; **and he shall be filled with the Holy Ghost, even from his mother's womb.**

Lu:1:16: And many of the children of Israel (Ruling with God) shall he turn to the Lord their God.

Lu:1:17: And he shall go before him in the spirit and power of Elias (God is god), to turn the hearts of the fathers to the children, and the disobedient to the wisdom of the just; to make ready a people prepared for the Lord.

Lu:1:18: And Zacharias (God is renowned) said unto the angel (messenger), Whereby shall I know this? for I am an old man, and my wife well stricken in years.

Lu:1:19: And the angel (messenger) answering said unto him, I am Gabriel (God is mighty), that stand in the presence of God; and am sent to speak unto thee, and to shew thee these glad tidings.

Lu:1:20: And, behold, thou shalt be dumb, and not able to speak, until the day that these things shall be performed, because thou believest not my words, which shall be fulfilled in their season.

Lu:1:21: And the people waited for Zacharias (God is renowned), and marvelled that he tarried so long in the temple.

Lu:1:22: And when he came out, he could not speak unto them: and they perceived that he had seen a vision in the temple: for he beckoned unto them, and remained speechless.

Lu:1:23: And it came to pass, that, as soon as the days of his ministration were accomplished, he departed to his own house.

Lu:1:24: And after those days his wife Elisabeth (God is Swearer) conceived, and hid herself five (veil of God) months, saying,

Lu:1:25: Thus hath the Lord dealt with me in the days wherein he looked on me, to take away my reproach among men.

We see that the angel or messenger of god that spoke to Zacharias (God is renowned) when he was in the church preparing the incense was probably a Levite sent to make an agreement or oath or swearing in of John his predicted son.

This oath that Zacharias made with the Levite messenger of God is not unlike the same oath made by Mary for Jesus' life.

> Lu:1:26: And in the sixth (idolatry) month the angel (messenger) Gabriel (God is mighty) was sent from God unto a city of Galilee (Circle), named Nazareth (separated),

> Lu:1:27: To a virgin espoused to a man whose name was Joseph (he will add), of the house of David (beloved); and the virgin's name was Mary (rebellious).

> Lu:1:28: And the angel (messenger) came in unto her, and said, Hail, thou that art highly favoured, the Lord is with thee: blessed art thou among women (out of man).

> Lu:1:29: And when she saw him, she was troubled at his saying, and cast in her mind what manner of salutation this should be.

> Lu:1:30: And the angel (messenger) said unto her, Fear not, Mary (rebellious) : for thou hast found favour with God.

> Lu:1:31: And, behold, thou shalt conceive in thy womb, and bring forth a son, and shalt call his name JESUS.

> Lu:1:32: He shall be great, and shall be called the Son of the Highest: and the Lord God shall give unto him the throne of his father David (beloved):

> Lu:1:33: And he shall reign over the house of Jacob (supplanter) for ever; and of his kingdom there shall be no end.

> Lu:1:34: Then said Mary (rebellious) unto the angel (messenger), How shall this be, seeing I know not a man?

Lu:1:35: And the angel (messenger) answered and said unto her, **The Holy Ghost (Holy Atheism) shall come upon thee, and the power of the Highest shall overshadow (veil of god) thee: therefore also that holy thing (idea) which shall be born (conception) of thee shall be called the Son of God. (by adoption)**

Lu:1:36: And, behold, thy cousin Elisabeth (god is swearer), she hath also conceived (idea) a son in her old age: and this is the sixth (idolatry) month with her, who was called barren.

Lu:1:37: For with God nothing shall be impossible.

Lu:1:38: And Mary (rebellious) said, Behold the handmaid of the Lord; be it unto me according to thy word. And the angel (messenger) departed from her.

Lu:1:39: And Mary (rebellious) arose in those days, and went into the hill country with haste, into a city of Juda (Praise);

Lu:1:40: And entered into the house of Zacharias (God is renowned), and saluted Elisabeth (god is swearer).

Lu:1:41: And it came to pass, that, when Elisabeth (god is swearer) heard the salutation of Mary (rebellious), the babe leaped in her womb; and Elisabeth (god is swearer) **was filled with the Holy Ghost**: (Holy Atheism)

Lu:1:42: And she spake out with a loud voice, and said, Blessed art thou among women (out of man), and blessed is the fruit of thy womb.

Lu:1:43: And whence is this to me, that the mother of my Lord should come to me?

Lu:1:44: For, lo, as soon as the voice of thy salutation sounded in mine ears, the babe leaped in my womb for joy.

Lu:1:45: And blessed is she that believed: for there shall be a performance of those things which were told her from the Lord.

Lu:1:46: And Mary (rebellious) said, My soul doth magnify the Lord,

Lu:1:47: And my spirit hath rejoiced in God my Saviour.

Lu:1:48: For he hath regarded the low estate of his handmaiden: for, behold, from henceforth all generations shall call me blessed.

Lu:1:49: For he that is mighty hath done to me great things; and holy is his name.

Lu:1:50: And his mercy is on them that fear him from generation to generation.

Lu:1:51: He hath shewed strength with his arm; he hath scattered the proud in the imagination of their hearts.

Lu:1:52: He hath put down the mighty from their seats, and exalted them of low degree.

Lu:1:53: He hath filled the hungry with good things; and the rich he hath sent empty away.

Lu:1:54: He hath holpen his servant Israel (ruling with god), in remembrance of his mercy;

Lu:1:55: As he spake to our fathers, to Abraham (Father of a multitude), and to his seed for ever.

Lu:1:56: And Mary (rebellious) abode with her about three (atheistic truth) months, and returned to her own house.

Mary makes an oath with a Levite or messenger of god (angel) and then goes into the 'hill' country to visit Elizabeth (god is swearer) where the oath was consecrated. While there they discuss the Idea (conception) that each of them now holds. We know that they were informed of the truth because of the presence of the Holy Ghost (Holy Atheism) and also because the visit lasted three (atheistic truth) months (moon or truth cycle). While there these people (not actually two women but two groups (out of man) probably a secret faction of Levites, planned the path of grooming both John and Jesus for the task of repairing Israel (ruling with God). The observation here is that Israel (ruling with god) was committing idolatry by worshipping god. The concept was to introduce the Baptism for the remission of sin. This new concept of entering into the womb and being re-born as described by Nicodemus is shown below.

> Joh:3:1: There was a man of the Pharisees, named Nicodemus, a ruler of the Jews:

> Joh:3:2: The same came to Jesus by night, and said unto him, Rabbi, we know that thou art a teacher come from God: for no man can do these miracles that thou doest, except God be with him.

> Joh:3:3: Jesus answered and said unto him, Verily, verily, I say unto thee, Except a man be born again, he cannot see the kingdom of God.

> Joh:3:4: Nicodemus saith unto him, **How can a man be born when he is old? can he enter the second time into his mother's womb, and be born?**

The whole concept of idolatry (death through worshipping gods); Baptism for the remission of sin and being born again from the womb of religion which signifies resurrection to eternal life (not heaven - one is never resurrected to heaven) describes a very intricate and complex plan for the mission of John and Jesus.

Their mothers (Levite factions) adopting this extraordinary concept were more widespread than the Gospels hint at. Every thought that Jesus expressed had already been conceived by the mother faction. We know that such factions or separate groups of religious extremists existed by the evidence of Qumran and the Dead Sea Scrolls. Qumran was just one separate group but there were probably many because as religions age they have prophecies predicting the coming of a messiah; those who wait for the messiah begin to get impatient and hence frequently decide to force the issue by adopting the mission themselves.

This is how the whole mission was established in the first place. There are separate and identifiable steps that are recognisable. First the Mothers; Elizabeth (god is swearer) forms a vow or oath to provide the children that will be groomed for the task. Then there is the recognition that the time is right Mary (rebellious) notes the sixth (idolatry) month of being barren. Both (Mothers) are filled with the Holy Ghost (Holy Atheism) and are informed of the plan and all the devices of the new concept (Baptism) before the elected saviours are born. All this is recorded in code and hidden by the veil (And after those days his wife Elisabeth (God is Swearer) conceived, and hid herself five (veil of God) months.)

The children are taken at around the age of twelve for their new role and apprenticeship.

> Lu:2:42: And when he was **twelve years old**, they went up to Jerusalem (possession of peace) after the custom of the feast.

> Lu:2:43: And when they had fulfilled the days, as they returned, the child Jesus tarried behind in Jerusalem (possession of peace); and Joseph (he will add) and his mother knew not of it.

> Lu:2:44: But they, supposing him to have been in the company, went a day's journey; and they sought him among their kinsfolk and acquaintance.

> Lu:2:45: And when they found him not, they turned back again to Jerusalem (possession of peace), seeking him.

> Lu:2:46: And it came to pass, that after three (atheistic truth) days they found him in the temple, **sitting in the midst of the doctors, both hearing them, and asking them questions.**

> Lu:2:47: And all that heard him were astonished at his understanding and answers.

Lu:2:48: And when they saw him, they were amazed: and his mother said unto him, Son, why hast thou thus dealt with us? behold, thy father and I have sought thee sorrowing.

Lu:2:49: And he said unto them, How is it that ye sought me? wist ye not that I must be about my Father's (God the Ideal) business?

Lu:2:50: And they understood not the saying which he spake unto them.

This interview with the 'doctors' both hearing them and asking questions portrays his teaching session and we know that it pertains to His mission because He says "wist ye not that I must be about my Father's (God the Ideal) business?"

After this there is nothing recorded about John or Jesus until it is time for the mission to begin.

Lu:3:22: And the Holy Ghost descended in a bodily shape like a dove upon him, and a voice came from heaven, which said, Thou art my beloved Son; in thee I am well pleased.

Lu:3:23: And Jesus himself began to be **about thirty years of age**, being (as was supposed) the son of Joseph (He will add), which was the son of Heli, (High Priest)

The mission begins with John Baptising in the wilderness and Jesus coming to Him to be Baptised in order that the Holy Ghost can alight on Him as discussed above.

Lu:3:2: Annas (grace of God) and Caiaphas (depression) being the high priests, the word of God came unto John (grace) the son of Zacharias (god is renowned) in the wilderness.

Lu:3:3: And he came into all the country about Jordan (god is high), **preaching the baptism of repentance for the remission of sins;**

Lu:3:4: As it is written in the book of the words of Esaias (god is helper) the prophet, saying, The voice of one crying in the wilderness, Prepare ye the way of the Lord, make his paths straight.

Lu:3:5: Every valley shall be filled, and every mountain (religion) and hill (place of worship) shall be brought low; and the crooked shall be made straight, and the rough ways shall be made smooth;

Lu:3:6: And all flesh (doctrine) shall see the salvation of God.

The Baptism of Jesus but not of John; It is very strange that John is never baptised.

M't:3:13: Then cometh Jesus from Galilee to Jordan unto John, to be baptized of him.

M't:3:14: But John forbad him, saying, I have need to be baptized of thee, and comest thou to me?

M't:3:15: And Jesus answering said unto him, Suffer it to be so now: for thus it becometh us to fulfil all righteousness. Then he suffered him.

M't:3:16: And Jesus, when he was baptized, went up straightway out of the water: and, lo, the heavens were opened unto him, and he saw the Spirit of God descending like a dove, and lighting upon him:

M't:3:17: And lo a voice from heaven, saying, This is my beloved Son, in whom I am well pleased.

Lu:3:7: Then said he to the multitude that came forth to be baptized of him, O generation of vipers, who hath warned you to flee from the wrath to come?

Lu:3:8: Bring forth therefore fruits worthy of repentance, and begin not to say within yourselves, We have Abraham to our father: for I say unto you, **That God is able of these stones (spiritual house) to raise up children unto Abraham.**

Lu:3:9: And now also the axe is laid unto the root of the trees (places of worship or synagogue): every tree therefore which bringeth not forth good fruit is hewn down, and cast into the fire (argument).

Lu:3:10: And the people asked him, saying, What shall we do then?

Lu:3:11: He answereth and saith unto them, He that hath two coats, let him impart to him that hath none; and he that hath meat, let him do likewise.

Lu:3:12: Then came also publicans to be baptized, and said unto him, Master, what shall we do?

Lu:3:13: And he said unto them, Exact no more than that which is appointed you.

Lu:3:14: And the soldiers likewise demanded of him, saying, And what shall we do? And he said unto them, Do violence to no man, neither accuse any falsely; and be content with your wages.

Lu:3:15: **And as the people were in expectation, and all men mused in their hearts of John, whether he were the Christ, or not;**

Lu:3:16: John answered, saying unto them all, I indeed baptize you with water; but one mightier than I cometh, the latchet of whose shoes I am not worthy to unloose: **he shall baptize you with the Holy Ghost and with fire:**

Lu:3:17: Whose fan is in his hand, and he will throughly purge his floor, and will gather the wheat into his garner; but the chaff he will burn with fire unquenchable.

> Lu:3:18: And many other things in his exhortation preached he unto the people.
>
> Lu:3:19: But Herod the tetrarch, being reproved by him for Herodias his brother Philip's wife, and for all the evils which Herod had done,
>
> Lu:3:20: Added yet this above all, that he shut up John in prison.

We see that John's advice is exactly the same as that given by Jesus. It is interesting to note that people (in expectation) wondered whether John was in fact Jesus.

Having two people sent forward at the same time was confusing, but John's task was to introduce the Baptism which Jesus never did. Although Jesus' disciples also baptised after the manner of John and his followers, Jesus never baptised any-body.

> Joh:4:1: When therefore the Lord knew how the Pharisees had heard that Jesus made and baptized more disciples than John,
>
> Joh:4:2: (**Though Jesus himself baptized not, but his disciples,**)

This seems very strange because Jesus obviously knew the meaning behind the Baptism and spoke of it highly yet did not baptise any, even though it was promised that Jesus would baptise with the Holy Ghost and Fire.

> M't:3:11: I indeed baptize you with water unto repentance: but he that cometh after me is mightier than I, whose shoes I am not worthy to bear: **he shall baptize you with the Holy Ghost, and with fire:**

Jesus went throughout the country preaching that there are no such things as gods. We know this through the Baptism which introduces the Holy Atheism which is also called the Holy Ghost. It is a concept that slays a person in the spirit. They are then said to be dead but are then re-born into a new concept of god that god is an Ideal. This is a more perfect state of mind because it allows one to know that sin is deemed irrelevant. This is why it is called the baptism for the remission of sins.

Apart from this and other things Jesus basically taught good behaviour because the Ideal of God is to demonstrate such behaviour. This of course cannot happen if the mind is deluded by dogma.

Regardless of what was taught and who was taught Jesus always through His honesty revealed the other meaning to His parables and promises. For example He said that every time a miracle was worked that VIRTUE went out of Him.

> M'r:5:30: And Jesus, immediately **knowing in himself that virtue had gone out of him,** turned him about in the press, and said, Who touched my clothes?

And also in Luke;

> Lu:6:19: And the whole multitude sought to touch him: for **there went virtue out of him, and healed them all.**

> Lu:8:46: And Jesus said, **Somebody hath touched me: for I perceive that virtue is gone out of me.**

Virtue is defined as 'Moral goodness' and Jesus knew that each time somebody was misled by way of a miracle or some other aspect of His ministry He states that Virtue had left Him.

Beyond His actual confession of Truth; the slaying of spirit by the Baptism; His explanations of what God is and the testimonials of His disciples there was little else He could do. As if all that isn't enough! Nevertheless He needed help on the inside if He was to make prophecy happen as it was recorded. There were many prophecies that had to be met either in word or reputation or in real life action of the role of a Saviour.

John the Baptist is arrested, imprisoned and eventually beheaded by Herod leaving Jesus on His own to complete that which was begun. It was not enough to just have the disciples. They had to be taught everything including the mystery of god and indeed had no influence within the courts of the High Synagogue or with Pontus Pilate. Jesus needed the Pharisees and Sadducees and all the High Priests to move and take certain actions that would also conform to prophetic role playing. Even though Jesus was a high priest himself even called 'King of the Jews' He had no way of getting the Pharisees of the courts to behave and manoeuvre into prophetic roles. He needed people on the inside. Luckily there were certain people in the streets who knew His mission and were even called helpers. For example there was the incident over tribute money.

> M't:17:24: And when they were come to Capernaum, they that received tribute money came to Peter, and said, Doth not your master pay tribute?

> M't:17:25: He saith, Yes. And when he was come into the house, Jesus prevented him, saying, What thinkest thou, Simon? of whom do the kings of the earth take custom or tribute? of their own children, or of strangers?

> M't:17:26: Peter saith unto him, Of strangers. Jesus saith unto him, Then are the children free.

> M't:17:27: Notwithstanding, lest we should offend them, go thou to the sea, and cast an hook, and **take up the fish (spirit filled person) that first cometh up; and when thou hast opened his mouth, thou shalt find a piece of money**: that take, and give unto them for me and thee.

This inkling of inside help does not reflect the greater need Jesus had for influencing those people in power to bring about dramatic events such as His planned Crucifixion. He had to be tried as an innocent person and found guilty of nothing and then to be crucified for no real reason except to martyr Himself for the people. It had to look like He would die for the sins of the world because He preached the Baptism; that He was Son of God (by adoption) and that He was King of the Jews by reason that He bore the truth while the rest of the world was under idolatry. By this method He could fulfil prophecy; Set in place the Baptism for remission of sin; advertise the Holy Ghost (Holy Atheism) which slays people in the spirit even demonstrate what the Spirit of Truth really was. Nobody (apart from His helpers and co-conspirators) knew these things. Only His planned death (a physical enactment of the Baptism and Resurrection) could provide enough evidence to place Him as an ensign to the whole world.

> Joh:3:14: And as Moses lifted up **the serpent in the wilderness, even so must the Son of man be lifted up:**

Having discussed all these things above we are now able to introduce the angels (messengers of god) that assisted Jesus throughout His ministry. The first is introduced as Nicodemus.

> Joh:3:1: There was a man of the Pharisees, named **Nicodemus (innocent blood)**, a ruler of the Jews:

> Joh:3:4: Nicodemus (innocent blood) saith unto him, How can a man be born when he is old? can he enter the second time into his mother's womb, and be born?

> Joh:3:9: Nicodemus (innocent blood) answered and said unto him, How can these things be?

Of course we are already familiar with Nicodemus asking about the Baptism. This happens right at the beginning of Jesus' mission. Further into the Gospels Jesus is seen by the disciples to be in a meeting with two others supposed to be Moses and Elias.

> Lu:9:28: And it came to pass about an eight (righteousness) days after these sayings, he took Peter (spiritual house) and John (grace) and James (he who supplants), and went up into a mountain (religion) to pray.

> Lu:9:29: And as he prayed, the fashion of his countenance was altered, and his raiment was white and glistering.

Lu:9:30: And, behold, **there talked with him two men**, which were Moses (drawn out of the water) and Elias (God is god):

Lu:9:31: Who appeared in glory, **and spake of his decease** which he should accomplish at Jerusalem (possession of peace).

Lu:9:32: But Peter (spiritual house) and they that were with him were heavy with sleep: and when they were awake, they saw his glory, and the two men that stood with him.

Lu:9:33: And it came to pass, as they departed from him, Peter (spiritual house) said unto Jesus, Master, it is good for us to be here: and let us make three tabernacles; one for thee, and one for Moses (drawn out of the water), and one for Elias (God is god): not knowing what he said.

Lu:9:34: While he thus spake, there came a cloud (Veil of truth), and overshadowed (covered them spiritually) them: and they feared as they entered into the cloud (veil of truth).

Lu:9:35: And there came a voice out of the cloud, saying, This is my beloved Son: hear him.

Lu:9:36: And when the voice was past, Jesus was found alone. And they kept it close, **and told no man** in those days any of those things which they had seen.

This encounter is very important because they state that what was discussed was Jesus' decease or in other words how He was planning the end of His ministry and also the end of His life. It was clear that Jesus couldn't travel the Middle East forever administering to the sick and Baptising. His role had to end at some time in order for the disciples to set up the new church which eventually became known as Christianity. Even so there was a huge risk and a big gamble to take for Jesus needed to be crucified in dramatic circumstances in order to be effective. The whole ministry was heading toward an ending that Greek ideology at the time dictated was the correct pathos for a martyr.

Our next encounter with Nicodemus in John Chapter 7 reveals that Nicodemus is speaking in Jesus' defence.

> Joh:7:45: Then came the officers to the chief priests and Pharisees; and they said unto them, Why have ye not brought him?

> Joh:7:46: The officers answered, Never man spake like this man.

> Joh:7:47: Then answered them the Pharisees, Are ye also deceived?

> Joh:7:48: Have any of the rulers or of the Pharisees believed on him?

> Joh:7:49: But this people who knoweth not the law are cursed.

> Joh:7:50: **Nicodemus saith unto them, (he that came to Jesus by night, being one of them,)**

> Joh:7:51: **Doth our law judge any man, before it hear him, and know what he doeth**?

> Joh:7:52: They answered and said unto him, Art thou also of Galilee? Search, and look: for out of Galilee (Circle) ariseth no prophet.

Nicodemus whose name strangely means 'depression' is visited again this time at the Crucifixion of Jesus. Here he is also in the company of Joseph of Arimathaea and the two of them beg for Jesus' body off Pontus Pilate, then take Jesus' body down from the cross and wrap it and 'prepare it" with the ointments of healing and place Jesus in the tomb owned by Joseph of Arimathaea for recovery (resurrection). There is enough evidence here not only to suggest conspiracy but to show who, what, when, where, and how all these things were achieved.

> M't:27:57: When the even was come, there came a rich man of Arimathaea, named Joseph, **who also himself was Jesus' disciple:**

M't:27:58: **He went to Pilate, and begged the body of Jesus**. Then Pilate commanded the body to be delivered.

M't:27:59: And when Joseph had taken the body, he wrapped it in a clean linen cloth,

M't:27:60: And laid it in his own new tomb, which he had hewn out in the rock: and he rolled a great stone to the door of the sepulchre, and departed.

Jesus knew He had to die but these two men devised a way that Jesus might be able to cheat death and still be resurrected and conform to the philosophy of the Baptism. These men would coax the Pharisees into condemning Jesus to Pontus Pilate on trumped up charges. This had to be done at Passover (to go without God – atheism) in order to fulfil certain predictions. These men also were wealthy because they could afford to buy the aloes and myrrh.

Joh:19:39: **And there came also Nicodemus**, which at the first came to Jesus by night, and brought a mixture of myrrh and aloes, about an hundred pound weight.

This unguent was necessary in restoring Jesus back to health after He was removed from the cross. These men also had enough influence to convince Pontus Pilate to release Jesus into their custody.

M't:27:57: When the even was come, **there came a rich man of Arimathaea, named Joseph, who also himself was Jesus' disciple:**

M't:27:58: **He went to Pilate, and begged the body of Jesus**. Then Pilate commanded the body to be delivered.

M't:27:59: And when Joseph had taken the body, he wrapped it in a clean linen cloth,

M't:27:60: **And laid it in his own new tomb**, which he had hewn out in the rock: and he rolled a great stone to the door of the sepulchre, and departed.

Having obtained the body of Christ these two probably with the help of other Levites took Jesus' body away and wrapped Him in the clean linen and prepared the still breathing body of Jesus with the ointments and laid Him in the tomb owned by Joseph of Arimathaea.

It all fits together nicely as a scenario that the modern day church will hate to hear about. How could we treat Jesus death in such a mundane way as to represent a conspiracy? However this is not the end of the story. Jesus was to rise again in three (atheistic truth) days.

> M't:28:1: In the end of the sabbath, as it began to dawn toward the first day of the week, came Mary Magdalene and the other Mary to see the sepulchre.

> M't:28:2: And, behold, there was a great earthquake: for the angel of the Lord descended from heaven, and came and rolled back the stone from the door, and sat upon it.

> M't:28:3: His countenance was like lightning, and his raiment white as snow:

> M't:28:4: And for fear of him the keepers did shake, and became as dead men.

> M't:28:5: And the angel answered and said unto the women, Fear not ye: for I know that ye seek Jesus, which was crucified.

> M't:28:6: **He is not here: for he is risen,** as he said. Come, see the place where the Lord lay.

> M't:28:7: And go quickly, and tell his disciples that he is risen from the dead; and, behold, he goeth before you into Galilee; there shall ye see him: lo, I have told you.

Here Jesus is said to have risen on the third (atheistic) day of the burial. This completes the acting out of the Baptism. The resurrection or the re-birth into a new conception is the final and permanent part of the Baptism process.

Luke's account gives us a little more insight into what actually happened at the death bedside.

> Lu:24:1: Now upon the first day of the week, very early in the morning, they came unto the sepulchre, bringing the spices which they had prepared, and certain others with them.
>
> Lu:24:2: And they found the stone rolled away from the sepulchre.
>
> Lu:24:3: And they entered in, and found not the body of the Lord Jesus.
>
> Lu:24:4: And it came to pass, as they were much perplexed thereabout, behold, **two men stood by them in shining garments**:
>
> Lu:24:5: And as they were afraid, and bowed down their faces to the earth, they said unto them, **Why seek ye the living among the dead**?
>
> Lu:24:6: He is not here, but is risen: **remember how he spake unto you when he was yet in Galilee (the circle),**
>
> Lu:24:7: Saying, **The Son of man must be delivered into the hands of sinful men, and be crucified, and the third day rise again**.
>
> Lu:24:8: And they remembered his words,

Here we see that two men probably Levites (in white clothing) of the conspiracy (of the Circle) were waiting in the tomb where Jesus had been placed but now was missing (raised from the dead). They say "why seek ye the living among the dead" and this brings to mind Jesus' own words to the disciples "let the dead bury the dead". Jesus always spoke of worshippers of god who committed idolatry as the dead and of those who knew the truth as the living. This is the differentiation made by the Baptism also. Atheists are those who are considered to be living while idolatry ensured that those who fell under dogma were dead.

Jesus also was not dead in the physical sense. He had survived the crucifixion with the help of Nicodemus and Joseph of Arimathaea and some very expensive aloes and myrrh. He had been collected on the third day by at least two confederates and perhaps helped to leave the tomb.

There were reports of Him showing His face on some occasions after His resurrection in order to prove that He had indeed survived the crucifixion. There was at least one account where the guards that were guarding Him were paid off to not say anything to the Elders here recorded in Matthew.

> M't:28:10: **Then said Jesus unto them,** Be not afraid: go tell my brethren that they go into Galilee (circle), and there shall they see me.

> M't:28:11: Now when they were going, behold, some of the watch came into the city, and shewed unto the chief priests all the things that were done.

> M't:28:12: And when they were assembled with the elders, and had taken counsel, **they gave large money unto the soldiers,**

> M't:28:13: **Saying, Say ye, His disciples came by night, and stole him away while we slept.**

> M't:28:14: And if this come to the governor's ears, we will persuade him, and secure you.

> M't:28:15: So they took the money, and did as they were taught: and this saying is commonly reported among the Jews until this day.

In Mark however there is a different instruction after the resurrection. Having proved that the resurrection works, Jesus then gives the disciples instruction to go abroad and teach the whole world about the Baptism and the resurrection of the spirit.

> M'r:16:14: **Afterward he appeared unto the eleven** as they sat at meat, and upbraided them with their unbelief and hardness

of heart, because they believed not them which had seen him after he was risen.

M'r:16:15: **And he said unto them, Go ye into all the world, and preach the gospel to every creature.**

M'r:16:16: **He that believeth and is baptized shall be saved; but he that believeth not shall be damned.**

Basically those *who do not believe the truth* about the atheistic nature of the Baptism; the slaying of the Spirit by way of the revealing of the truth about the mystery of god; and the resurrection of the Spirit of Life via the new concept of truthful knowledge of the Ideal of God adopted as a Father figure, then they are damned by their own belief systems until such times as they change their minds.

Lu:24:45: **Then opened he their understanding, that they might understand the scriptures,**

Lu:24:46: And said unto them, **Thus it is written, and thus it behoved Christ to suffer, and to rise from the dead the third day:**

Lu:24:47: And **that repentance and remission of sins should be preached in his name among all nations, beginning at Jerusalem.**

Lu:24:48: And ye are witnesses of these things.

Lu:24:49: And, behold, I send the promise of my Father upon you: but tarry ye in the city of Jerusalem, until ye be endued with power from on high.

So in Luke also is the revelation that Christ's suffering was for the benefit of a demonstration of the Baptism "Thus it is written, and thus it behoved Christ to suffer, and to rise from the dead the third day that repentance and remission of sins should be preached in his name".

There are many more things that Jesus did and said that are worthy to be revealed as a testament to the truth.

> Joh:21:25: And there **are also many other things which Jesus did, the which, if they should be written every one, I suppose that even the world itself could not contain the books that should be written**. Amen.

Thus this little book finds an end. It is not necessary to labour the point by extracting every verse from the New Testament. There is no need to prove what was taught from the beginning; that there are no such things as gods. Our God is an Ideal and we adopt that Ideal as a Father figure, for our society to function as perfectly as it can. The Baptism is a public demonstration, that we follow after the like-kind of Jesus, being first slain in the spirit by the revelation of the mystery of god, then plunged into the service of humanity, and then to promise to promote goodness in all our activities; and finally to be raised up into newness of life, with a new appreciation of Jesus and the sacrifice He made in order to teach us this vow

The Bible confesses that there is no such thing as God. This is the core of truth, without this knowledge of truth only derision remains. The mind is easily corrupted by imaginations of what might be in heaven. Imagination of spiritual things is dangerous ground. From it breeds all manner of contrivances from cherubim to angels and from performing miracles to speaking to the dead spirits of others. All are fraudulent. The only remedy for such misconception is the little book spoken of in Revelations.

> Re:10:10: And I took the little book out of the angel's hand, and ate it up; and it was in my mouth sweet as honey: and as soon as I had eaten it, my belly was bitter.

Jesus taught and healed people from their misconceptions about God. He said God was not in a place called heaven but the kingdom of God was within us.

> Lu:17:21: Neither shall they say, Lo here! or, lo there! for, behold, the kingdom of God is within you.

The spirit of god was a sense of loyalty and dedication directed toward a deeper more significant meaning than somebody seated in heaven. God was humanity which the people served without want or need for reward especially heavenly rewards. Everlasting life was the gift one received from the Baptism. It was a new appreciation of life freed from the bonds or burden of sin. This could only come about through an understanding of the Holy Ghost or through adopting the spirit of prophecy when dealing with scripture. The Spirit of Prophecy is the Testimony of Jesus.

> Re:19:10: And I fell at his feet to worship him. And he said unto me, See thou do it not: I am thy fellowservant, and of thy brethren that have the testimony of Jesus: worship God: **for the testimony of Jesus is the spirit of prophecy.**

Through this new language of the spirit the person was able to appreciate a type of atheism but also remain true to God's first principle to 'love one another'.

There is another spirit that being the spirit of truth. Jesus proclaimed that the Spirit of Truth would come into the world but this was impossible while the world was dominated by the dogma of the church.

> Joh:14:16: And I will pray the Father, and he shall give you another Comforter, that he may abide with you for ever;

> Joh:14:17: Even the Spirit of truth; whom the world cannot receive, because it seeth him not, neither knoweth him: but ye know him; for he dwelleth with you, and shall be in you.

Whilst it is true that the early Christians spoke out against the Pharisees and Sadducees of the day for corrupting the Word of God it is also known that the new Christian faith soon followed the same path into idolatry. They fell into the same dogma only under a new title. Good sense and knowledge went begging whilst this happened because people who spoke out were condemned of heresy and put to death. Such things cannot be understood unless the person is privy to the truth of what constitutes God.

Ro:3:1: What advantage then hath the Jew? or what profit is there of circumcision?

Ro:3:2: Much every way: chiefly, because that unto them were committed the oracles of God.

Ro:3:3: For what if some did not believe? shall their unbelief make the faith of God without effect?

Ro:3:4: God forbid: yea, let God be true, but every man a liar; as it is written, That thou mightest be justified in thy sayings, and mightest overcome when thou art judged.

Ro:3:5: But if our unrighteousness commend the righteousness of God, what shall we say? Is God unrighteous who taketh vengeance? (I speak as a man)

Ro:3:6: God forbid: for then how shall God judge the world?

Ro:3:7: For if the truth of God hath more abounded through my lie unto his glory; why yet am I also judged as a sinner?

Ro:3:8: And not rather, (as we be slanderously reported, and as some affirm that we say,) Let us do evil, that good may come? whose damnation is just.

Ro:3:9: What then? are we better than they? No, in no wise: for we have before proved both Jews and Gentiles, that they are all under sin;

For whilst the New Testament says there is but one god it implies there is none through the knowledge of this lie. The lie is the misleading statement that god exists, and so it does, but the insinuation is that God is a person in heaven which is not true. God is a spirit

Joh:4:24: God is a Spirit: and they that worship him must worship him in spirit and in truth.

So it was impossible for the Spirit of Truth to be recognised under such dogma.

> 2Th:2:5: Remember ye not, that, when I was yet with you, I told you these things?

> 2Th:2:6: And now ye know what withholdeth that he might be revealed in his time.

> 2Th:2:7: For the mystery of iniquity doth already work: only he who now letteth will let, until he be taken out of the way.

> 2Th:2:8: And then shall that Wicked be revealed, whom the Lord shall consume with the spirit of his mouth, and shall destroy with the brightness of his coming:

> 2Th:2:9: Even him, whose coming is after the working of Satan with all power and signs and lying wonders,

> 2Th:2:10: And with all deceivableness of unrighteousness in them that perish; because they received not the love of the truth, that they might be saved.

> 2Th:2:11: And for this cause God shall send them strong delusion, that they should believe a lie:

This mystery of iniquity which is already at work in Thessalonians is the very issue of worship under dogma. To worship god or anything at all is idolatry and such prevents knowledge of the truth from being seen and appreciated. All knowledge is given by god.

> 2Tm:3:16: All scripture is given by inspiration of God, and is profitable for doctrine, for reproof, for correction, for instruction in righteousness:

So we are introduced to the Spirit of Truth by Jesus

> Joh:16:12: I have yet many things to say unto you, but ye cannot bear them now.

Joh:16:13: Howbeit when he, the Spirit of truth, is come, he will guide you into all truth: for he shall not speak of himself; but whatsoever he shall hear, that shall he speak: and he will shew you things to come.

Joh:16:14: He shall glorify me: for he shall receive of mine, and shall shew it unto you.

In the light of all this knowledge and the lie of god the early Christians were asked to confess these things as part of the Baptism knowledge.

Ac:24:14: But this I confess unto thee, that after the way which they call heresy, so worship I the God of my fathers, believing all things which are written in the law and in the prophets:

This is the confession of truth which can only be made by a person whom has the insight of God. When this insight comes, it is the thing called the Holy Ghost which reveals it. For according to Jesus there are no such things as gods. Accompanying this insight is the knowledge that sin is irrelevant and does not exist. Neither are there heavens and rewards in heaven because if we love one another all our rewards are reflected in our actions.

Re:22:12: And, behold, I come quickly; and my reward is with me, to give every man according as his work shall be.

When we are baptised we are informed of the mystery of god. The insight that is god, slays us in spirit and we become atheists and by this are then said to be dead to worship. We are then buried under the water, in which is the spirit of life. The insight of truth then reveals to us a new appreciation of secular life in truth, which is everlasting life that cannot be taken away. We are then resurrected into a new identity knowing that God is an ideal and as such is the ideal god we then pledge our vow to love thy neighbour.

We therefore can never be robbed again of our sobriety through the word.

Re:21:1: And I saw a new heaven and a new earth: for the first heaven and the first earth were passed away; and there was no more sea.

We thank you for reading this book.

Howbeit when he, the Spirit of truth, is come, he will guide you into all truth: for he shall not speak of himself; but whatsoever he shall hear, that shall he speak: and he will shew you things to come.
Joh:16:13

And I took the little book out of the angel's hand, and ate it up; and it was in my mouth sweet as honey: and as soon as I had eaten it, my belly was bitter. Re:10:10:

THE END